M. French Sheldon

Salammbo Of Gustave Flaubert

M. French Sheldon

Salammbo Of Gustave Flaubert

ISBN/EAN: 9783742848987

Manufactured in Europe, USA, Canada, Australia, Japa

Cover: Foto ©Andreas Hilbeck / pixelio.de

Manufactured and distributed by brebook publishing software (www.brebook.com)

M. French Sheldon

Salammbo Of Gustave Flaubert

TO MY FRIEND

HENRY M. STANLEY,

THE GREAT EXPLORER, WHO FOUND DR LIVINGSTONE;
FIRST CIRCUMNAVIGATED THE GREAT LAKES OF CENTRAL AFRICA,
FIRST REVEALED THE EXTREME SOUTHERN SOURCES OF THE NILE;
FIRST TRACED THE CONGO TO THE SEA,
AND CREATED THE CONGO FREE STATE, WHICH IS DESTINED SOME DAY TO
OUTRIVAL ANCIENT PHŒNICIA
TO HIM WHOSE EXALTED NOBLE ATTRIBUTES AS MAN AND FRIEND EXCEL,
IF POSSIBLE, THE GREATNESS OF HIS FAME,
IT IS MY HONOUR AND PLEASURE TO DEDICATE THE
TRANSLATION OF SALAMMBÔ

M. FRENCH SHELDON.

London, 1885.

CONTENTS.

		PAGE
	INTRODUCTION	ix
I.	THE FEAST	1
II.	AT SICCA	26
III.	SALAMMBÔ	55
IV.	UNDER THE WALLS OF CARTHAGE .	66
V.	TANIT	91
VI.	HANNO	112
VII.	HAMILCAR BARCA . . .	140
VIII.	THE BATTLE OF THE MACAR .	192
IX.	THE CAMPAIGN	218
X.	THE SERPENT	239
XI.	IN THE TENT	256
XII.	THE AQUEDUCT . . .	282
XIII.	MOLOCH	309
XIV.	THE DEFILE OF THE BATTLE-AXE .	358
XV.	MÂTHO	409

INTRODUCTION.

THE French man of genius whose masterpiece is now for the first time presented in English to the attention of the Anglo-Saxon world was thirty-six years of age before he had published anything, and had attained the ripe age of forty-one when *Salammbô* made its appearance. Gustave Flaubert was born in the old town of Rouen, in Normandy, on the 12th of December, 1821. Both his father and his brother were noted physicians and surgeons, a fact which probably prompted Sainte-Beuve, when he came to criticise and to praise Gustave Flaubert, to remark that the author handled his pen as others handled the scalpel. The father was for more than thirty years chief surgeon of the Hôtel Dieu in Rouen, and was the author of many valuable treatises on medical science. The son Gustave, who had a passionate admiration for his elder brother, had determined to study medicine; but he soon perceived, says an acute biographer, that the observation of the phenomena of the moral order was better suited to his character, and he abruptly closed his scientific studies and turned to literature.

There are few instances in letters of a career so tardily begun ripening so quickly into renown, or concentrating into a few years so many excitements, struggles, debates, and victories. As soon as he had taken his great resolve, Flaubert

INTRODUCTION.

devoted his entire life and his phenomenal energy and persistence to the art which he had chosen to pursue. His life was thenceforward a consecration. The changes and the battles of 1848 did not affect him. He seems, to the very close of his life, save when the anguish of the war of 1870-71 wrested from him some outbursts of patriotic wrath, to have remained a stranger to political strife, and to have felt a kind of contempt for it. When he was at the height of his glory, he went one evening into Imperial society, where he met the highest dignitaries of the land. He returned home quite disgusted, and recorded his disgust in a letter written the next morning to a friend, in which letter he said: "The evening was filled with platitudes and nonsense. These people actually talked of nothing else but M. de Bismarck and the Luxemburg."

In 1849, while France was still tremulous from the shock of the recent explosion, Flaubert set out on a journey up the Nile, through Egypt and Nubia, along the borders of the Red Sea, into Palestine and Syria, into Cyprus and Rhodes; then to Asia Minor, Turkey in Europe, and Greece, all the while accompanied by his faithful and amiable friend, M. Maxime Du Camp, who still survives him, and who has left us a noble and impressive monograph of the great author. All these years the talent, which had been of slow and subtle development, was crystallising; the minute and careful observation for which Flaubert was so noted among his friends was destined to bear splendid fruit in the masterly pages of *Salammbô*. Flaubert was a thorough convert to the idea that every material thing the description of which is permanent in literature must have been seen, grappled with, handled, lived; and out of this intense conviction was distilled the alembic of his style: out of it came the immortality of his best work.

These years of travel were merry and happy as well as profitable, and they were studded with picturesque adventures,

INTRODUCTION.

which Lamartine would have woven into a dozen fascinating volumes, but which Flaubert sternly compressed into the great volume of his experience, keeping the combined education and remembrances for the atmosphere of the work which he meant to make abiding. Maxime Du Camp has given us many charming accounts of Flaubert's wanderings among the hills of Greece; his frolics at Corinth or in the plain of Argolis; his fantastical pilgrimage to the fountain between Argos and Nauplia, where Juno went each year in search of new youth and beauty; and his furious digging in Mycenæ before Dr. Schliemann had been able to undertake his excavations. Those critics who unadvisedly attacked Flaubert after the publication of *Salammbô*, as to the depth and extent of his archæological studies, might have acted with more caution had they known how, during those years of travel, Flaubert read, investigated, unearthed, and ransacked in museums, and with what earnestness he verified even the smallest details which were to be of use to him in his future work. At Pompeii, at Rome, in Sicily, tracked by *gendarmes*, arrested by suspicious inhabitants and haled before country justices, Flaubert continued his researches. "The police followed us," says Maxime Du Camp, "into the trenches of Herculaneum and on to the rocks of Cape Misenum." To his long wanderings in Phœnicia, in 1850, is due much of the subtle charm which exhales from the pages of *Salammbô*, in which the author has resurrected for us the life of that ancient world where the Hebrew fugitives from Egypt, the dauntless merchant-warriors, were supreme until the final triumph of that Rome which they had defied with the arrogance of success for so long a time.

After his return to France, Flaubert settled down in the parental home at Croisset, near Rouen; "and," says M. Du Camp, "as in the Orient he had been homesick for Normandy, so in Normandy he was homesick for the Orient.

INTRODUCTION.

Poor great man! whose mind was always grasping after that which was past, and always regretting and never enjoying." While his friends were founding the *Revue de Paris*, with which his name was in later days to be connected, he was writing and re-writing, passing long months in doubt and depression, followed by periods of literary enthusiasm, when the hundred projects boiling in his brain seemed each to get in the way of the other. "Before a pleasant fire, by the genial light of the lamps," says M. Du Camp, describing his friend at that time, "Flaubert seemed to grow intoxicated with the sound of his own voice. The lyric force which filled him seemed to overflow. At such moments, he swore that he would at once publish his books, and delighted in the prospect of frightening the *bourgeois* with new ideas, and newer forms of expression." But the next morning, Flaubert would appear quite exhausted, and given up to despair, and would say to the same friends who had listened with astonishment to his declarations of the previous evening, "I shall never publish anything." These alternate periods of exalted enthusiasm and of discouragement lasted, says M. Du Camp, about fifteen days, after which Flaubert would settle down to work once more. Finally, he decided that he would go up to Paris, and consult Théophile Gautier, who was in those days a great authority; and his friend Bouilhet, the poet, said to him laughingly, "You remind me of Panurge going to consult the oracles."

Flaubert took to Théophile Gautier the manuscript of the *Temptation of St. Anthony*, a strange volume, into which he had put so much of the force alluded to by M. Du Camp, and of his pronounced hatred for the Philistines. The gentle Gautier smiled at the excess of conscience displayed by Flaubert, and at his doubts of his own work. He reminded him that a writer wrote works for the purpose of publishing them; that he should not sit musing over them year after year, but should give them to the public, and

INTRODUCTION.

abide by the public's verdict. Flaubert, however, was like those good people who ask financiers for advice as to investment, and then take a contrary decision. He put the *Temptation of St. Anthony* back in his portfolio, and it was not until a lengthy period had elapsed that he drew therefrom another and a singular book, destined to create a marked impression, and published it in the *Revue de Paris*, which had been founded by Maxime Du Camp. This book was *Madame Bovary*, with which Flaubert's name has unluckily been more closely associated in the minds of English-speaking peoples than with the glowing and majestic pages of his great historical romance.

The mention of *Madame Bovary* brings us naturally to the contemplation of certain peculiarities in Flaubert's literary method, and especially in his style, methods which have been the subjects of hundreds of essays, and of some bitter polemics by continental critics during the past generation. Flaubert has been called by some the "father of naturalism," and was even wont to allude to himself as a disciple of the realistic method in literature. But to my thinking he is more accurately described, in the phrase of a recent writer, as "that lingering lover of the romantic school, elevated, despite himself, to the high post of pontiff of realism." He was certainly the originator in France of the school to which belong the De Goncourts, Emile Zola, and other men, who have had far greater pecuniary successes than Flaubert. Many careless observers of the French literary movement have fancied that they could directly trace the inspiration of Emile Zola in his most unbridled and erotic effusions to *Madame Bovary* and the spirit which presided at the writing of such a book.

But the truth is that Zola and the men of his type are seceders from the school which Flaubert founded. They have gone to an extreme at which Flaubert's wisdom, his dignity, and his devotion to literature, would never have permitted him to arrive. His disdain for the conventional restrictions of the cold and classical school was not so great as to lead him to indecencies, or to pervert his imagination. *Madame Bovary* was a daring book, but its atmosphere was not impure. Here Flaubert truly handled the pen as if it were a scalpel. A *bourgeois* himself, and the son of *bourgeois* parents, he wrote down with masterly skill and frankness the petty vices of the *bourgeois* world, and with unerring finger pointed out their causes and their fatal results. *Madame Bovary* caused a profound sensation. The Imperial Government thought it necessary to prosecute its author for immorality. The *Revue de Paris* gained from this suit against Flaubert a fame which it might otherwise never have attained, and Flaubert emerged from the obscurity of Croisset into the full glare of Parisian celebrity, and at the same time found himself triumphantly acquitted of the charge brought against him. Many years afterwards, when he was ill, dispirited, sorely tried by fortune, and saw no companions save the few of the faithful in the little circle in Paris, he was wont mockingly to allude to Zola and the others as people whom he had invented, and who had won fortunes and honours ten times greater than those accorded the inventor.

"By means of this book alone," says a French critic, alluding to *Madame Bovary*, "one might form an accurate conception of the poesy of realism as Flaubert understood it. The pen is an instrument destined to reproduce all the plastic combinations of human existence. The moral world offering to imitation neither form nor colour, an imagination which need not occupy itself with the saving of souls is supposed to confine itself to the physical world, as an immense studio filled with models, all of which have the same value in its sight, for it would be almost like blaming the Creator if one were to set aside or correct any of his creatures, as unworthy of exact reproduction. The school even requires that we should abstain from judging people, making *form*

INTRODUCTION.

everything, and conclusions and the moral nothing; in other words, this attractive school has neither sentiment nor idea, but execution."

This may have been a correct statement of Flaubert's school, and of his method when *Madame Bovary* was published, but it would not serve to describe the spirit which dictated *Salammbô*. Shortly after the publication of *Madame Bovary,* Flaubert published in the *Artiste* a series of studies of fragmentary character, the remnants of that manuscript of the *Temptation of St. Anthony* which he had shown to Gautier. The characterisation of this work I leave to more competent hands. It is sufficient here to say that it shows, perhaps in greater degree than any other of Flaubert's works, his wonderful knowledge of the French language. "He has," says one of his countrymen, "the whole French dictionary in his head, and possibly a good many other dictionaries as well. He knows the terms which fix the idea most strongly in the mind. There is nothing floating or indecisive in his expression; but the word invariably conveys delicate shades of meaning."

In 1858 Flaubert set out on the journey which was to be the crown of his life, and which resulted in the creation of *Salammbô*. He went first to Tunis, and thence to the ruins of Carthage, where he remained for a long time, groping with the ferocious industry of an archæologist in the mysterious ruins of the proud city swept away by Scipio, and of the pathetic fate of which there are no minute chronicles, save that of the Greek Polybius, renowned among the "special correspondents" of the elder world.

It was well to call the story of *Salammbô* the "resurrection of Carthage"; and for those who doubt the skill of the magician, as some were found to doubt when the work was first published, they have only to turn to the simple narrative of the truceless war between the Carthaginians and those barbarian mercenaries whom they could not or would not pay for their

INTRODUCTION.

long services, to see how grand a spectacle has been grouped about the war which historians regarded as uninteresting. Flaubert follows the historic facts with the closest fidelity, save in the two or three simple cases in which he has changed the date of an occurrence in order to heighten the dramatic force of the narrative. The great Hamilcar Barca, the father of Hannibal, had sent home the Barbarian followers with whom he had been waging his difficult war in Sicily, with instructions that they be paid off by detachments. But the Carthaginians, who had grown covetous after the many privations which their foreign campaigns had cost them, declined to pay the mercenaries, but let them rest in idleness and feasting, until they were thoroughly angered and mutinous, and then sent them to another town, with instructions to await the money. Here, Greeks and Iberians, Libyans and Ligurians, Balearic slingers and run-away slaves, finally revolted, and headed by Spendius, the crafty Greek, Mâtho the Libyan, and Autharitus the Gaul, marched back to Carthage to begin the stupendous siege which Hamilcar finally crushed by his gigantic efforts, and which he punished with a cruelty almost without parallel. Spendius and Autharitus, and the other minor chiefs, were crucified; but Mâtho was taken prisoner and put to death, being led in triumph through the streets of the Carthage which he had so long threatened and defied during the score of years separating the first from the second Punic wars. Polybius characterises the struggle as more cruel and inhuman than any other of which he had heard.

Upon this Flaubert has grafted the bewitching tale of the fierce and sensuous passion of Mâtho, the Libyan chief, for Salammbô, the daughter of Hamilcar. Mâtho, aided by Spendius, penetrates into Carthage by night during the siege, enters the temple of Tanit, and carries off the mysterious veil of the goddess, whom the Carthaginians held in a special and peculiar veneration. Clad in this mantle, which to look upon was profanation for the worshippers, he passes into the private apartments of Salammbô, there declares his passion, and then retires, serene and composed before the mob which comes to kill him, but dares not touch him because of the sacred veil or mantle. He carries this talisman into the camp of the Barbarians, and thither Salammbô, commanded by the priests, comes to rescue it at whatever risk of life or of virtue. Mâtho delivers it up. The consecration of the loves of the barbarian and the daughter of Hamilcar is the fruit of this interview; and thenceforward the story moves nobly through a succession of grand military scenes, interspersed with delightful pictures of the intimate and familiar life within Carthage, until it arrives at its tragic close, serene as that of an epic, in which Salammbô dies after she has seen the captured Mâtho slain at her feet while she stands on the throne beside the bridegroom to whom her father has given her.

The exquisite humanity of all the central figures in this book, which would make an illustrious play, is here and there almost Shakespearean. It is true that Flaubert, with his exaggerated dread of a display of sensibility, has sometimes so hurried along the impetuous torrents of the narrative that one experiences a feeling of breathlessness, a desire to catch at something, and linger by the way. So, too, the French critics have accused him of insufficient sense of contrast, of making all his pictures too imposing. Singularly striking as the figure and character of Salammbô are, poetic and sensuous as are the descriptions of her worship on the housetops, her communion with the sacred serpent, and her adoration of Tanit, and the other false goddesses and gods of Carthage, the great figure in the book is that of the veteran father, Hamilcar, the admiral of the seas, the master of slaves and of the lives of men, the politician and leader, the prince of expedients and of strategy, the father of the general who was to cross the Alps and fall with his army upon bewildered Italy like a storm of fire. From the first entrance of

Hamilcar into the story we breathe a larger air; we feel the impression of truth, and of transcript from the truth. It is as if Flaubert himself were one of the ancients, and had written what he said and knew, even as Polybius did. There is something infinitely touching and frightful at the same time in the portrait of Hamilcar, in his passionate admiration and love for the little Hannibal, in the grand description of his mastery of the Elders and Patricians when he returns from Sicily, in his pilgrimages through his farms, and among his slaves, in his contemplation of his almost countless treasures, and finally in his semi-barbaric sacrifices to Moloch and the ferocious joy with which he seizes upon Spendius and the other dying chiefs when he has enticed them into their death-trap.

Yet Salammbô is noble as a daughter of the gods; noble in her maiden contemplation of mysteries which she dare not even think of fathoming; noble in her self-sacrifice for Carthage; noble in her father's wrath at what he thinks her fall from the high virtue befitting a daughter of Hamilcar; noble in the midst of those patrician splendours which Flaubert describes with such wealth of detail; and there are certain bits of descriptive writing showing Salammbô and her attendants in their various avocations, which give, in the highest sense of the term, the "colour compressed in words," which the critic found in the famous line in *Iphigenie*, where Racine, in a dozen words, depicts the sleeping sea with the sleeping fleet crowded with sleeping men. Such effects cost Flaubert infinite anguish—the word is not too strong, for he struggled with his phrases as with a nervous malady. There is something of Meissonier in the elaboration of his pictures, while oddly enough there is also in his work the same grand and thrilling sense of combination of vast subjects to be found on the canvases of Rubens. In fact, Flaubert was like a painter trying to cover a canvas worthy of Rubens with the excessively minute and perfect finish of Meissonier. What wonder that his life was filled with unremitting study and toil, and that the practice of his art almost broke his spirit?

Flaubert had much trouble with the critics. Sainte-Beuve administered to him one of his amiable but somewhat pretentious scoldings, to which Flaubert responded in December of 1862 with commendable promptness and almost a complete refutation. Sainte-Beuve, like lesser men, presumed to doubt the wisdom of applying to antiquity the processes of the modern novel, whereupon Flaubert entered into one of his fine rages, in which he sometimes forgot his purity of style, and scolded, railed, and battled like the Frenchmen of his time. But as one said of him, shortly after this cudgelling with the critics: "he comes out of it a much greater person than before." Did a writer presume to criticise a single description of Carthaginian archæology or religion, as it appeared in *Salammbô*, Flaubert instantly brought up an authority to crush the unhappy wight. Even for the pardonable changes in the spelling of names, to reconcile them to corrupt modern usage, Flaubert had his defensive reasons. Whenever he had taken a liberty, he admitted it, as in his expressed opinion that there was really no aqueduct leading to ancient Carthage, although the ruins of an aqueduct may be seen to-day. That Hanno was crucified in front of Tunis he admits to be untrue, and says that the execution took place in Sardinia. M Frœhner, the editor of the *Revue Contemporaine*, had violently attacked *Salammbô*, as false in its pretended erudition; but Flaubert in a dozen pages made short work of him. In fact, M. Frœhner, although he returned to the attack, was at last completely crushed.

Even had Flaubert paid less attention to the perfection of detail in his description of these ancient battles, and these imagined or somewhat idealised loves and lives in the midst of the truceless war's long and gloomy course, his work would have been certain to endure. There is a magic in the atmosphere, a truth in the delineation of passion, so abundant a sympathy in the accounts of the battles and the privations of the combatants, and such a simplicity and strength in the hundreds of *genre* pictures scattered through the book, that it must be accounted a masterpiece. So long as men battle and women love, so long as human nature suffers no change in its great attributes, so long will the story of Hamilcar and of Spendius, of Mâtho and of Salammbô, of the leprous Hanno and the fiery Narr' Havas, be read with strong emotion and with avidity. It awakens only noble thoughts, despite its sensuous setting. It is like an exquisite piece of Greek sculpture, mighty, yet too ethereal in its beauty for modern hands to create, set against a back-ground flooded with sumptuous colour.

The great scenes in the book, the banquet and riot of the barbarians, their contemplation of the crucified lions on the road to Sicca, the preaching of the revolt by Spendius, the entrance into the temple of Tanit by night, the contemplation of Mâtho enshrouded in the veil by Salammbô, the arrival of Hamilcar from Sicily, the interview in the tent, the Carthaginian prisoners in the ditches filled with water, the woes of Hanno, the deaths of the barbarians entrapped into the defile, the sacrifices to Moloch, and the death of Salammbô, are every one genuine works of art, imperishable as diamonds ; and if the French critics did not at first find sufficient contrast in these paintings on the sublimely sculptured portico, they discovered them when they had bestowed proper attention upon the work.

The originality of Flaubert's character is shown in all his subsequent works, as well as in those preceding *Salammbô*, in different vein from that adopted in the Carthaginian tale. In this latter, Flaubert rises to his completest dignity as an artist : in the others he is the *rageur*, the battler, the beater of bucklers, and is evidently very often ill at ease with himself. Fond of discussion of theories, he maintained an immense correspondence with George Sand, in which he pilloried everything commonplace, classing as such her notion that one might preach in books. His *Sentimental Education*, and other books of lesser importance from his pen, were written with all his determined straining after effects of words. He even graduated his sentences to musical notes. "Phrases," he cried, "which make me enthusiastic with admiration, appear to others very ordinary. I would give all the legends of Gavarni for certain expressions and certain masterly cuts of style." He was tempted once, in 1874, to try for success upon the stage, where so many brilliant men, amply successful in their own lines, have insisted upon coming to grief. His piece of *The Candidate*, a comic sketch of manners during an election, was a complete failure. At the end of the fourth representation at the Vaudeville, Flaubert was himself convinced, and admitted, not without rage, that he had made a mistake. It was, in fact, an excursion into light literature for which he had not sufficiently prepared himself. A comedy written in six weeks could not hope to compare with *Salammbô*, which was the work of such laborious years. Later on, in his three tales, *Herodias*, *St. Julien l'Hospitalier*, and *Un Cœur Simple*, he showed the great analytic force which had done so much to secure the success of *Madame Bovary*. These tales were little lyrics in prose. They were published in 1877, and brought popular interest again to bear upon Flaubert, who would better have paused there, and never have written the adventures of Bouvard and Pecuchet, the chronicles of the useless life of two *bourgeois* imbeciles, whom he intended as two characters typical of that human folly and weakness which he so much derided.

With his closing years came the trials from which few are exempt. The death of his mother was a severe blow to one who raised his family affection to the height of a veritable religion, and who had always been delightful and delicate in the exercise of his friendships with men and women. Then, by a stroke of generosity, he swept away nearly all that he had, except the right to live in the old house at Croisset, with the knowledge that it belonged to another heir. The Government gave him a small sinecure, which he was with difficulty persuaded to accept, and from March of 1879 until early in May of 1880, he passed an agitated and wearied existence. The solitude which he once so loved in his retreat at Croisset now alarmed him, and he sought for company. The nervous malady with which he had been all his life afflicted finally manifested itself in frequent crises, which he tried in vain to dispel by breathing ether. He had a fatal apoplectic attack, battling against it to the last moment, like the vigorous and lusty being that he was, as if clinging to the life which still possessed many tortures for him, yet out of which he had carved an immortal reputation, founded on at least two works of singular genius and one of surpassing beauty. Shortly after his death the old house at Croisset was sold, and to-day a distillery is erected on the site of the rustic retreat to which Tourgueneff loved to find his way, and where Flaubert had passed many profitable years.

Between Tourgueneff and Flaubert the affection was entirely mutual. Each recognised in the other a consummate artist; each knew the other gifted with the so rare capacity of making true pictures with noble and elevated language. Each had the requisite proportion in his literary character to enable him to avoid falling into the excesses of the naturalist school and to remain capable of practising an eclecticism, founded on what is true in the romantic and in the realistic schools.

Flaubert and Tourgueneff shared each other's deep human sympathies; yet each scoffed at the folly of the conventional men and women. Each wrote bitter pages of satire, and each held pure and elevated ideals of politics. Each, too, had the wonderful faculty of reproducing with words the sounds of the boughs moved by the wind, the effect of summer moonlight on the quiet waves, the rhythmic swaying of grasses on the virgin prairie—and all those manifestations of nature which touch the hearts of all men in common, whatever be their station or education ; and this was one of the secrets of their success. By their conscientious study of nature they came to know how to interpret her. The cold classicists of the eighteenth century knew little of these things, nor can they ever hope to be loved like Flaubert and Tourgueneff, the two great rugged twins of the new method in literature.

EDWARD KING.

Villa des Ternes, Paris.

SALAMMBÔ.

CHAPTER I.

THE FEAST.

It was at Megara in the suburbs of Carthage in Hamilcar's gardens.

The soldiers whom he had commanded in Sicily had been accorded by the Grand Council a great feast, to celebrate the anniversary of the battle of Eryx.

The captains, wearing bronze cothurnes, were seated in the central avenue, beneath a purple canopy fringed with gold, extending from the stable walls on one side to the first terrace of the palace on the other; while the majority of the common soldiers were out under the trees. Farther on in the gardens appeared a number of flat-roofed structures, comprising wine-presses, wine-cellars, bakeries, warehouses, and arsenals. The park also environed a court for elephants, pits for ferocious animals, and a prison for slaves.

Fig-trees surrounded the kitchens; beyond, a sycamore grove extended to masses of verdure, wherein the pomegranates shone resplendent in the midst of white tufts of cotton plants; vines laden with clusters of grapes interwove through pine branches; under plane trees a field of roses bloomed, and here and there interspersing the green turf, lilies waved gracefully. The pathways were strewn with black sand mixed with powdered coral, and through the centre, from end to end of this vast park, an avenue of cypress trees formed a double colonnade of green obelisks.

Hamilcar's palace, built of yellow-spotted Numidian marble, of four terraced stories, towered above a substructure of huge courses of stone; its grand, straight, ebony stairway, bearing on the corner of each step the prow of a vanquished galley; its red doors quartered by a black cross, protected at the base from scorpions by brass grillages, and the openings at the top masked by trellisses of golden baguettes,—seemed to the soldiers, in its display of barbaric opulence, as solemn and impenetrable as Hamilcar's face.

At early dawn the convalescents who had slept in the temple of Eschmoûn set out to attend the feast, and dragged themselves on their crutches to the gardens.

By all the diverse pathways soldiers poured forth incessantly, like torrents precipitated from heights into a lake. Bewildered kitchen-slaves, half-naked, could be seen running about between the trees in confusion, and the startled gazelles bleated as they scampered over the lawns.

The setting sun and the perfumes of the lemon-trees rendered even heavier and more oppressive the exhalations of this sweating, seething crowd. Here, upon this festal occasion, were gathered men of all nations: Ligurians, Lusitanians, Balearic warriors, Negroes, and Roman fugitives. Here could be heard, mingled with the heavy Dorian patois, the Celtic syllables, rattling like battle-chariots; and the Ionian terminations, clashing with the consonants of the desert, harsh as the yelpings of jackals. Greeks could be recognised by their slender figures; Egyptians by their high, square shoulders; Cantabrians by their broad, muscular legs; Carians swayed proudly the plumes on their helmets; Cappadocian archers were conspicuous by the large flowers painted over their entire bodies; and some Lydians feasted arrayed in the robes, slippers, and earrings of women; others, for the sake of pomp, had daubed themselves with vermilion, resembling, as they moved about, animated coral statues.

To partake of the feast these men stretched themselves out upon cushions, or ate as they squatted on their haunches around large plateaus; or even lay flat on their bellies, and pulled towards themselves pieces of meat, which they munched, leaning on their elbows, in the pacific attitude of lions dismembering their prey. The late comers, standing against the trees, looked wistfully at the low tables, half concealed beneath scarlet cloths, and the sumptuous repast, eagerly awaiting their turns.

Hamilcar's kitchens being insufficient for this occasion, the Grand Council had supplied slaves, utensils, and couches. Bright, huge fires blazed in the centre of the gardens, before which beeves were roasting, imparting to the vicinity the appearance of a battle-field upon which the dead were being burned. On the tables were placed loaves of bread sprinkled with aniseseed, alternating with large cheeses, heavier than discs. Bowls of wine, and canthari filled with water, were placed by the side of gold filigree baskets containing flowers.

The delight experienced in being able at last, after prolonged privations, to gorge themselves at will, dilated the eyes of these starving warriors, and here and there songs burst forth. Hamilcar's absence contributed to the freedom with which the multitude ate, drank, and caroused.

First—birds, covered with green sauce, were served in red clay dishes embellished with black designs; then all species of shell-fish caught on the Punic coast, followed by broths of barley, wheat, and beans; and snails with cumin, on yellow amber plates. Afterwards the tables were covered with every variety of meats: roasted antelopes, garnished with their horns—peacocks in their plumage—whole sheep cooked in sweet wine—legs of camels and buffaloes—hedgehogs, with garum sauce—fried grasshoppers, and preserved dormice. In Tamrapanni wooden bowls, large pieces of fat floated in the midst of saffron—every dish overflowed with pickle, truffles, and assafœtida; pyramids of fruit rolled over honey-cakes; nor were forgotten some of the red-haired, big-bellied little dogs fattened on olive-marc; the Carthaginian practice of eating which was loathed by all other people.

The surprise of these new dishes to this rude multitude excited the greed of their stomachs. Gauls, with their long hair coiled up on the top of their heads, snatched from each other water-melons and lemons, which they crunched, rinds and all ; Negroes, who had never before seen lobsters, tore their faces with the red claws ; shaven-faced Greeks, whiter than marble, threw behind them the pickings-off from their plates, and herdsmen of Bruttium clothed in wolves' skins silently devoured their portions with their faces buried in their dishes.

Night fell. The canopy that had been spread over the cypress avenue was now withdrawn, and torches were brought forth. The vacillating petroleum lights, burning in porphyry vases, frightened in the tops of the cedars the apes consecrated to the moon ; the terrified chatterings of these animals filled the soldiers with great glee. Oblong flames trembled over the brazen cuirasses ; all manner of scintillations flashed from the dishes incrusted with precious stones. Bowls bordered with convex mirrors multiplied the reflected images, enlarging every object so strangely as to attract the attention of the soldiers, who, in astonishment, crowded around, gazing at themselves, or making grimaces to provoke the laughter of their comrades by the grotesque reflections. Becoming boisterous, they threw at each other across the tables the ivory stools and the gold spatulas. They swallowed, in gluttonish mouthfuls, all the Greek wine contained in wine skins ; all that from Campania held in amphoras, and that from Cantabria, which was drawn from hogsheads ; as well as the jujube, cinnamon, and lotus wines. All were drunk, or wastefully spilled upon the ground, forming puddles in which the rioters would slip. In dense vapours, the fumes of the viands, mixing with the heavy breaths, rose in the foliage. In a nameless clatter mingled the crunching of jaws, din of words, outburst of wassail songs, clinking of cups, shattering of Campanian vases—scattered in a thousand fragments—and the limpid ring of large silver plates. As the drunkenness of the soldiers augmented, they recalled to memory more vividly the injustice Carthage had put upon them.

The Republic, drained by the war, had permitted all the returning troops to congregate in the city, despite the fact that General Gisco had taken the precaution to send them back in detachments, in order to facilitate their speedy payment and discharge; but the Council, believing that they would succeed in getting these warriors to consent to some diminutions, detained them. However, at present they were desirous not to be obliged to pay them. This war debt was confused in the minds of the people with the three thousand two hundred Eubœan talents exacted by Lutatius; hence these soldiers, like the Romans, were considered enemies to Carthage. The Mercenaries comprehended this feeling, therefore their indignation burst forth in menaces and irruptions. Finally, they demanded a reunion, to celebrate one of their victories: the peace party yielded, hoping at the same time to revenge itself upon Hamilcar, who had so strongly supported the war. It had been terminated contrary to his policy and efforts; so much so that despairing of help from Carthage, he placed Gisco in command of the Mercenaries, himself continuing to march towards the amber country. The Council, desirous of attracting upon Hamilcar some of the hatred the soldiers bore them, designated his palace gardens for the festival. Notwithstanding the excessive expense, Hamilcar would have to submit individually to defray the greater part of it.

Proud of having made the Republic comply with their demands on this score, the Mercenaries believed that they would also ultimately return to their native countries, with the payment for their blood in the hoods of their cloaks. But now their recent hardships, reviewed through the vapours of their present drunkenness, seemed prodigious, and too poorly recompensed at best. To one another they displayed their wounds, recounted their combats, their journeys, and the hunts peculiar to their various countries; imitating the cries and leaps of ferocious animals. They made indecent wagers, immersing their heads in amphoras of wine, there remaining drinking like thirsty dromedaries, without intermission. A Lusitanian, of gigantic height, carrying a man upon each arm, stalked about the tables, the while spurting fire from his nostrils. Lacedemonians who had not removed their cuirasses leaped about with heavy strides; others came forward like lewd women making obscene gestures; some, stripped naked, wrestled like gladiators in the midst of the feast; and a company of Greeks danced around a vase upon which they chanced to see the figures of the nymphs that ornamented it; meantime a negro pounded lustily on a brass buckler with a beef-bone.

Suddenly a plaintive chant was heard, a chant strong and soft, rising and falling on the air like the fluttering wings of a wounded bird. It was the voice of the slaves in the *ergastulum*, where they were imprisoned.

A group of soldiers bounded off, disappearing in the direction of the voices, bent upon liberating these captives. Presently they returned, chasing before them amid yells, through the dust, a score of men, distinguishable by the paler hue of their faces. These slaves wore on their shaven heads little, conical-shaped, black felt caps; their feet were shod in wooden sandals, and as they ran, their chains clattered like the iron felloes of a moving chariot. Thus driven, they finally reached the cypress avenue, where they were lost in the crowd that surrounded and interrogated them.

One of these slaves remained standing apart from the others. Through his tattered tunic could be seen on his shoulders the weals of long gashes; with chin lowered he looked suspiciously about him as he half-closed his eyelids, in the glare of the torches; but, so soon as he seemed convinced in his own mind that none of the armed men wanted to harm him, a deep sigh of relief escaped from his breast, and he stammered and mouthed, while tears bathed his face; then, abruptly seizing a full cantharus by its rings, he raised it at arm's-length on high, straight in the air, revealing chains dangling from his wrists.

He looked up to the sky, still holding the cup, as he cried :—"All hail! first, to thee, Baal Eschmoûn, liberator, whom the people of my country call Æsculapius! Hail! ye, spirits of the springs! of the light! and of the woods! and ye, Gods, hidden beneath the mountains and in the caverns of the earth! and ye strong men in shining armour, who have delivered me!"

He dropped the cantharus, and told his story.

His name was Spendius; he had been captured by the Carthaginians during the battle of the Ægatian islands. He spoke Greek, Ligurian, and Phœnician. Once again he thanked the Mercenaries, kissed their hands, felicitated them on their feast; but expressed great astonishment that he did not see the golden cups of the Sacred Legion. These cups were embellished on each of their six golden faces by an emerald vine, and belonged to a militia exclusively comprised of young patricians of the tallest stature. To see them was a privilege, considered almost a sacerdotal honour, and nothing in the treasury of the Republic was so coveted by the Mercenaries. They detested the Legion because of this possession, and had been known to risk their lives for the ineffable pleasure of merely drinking out of these cups. Instigated by what this slave said, the soldiers commanded that the cups should be fetched to them. The slaves said that they were deposited with the Syssites, companies of merchants who ate in common; but at this hour all the members of the Syssites slept.

"Let them be wakened!" responded the Mercenaries.

After a second evasion, one of the slaves explained that the cups were locked up in a temple.

"Let the temple be opened!" replied the soldiers; and when the slaves trembled, avowing that veritably the cups were in the custody of General Gisco, they yelled, "Let him bring them!"

Presently Gisco appeared at the end of the garden, with an escort of the Sacred Legion: his ample black mantle was adjusted on his head by a gold mitre starred with precious stones; its folds falling all around him, reached down to his horse's hoofs and blended in the distance with the shadows of night. Nothing could be seen of him but his white beard, the radiancy of his coiffure, and his triple collar of wide blue plaques, which, agitated by the motion of his horse, struck against his breast.

As he entered the gardens, the soldiers saluted him with great cheers, crying out:—"The cups! The cups!"

He commenced by declaring "that if one only considered their courage, they certainly merited the cups,"—at which the crowd fairly howled with joy in applauding him. "He knew it well, he who had commanded them, and had returned with the last cohort, on the last galley!"

"It is true! it is true!" they cried out.

"Nevertheless," continued Gisco, "the Republic respects the divisions of the people, their customs, and their religions; at Carthage they are all free. As to the gold cups of the Sacred Legion, they are personal property."

Suddenly, from beside Spendius, a Gaul darted across the tables, making straight for Gisco, whom he threatened by brandishing two naked swords. Without interrupting himself, the General struck this man over the head with his heavy ivory baton, felling him to the ground; at this the Gauls all shrieked, and their fury communicating itself to the other soldiers, they turned upon the Legionaries.

Gisco shrugged his shoulders as he saw his escort grow pale: his courage would be vain against these foolish, exasperated brutes; whereas, later on perhaps he might avenge himself if he should at present check them by some strategy; so he made a sign to his guards, and they all slowly moved away. When under the entrance, he turned towards the Mercenaries, and cried out:—" You shall repent this!"

The feast recommenced; but the revellers were disturbed by the idea that Gisco might return, and invest the suburb that impinged on the last ramparts, and thus crush them against the walls. They felt alone, despite their multitude; and the vast city, with its massive piles of stairways and lofty black mansions sleeping under them in the shadow, filled them with terror: but yet more ferocious than the city, or its people, seemed its mysterious Gods. In the distance lanterns glided about the harbour, and lights could be seen in the temple of Khamoûn. Their troubled thoughts reverted to Hamilcar. Where was he? Why had he abandoned them just as peace was declared? Doubtless his dissensions with the Council had been a trick planned for their destruction. They exasperated each other by the recital of their personal wrongs, and their insatiable hatred now fell in curses upon him.

At this stage of discontent a crowd assembled under the plane trees, attracted thither by a negro who rolled about beating the ground frantically with his arms and feet, his eyes fixed, his neck contorted, and foaming at the mouth. Some one cried out that the man had been poisoned; then they all likewise believed themselves poisoned, and fell upon the slaves. A vertigo of destruction whirled over this drunken army; they struck at random, breaking, maiming, killing. Some, moved by diabolical impulse, threw lighted torches among the foliage; others leaned over the balustrade of the lions' pit, ruthlessly killing the animals with arrows; and the most venturesome recklessly ran among the elephants, and sought to hew off their trunks and destroy their tusks.

Meanwhile a group of Balearic slingers, with a view to pillage more conveniently, turned a corner of the palace, but were hindered from proceeding by a high barrier constructed of malacca-cane. However, not to be thus daunted, they severed, by the aid of poniards, the leather thongs holding the hedge together. This obstacle surmounted, they found themselves under the façade that looked towards Carthage, in another garden filled with tall vegetation. Rows of white flowers succeeded one after another, describing on the azure-coloured ground long parabolas, like the trails of shooting stars. Shadowy bushes exhaled honey-sweet, warm odours; and the trunks of trees, daubed with cinnabar, resembled blood-stained columns. In the centre were twelve copper pedestals, each one supporting a large glass bowl; the ruddy gleams filled and flickered confusedly in these hollow bowls, which simulated enormous throbbing eye-balls. The soldiers by torchlight stumbled down a deeply furrowed declivity. They descried a little lake, divided into numerous basins by partitions of blue stone. The water contained therein was so limpid, that the reflected torch flames quivered to the very bottom, striking on a bed of white shells and gold dust. All at once the water set up a bubbling, and luminous spangles glistened, as large fish, wearing precious stones in their gills, came swimming to the surface.

The soldiers, laughing immoderately, thrust their fingers through the fishes' gills, and carried them thus to the tables. These fish belonged to the Barca family, and were reputed descendants of the primordial eel-pout, which had brought to light the mystic egg wherein was hidden the Goddess.

The idea of committing a sacrilege reanimated the gluttony of the Mercenaries, which found quick vent by their kindling fires under the brass vases, and they evinced vast amusement as they watched the beautiful fish flounder about and perish in the boiling water. The throng of soldiers surged forward. Fear no longer possessed them. They again commenced their carousal and drinking. Perfumes trickled down over their foreheads, falling in large drops, moistening their tattered tunics. They leaned their fists on the tables, that seemed to them to oscillate like ships; while their large, drunken eyes turned and roved about as though seeking to devour with their glances all that they had not the power to take away. Others walked about in the midst of the plates on the crimson table-covers, breaking, with wanton kicks, the Tyrian glass phials and the ivory benches. Festal songs intermingled with the death-rattle of the attendant slaves, in their last agonies among the shattered cups. Still the soldiers demanded more wine, more meat, and gold, and shouted for women—raving deliriously in a hundred languages. Many believed themselves in the baths, deceived by the fumes floating about them; or even, whilst observing the foliage, fancied that they were engaged in hunting, and thus deluded, would rush violently upon their comrades, thinking them to be ferocious beasts.

Slowly the torches ignited the trees: the fire spread from tree to tree, until the tall mass of verdure resembled a volcano beginning to smoke. The clamour redoubled, the wounded lions roared, and the elephants trumpeted, through the darkness.

By a single flash the palace was illuminated from the bottom to its highest terrace: the centre door at the top opened, and a woman—the daughter of Hamilcar—robed in black appeared on the threshold. She came down the stairway that traversed obliquely the third story, then the second and the first; pausing on the lowest terrace at the top of the stairway of the galleys, motionless, head downcast, looking down upon the soldiers. Behind her on both sides were two long processions of pale men, clothed in white robes fringed with red, hanging straight down to their feet; their heads and eyebrows were shaven; their hands, in which they carried enormous lyres, glittered with rings. They all chanted in a shrill voice a hymn to the divinity of Carthage. These were the eunuch priests of the temple of Tanit, often summoned by Salammbô to her palace.

Finally she descended the stairway of the galleys, followed by the priests; and moved forward with her retinue under the cypress trees, between the tables at which the captains were seated, who drew back slightly to watch her as she passed. Her hair was powdered with violet dust, and, according to the fashion of Canaanite maidens, it was gathered up in the form of a tower on the crown of her head, making her appear taller: strands of pearls attached to her temples fell down to the corners of her mouth—as rosy as a half-opened pomegranate; on her neck she wore a collection of luminous gems, which imitated in their medley the scales of a sea-eel; her sleeveless tunic, made of a black tissue, starred with red flowers, exposed her bare arms, bedecked with diamonds. Between her ankles she wore a gold chainlet to regulate the length of her steps; and her voluminous dark purple mantle, of an unknown fabric, trailed, making at each step a wide billow behind her.

From time to time the priests thridded on their lyres harmonious, almost soundless, tones. During the intervals of the music could be detected a faint noise produced by her gold chainlet accompanying the measured patter of her papyrus sandals. At first no person recognised her. It was only known that she lived secluded, devoted to pious practices. During the nights the soldiers had seen her between the curling smoke arising from fuming censers, kneeling before the stars, on the top of the palace.

At this moment the moon made her appear very pale, and something of the gods seemed to envelope her like a subtle mist. Her eyes appeared to penetrate far away in the distance beyond terrestrial spaces. She advanced with her head inclined downward, holding in her right hand a small ebony lyre. They heard her murmur:

"Dead! all dead! you no longer will obey my voice when I sit on the lake shore and throw pips of water-melons into your jaws! In the depths of your eyes, more limpid than drops of the streams, rolled the mystery of Tanit!" Then she called her fish by their several names, which were the names of the months—" Siv! Sivan! Tammoûz! Eloul! Tischri! Schebar!—Ah! Goddess, pity me!"

Without comprehending her, the soldiers crowded around her, much amazed by her attire. She cast upon them a long, frightened look; then, burying her head in her bosom, she threw out her arms, repeating many times:—"What have you done? What have you done? For your enjoyment bread, meat, oil, and malobathrum were provided from the storehouses; I even had beeves fetched from Hecatompylus, and sent hunters into the desert to procure all sorts of game."

Her voice grew louder, her cheeks blazed, as she continued: "Where then do you think you are? Is this a conquered city, or the palace of a master? And what a master! The Suffete Hamilcar, my father, servitor of the Baalim! Your weapons now reek with the blood of his slaves, when it was he who refused them to Lutatius! Do you know of one in your native countries who understands better than he how to conduct battles? Behold! the steps of our palace are laden with the trophies of our victories! Go on, burn it to the ground! I will take with me the genius of our mansion—my black serpent—who sleeps up there in the lotus leaves; for when I whistle he will follow me, and when I enter my galley he will glide in the wake of the vessel on the foam of the waves."

Her thin nostrils palpitated. She crushed her finger nails against the jewels on her bosom. Her eyes became suffused as she continued: "Alas! poor Carthage! lamentable city! you no longer have for your defence the strong men of former times, who went beyond the oceans to build in your honour temples on foreign shores. All the countries about have been cultivated by you, and wave with your harvests, and the plains of the seas are furrowed by your oars!"

Then she began to chant the adventures of Melkarth, the God of the Sidonians and founder of her family. She told how he had ascended the mountains of Ersiphonia, journeyed to Tartessus, and waged war against Masisabal to avenge the Queen of Serpents.

"He pursued in the forest the female monster, whose tail undulated like a rivulet of silver over dead leaves; and he came to a prairie, over which the moon, the colour of blood, shone refulgent in a pale circle; and there he found women, half dragons, grouped around a huge fire, poised erect on their tails, thrusting out and curving their scarlet tongues, forked like fishermen's harpoons, to the very edge of the flames."

Then, without ceasing Salammbô recounted how Melkarth, after vanquishing Masisabal, had put the decapitated head of his victim at the prow of his ship: "At each surge of the waves it was plunged under the foam; and was embalmed by the sun until it became more enduring than gold, yet tears never ceased flowing from the eyes, but constantly dropped into the water." All this she chanted in old Canaanite dialect, which the Barbarians did not understand.

They demanded of one another what she could be saying to them, accompanying her words with such frightful gestures. Mounting upon the tables, the benches, and the branches of sycamores, with open mouths and outstretched necks, they endeavoured to grasp the vague stories that floated before their imaginations, through the obscurity of the theogonies, like phantoms in the clouds.

Only the beardless priests understood Salammbô. Their shrivelled hands tremblingly clutched the strings of their lyres, upon which from time to time they pulled a lugubrious chord; they were weaker than old women, and quaked as much from fear as with mystic emotion, not knowing what the soldiers might be tempted to do. However, the Barbarians did not notice the priests, for they were absorbed in listening to the chanting maiden.

No one watched her more attentively than a young Numidian chief who sat among the captains, surrounded by the soldiers of his own nation. His girdle bristled so full of darts that it made a protuberance beneath his wide mantle, fastened to his temples by a leather lacing; this garment divided and swung down over his shoulders in such a manner as to effectually hide his face in shadow, concealing all but his gleaming eyes. It was by chance that he attended this feast. His father, conforming to the custom adopted by kings of sending their sons to live in noble families in other dominions, in order to prepare future alliances, had sent him to abide with Barca. During the six months that Narr' Havas had sojourned in Carthage, he had never before seen Salammbô; and now sitting on his heels, his beard flowing down over the shafts of his javelins, he contemplated her with nostrils distended, like a leopard crouching in a jungle.

At the other side of the tables was a Libyan of colossal stature, with short, curly black hair. He was unarmed, save for his military jacket, the brass plates of which frayed the purple covering of the couch upon which he sat. A collar with a silver moon was entangled in the hairs on his breast; splashes of blood spotted his face; he leaned on his left elbow, mouth wide open, and smiled.

Salammbô ceased to employ sacred rhythm, resorting successively to the various barbaric dialects, and with delicate tact sought to soften their anger, speaking Greek to the Greeks; then turning towards the Ligurians, the Campanians, and the Negroes in turn, each, in listening, found in her voice the sweetness of his own native language.

Carried away by the memories of Carthage, she chanted the old battles against Rome, thus winning their applause. Becoming excited by the flashing of the naked swords, she cried out, with open arms. Her lyre fell, then relapsing into silence, she pressed her heart with both hands, thus resting for some minutes with closed eyes as though to relish the agitation of all these warriors.

Mâtho, the Libyan, leaned towards her; involuntarily she approached him, and urged by recognition of his pride, she poured out for him into a gold cup a long stream of wine as her reconciliation with the army.

"Drink!" she said.

He took the proffered cup, and was carrying it to his lips, when a Gaul, the same man Gisco had wounded, slapped him across the shoulders, uttering in a jovial manner insinuating pleasantries in the language of his own country. Spendius, who was not far off, volunteered to interpret.

"Speak," said Mâtho.

"The Gods patronise you, for you are about to become rich. When will the marriage be?"

"What marriage?" asked Mâtho.

"Thine; for with us," says the Gaul, "when a woman offers to drink with a warrior she proffers him her couch."

No sooner had Spendius interpreted this speech, than Narr' Havas sprang forward, pulling from his belt a javelin, poised his right foot on the edge of a table, and hurled the weapon at Mâtho. The javelin whirred between the cups, and passed through the Libyan's arm, nailing it firmly to the table, with such momentum as to cause the shaft to vibrate swiftly in the air. Mâtho quickly jerked it out; but as he was without weapons, in his rage he lifted up in his arms the heavily laden table, and pitched it against Narr' Havas. In the midst of the crowd that rushed between the two infuriated men, Numidians and the soldiers pressed so closely that they could not draw their swords. Mâtho moved forward, dealing heavy blows with his head. Finally, when he lifted his face to look about, Narr' Havas had disappeared, and Salammbô had also fled. Turning his eyes towards the palace, he noticed that the red door at the top quartered with a black cross was just closing: at once he darted off in that direction. He could be seen running between the prows of the galleys, hidden and reappearing successively the length of the three stairways till he at last reached the red door; this he fruitlessly threw himself against with all his weight. Panting, breathless, he leaned against the wall to keep from falling.

A man had followed him, and as he crossed the

shadows—for the lights of the feast were obscured by an angle of the palace,—he recognised Spendius.

"Go back!" exclaimed he to the intruder.

The slave, without answering, began to tear his tunic with his teeth; then kneeled beside Mâtho and took hold of his arm, delicately feeling in the dark, to discover the wound he had so recently received. Under a ray of moonlight that just then shimmered between the clouds, Spendius perceived in the middle of the arm a gaping wound; he rolled around it the strips he had torn off from his tunic; but Mâtho, with irritability, said:

"Leave me! leave me!"

"No!" replied the slave "you delivered me from the *ergastulum*. I am yours! you are henceforth my master! Command me!"

Hugging close the wall, Mâtho made the circuit of the terrace, attentively listening at every step; darting at intervals glances through the golden trellisses into the silent apartments. At last he paused in a despairing manner. The slave said to him:

"Listen—Oh! do not despise me for my weakness; I have lived in this palace, I can crawl like a viper between its walls. Come, there is in the Chamber of the Ancestors an ingot of gold under each slab, and a subterranean passage leading to their tombs."

"Well, what of that?" asked Mâtho.

Spendius was silent.

Thus, standing on the terrace, an immense expanse of shadow spread out before them that seemed full of vague masses, like the gigantic billows of a black, petrified ocean. But on the eastern horizon a luminous streak appeared; and to the left, the canals of Megara began to ray with their white sinuosities the verdant gardens. The conical roofs of the heptagonal temples, the stairways, the terraces, the ramparts, all became gradually defined in the pale dawn; and surrounding the peninsula of Carthage a girdle of white foam fluctuated, and the emerald sea seemed congealing in the coolness of morning. In proportion as the rosy sky widened, the tall mansions climbing up the slope rose higher and massed together, resembling a herd of black goats descending the mountains. The deserted streets stretched out; palm trees here and there jutting beyond the walls did not stir; the full cisterns appeared like silver shields lost in the courtyards; on the promontory of Hermæum the lighthouse beacon grew fainter. On the summit of the Acropolis in the cypress-groves the horses of Eschmoûn, just seeing the light, placed the hoofs of their forefeet upon the marble parapet, neighing shrilly as they faced the rising sun. The sun arose. Spendius lifted his arms and uttered a cry of adoration.

All was pulsating in a ruddy flood, as though the God, rending himself, poured forth in full rays upon Carthage the golden rain of his veins. The prows of the galleys sparkled, the roof of Khamoûn appeared ablaze, and through the open doors lights could be descried in the interior of the temple. The wheels of large chariots coming from the country to the city marts rumbled over the pavements; dromedaries loaded with baggage descended the slopes; money-changers in the thoroughfares took down the weather-boards from their shops; storks flew, and white sails fluttered athrill with day.

In the groves of Tanit could be heard the tambourines of the sacred courtesans; and at the point of Mappals the furnaces used for baking clay coffins began to smoke.

Spendius leaning over the terrace, gnashed his teeth, repeating "Ah, yes,... .yes,... master, I comprehend why you just now disdained to pillage the mansion."

Mâtho was aroused by the whisper of this man's voice, yet he did not seem to understand.

Spendius resumed, "Ah, what wealth! and the men who possess it have not even the weapons to protect it." Then, with his right hand extended, he pointed out to Mâtho some people outside of the pier, crawling on the sand seeking for gold dust.

"Look!" he exclaimed "the Republic is like those wretched ones grovelling on the sea-beach. She also plunges her avaricious arms into the sea-sands, and the roar of the billows so fills her ears, that she would not hear the step of a master coming up behind her!"

Drawing Mâtho along to the end of the terrace, the slave pointed out the garden wherein the sun shone on the soldiers' swords that were hanging up in the trees.

"But here are strong men who are exasperated by hatred; and nothing attaches them to Carthage, neither families, nor oaths, nor gods!"

Mâtho remained leaning against the wall. Spendius drew nearer to him, pursuing in a low voice:

"Do you comprehend me, soldier? We shall go

about arrayed in purple like satraps. We shall bathe in perfumes. I shall in turn have my slaves! Are you not weary of drinking camp vinegar, and of always hearing the trumpets? You will repose perhaps later on, will you not? When some one pulls off your cuirass to throw your body to the vultures! or possibly when leaning on a staff, blind, feeble, lame, you hobble about from portal to portal and recount to the pickle vendors and to the little children the tale of your youth! For one moment recall all the injustice of your chiefs, the encampments in the snow, the forced marches, exposure to the sun, the tyrannies of discipline, and the eternal threat of the cross! After so much misery, a collar of honour is given to you, as one hangs a girdle of bells around asses' necks to divert them on their toilsome marches and render them insensible to their fatigue. A man like you, braver than Pyrrhus! If you desire all that, very good! Ah, but you would be happy in the grand, fresh halls, listening to the sound of lyres as you lie on flowers, amused by buffoons and women! Do not tell me that the undertaking is impossible! Have not the Mercenaries already taken possession of Rhegium and other strong places in Italy? Who hinders you? Hamilcar is absent; the people execrate the Rich; Gisco has no power over the cowards who surround him; but you are brave, the soldiers will obey you. Command them! Carthage is ours; let us fall upon her!"

"No!" said Mâtho; "the malediction of Moloch weighs upon me. I felt it in her eyes, and just now I have seen a black ram recoil in the temple!" then adding, as he looked around him: "Where is she?"

THE FEAST.

Spendius now perceived that an immense inquietude absorbed Mâtho, and he dared not speak.

Behind them the trees yet smoked; and from the charred branches carcasses of half-burned apes tumbled down from time to time among the dishes; drunken soldiers with open mouths snored by the side of corpses; and those who were awake lowered their heads, dazzled by the glare of daylight. The trampled earth was covered with bloody pools. The elephants swayed their bleeding trunks between the pickets of their paddocks. In the open granaries could be seen sacks of wheat scattered about, and under the gateways a compact line of chariots heaped up by the Barbarians; in the cedars, peacocks perched, spread their tails and squawked.

Mâtho's immobility astonished Spendius. He was now even paler than before, and his eyes fixedly followed some object visible on the horizon, as he leaned with both hands on the edge of the terrace. Spendius also, leaning over, discovered what thus occupied him. In the distance a point of gold turned in the dust on the road leading to Utica. It was the axle of a chariot drawn by two mules, guided by a slave who ran at the end of the pole, holding the bridle. Two women were seated in the chariot. The manes of the mules were puffed out in Persian fashion between their ears, under a netting of blue pearls.

Spendius, recognising them, suppressed a cry. Behind, a wide veil floated on the breeze.

CHAPTER II.

AT SICCA.

Two days later the Mercenaries left Carthage. To each soldier was given a piece of money, upon the stipulated condition that he should go into camp at Sicca, and they were told, upon their departure from the city, with all manner of fawning:

"You are the saviours of Carthage, but you will certainly starve her if you remain here, for the city will become insolvent. You must, for your own preservation, withdraw; but by such a concession you will secure the Republic's goodwill. We will immediately levy taxes to complete your payment, and equip galleys to conduct you to your native countries."

The soldiers did not know what response to make to such discourses. These men, accustomed to war, becoming weary of sojourning in the city, were not difficult to convince. The entire populace of Carthage mounted on the city walls to watch the departing soldiers, as they defiled through the street of Khamoûn by the gate of Cirta, pell-mell—archers with hoplites, captains with common soldiers, Lusitanians with Greeks. They marched boldly, making their heavy cothurnes ring on the pavements. Their armour was defaced by dents made by the catapults, their faces were sunburnt from long exposure on battle-fields. From their mouths, covered with heavy beards, rasping yells escaped; their torn coats of mail rattled upon the hilts of their swords, and through the rents in the metal were revealed bare limbs as terrific as war-engines. Sarissas, spears, felt-caps, and bronze helmets all swayed as by a single rocking movement. This long array of armed men poured forth between the high six-storied mansions daubed with bitumen, making the very walls crack as they overflowed the street. From behind iron or wicker grills, veiled women silently watched them pass.

The terraces, the fortifications, and the walls were fairly hidden under the throng of Carthaginians attired in black, and the sailors' tunics looked like spots of blood amongst this sombre multitude. Children, almost naked, gesticulated in the foliage of the columns, or between the branches of the palm-trees. The Elders posted themselves on the platforms of the towers; and no one knew why a man with a long beard kept moving from place to place, in a thoughtful attitude. In the distance, he seemed indistinct as a phantom, and at times as motionless as the stones.

All were oppressed by the same disquietude, fearful lest the Barbarians, who now perceived themselves to be so strong, might take a whim and desire to remain. But they departed with such assurance that the Carthaginians were gradually emboldened to mingle with the soldiers, overwhelming them with gifts and promises. Some with exaggerated cunning and audacious hypocrisy, entreated them not to leave the city. Some threw to them flowers, perfumes, and pieces of money; others gave away their amulets, worn to ward off illness and harm, but first spat upon them three times in order to dispel their intrinsic charm, and attract upon the new possessors death; or, to make the hearts of the recipients cowardly, they enclosed jackal's hair in the talismans; others would invoke aloud the blessing of Melkarth, but in a whisper implore his malediction.

Hard upon the soldiers came the crush of baggages, beasts of burden, and the stragglers; the sick groaned upon the backs of dromedaries, others limped along, supporting themselves on broken spears. The bibulous carried wine-skins, the gluttonous took quarters of meat, cakes, fruits, and butter done up in fig-leaves, and snow packed in canvas-bags. Some were observed holding parasols, and others had parrots perched on their shoulders, or were followed by dogs, gazelles, or panthers. Libyan women, mounted on asses, heaped invectives upon the negresses who had forsaken the brothels of Malqua to go with the soldiers; many suckled their infants suspended from their breasts in a leather leash. Mules, goaded by their drivers with the points of spears, bent under the burden of the heavy tents heaped on their backs. The train also comprised a number of varlets and water-carriers, emaciated and yellow from fevers, filthy with vermin, the scum of the plebeian Carthaginians who had attached themselves to the Barbarian troops.

As soon as they had all passed out, the gates were fastened behind them. Still the people did not descend from the walls, but tarried to watch the army. It spread quickly over the width of the isthmus, and divided in unequal detachments, until presently the lances appeared only like tall blades of grass; finally all were lost to view in clouds of dust, and the soldiers, looking back at Carthage, could only distinguish the long walls with the vacant battlements outlined against the sky.

The Barbarians heard a great outcry; not knowing the exact number of their troops, they believed some of their comrades had lingered behind in the city to amuse themselves by plundering a temple: they laughed heartily over this idea as they continued on their way. Once more marching together through the open country, all were as joyous as formerly, and the Greeks sang the old song of the Mamertines:

> "With my lance and my spear I sow
> And I reap : I am master of the house!
> The disarmed man falls at my feet,
> Calling me 'Signor!' and 'Great King!'"

They shouted, jumped, and the gayest narrated stories, as now the period of their miseries seemed to be at an end. Upon reaching Tunis, some of the soldiers noticed that a troup of Balearic slingers were missing; but assuming that they could not be far behind the army, no more was thought about them.

At Tunis some lodged in the houses, others camped at the foot of the walls, and the people of the city came thither to chat with them. During the entire night fires blazed on the horizon in the direction of Carthage, and the flames, like gigantic torches, cast shaft-like reflections over the surface of the motionless lake: yet no one in the army could divine what feast was there being celebrated.

The next day the Barbarians crossed over a tract of country under complete cultivation. Patricians' farm-houses succeeded one after another on the edge of the road, irrigating ditches flowed through palm-groves, olive-trees formed long green rows, while rosy vapours floated in the gorges of the hills, and blue mountains towered up behind. A warm wind blew. Chameleons crawled over large cactus-leaves. With slackened speed the Barbarians marched in isolated detachments one after another, at long intervals. They ate grapes from the vines, slept on the grass, and looked in marked astonishment at the large artificially distorted horns of the cattle, and the sheep encased in skins to protect their wool; or, in surprise examined the furrows, intercrossing in a manner to make lozenge-like spaces; then scanned the ploughs, with shares like the flukes of a ship's anchor, and the pomegranates watered with silphium. The prevailing opulence of the earth, and the wisdom of all these strange agricultural inventions, truly amazed them.

At night, with faces upturned to the stars, they stretched themselves upon their unfolded tents, still yearning for the delights of Hamilcar's feast as they fell asleep.

In the middle of the subsequent day they halted

amid laurel-rose bushes, on the banks of a river. They quickly threw aside their lances, bucklers, and belts, and plunged into the water, yelling as they bathed, drinking out of their helmets or from the stream as they lay flat on the ground, surrounded by the beasts of burden from whose backs the baggage was falling.

Spendius, sitting on a dromedary stolen from Hamilcar's parks, spied Mâtho at a distance, allowing his mule to drink, while he steadily looked in the running water. His wounded arm was suspended against his chest, he was bareheaded, and his face was downcast. The slave ran through the crowd, calling out: "Master! Master!"

Mâtho did not trouble himself to thank him for his benediction. Spendius, thus repulsed, cautiously moved on behind him, and from time to time turned his eyes anxiously towards Carthage. He was the son of a Greek rhetorician and a Campanian courtesan. He grew rich by selling women: then was ruined by a wreck; after which, with the Samnite shepherds, he made war against the Romans, was captured, effected his escape, and was then retaken. During his captivity he had worked in the quarries, panted in the sweating-baths, groaned in the tortures, passed into the hands of various masters, and experienced all their fury. One day, in despair, he plunged into the sea off a trireme, in which he was one of a squad pulling the oars. The sailors picked him up as drowning, and took him to Carthage to the *ergastulum* of Megara; but as the fugitives were eventually to be delivered back to the Romans, he had profited by the prevailing confusion to fly with the soldiers. During the entire march he remained beside Mâtho bringing him his food, assisting him to mount or dismount, and at night placing a rug under his head; until finally, touched by such persistent attentions, Mâtho became gradually less reserved.

Mâtho was born on the Gulf of Syrtes; his father had conducted him on a pilgrimage to the temple of Ammon; he had hunted elephants in the forests of the Garamantes; and afterwards had engaged himself in the service of Carthage. After the capture of Drepanum he had been named tetrarch. The Republic was in Mâtho's debt for four horses, twenty-three *medimni* of wheat, and his pay for one winter. He feared the Gods, and wished to die in his native country.

Spendius talked to him of his own voyages, his people, and the temples that he had visited; he was familiar with many things: knew how to make sandals, boar-spears, and nets, as well as how to tame wild animals, and the manner of curing fish. From time to time he interrupted his narration by giving utterance from the depths of his chest to a sharp cry, whereupon Mâtho's mule quickened its pace and the others hastily followed; then Spendius would resume, always agitated by his grief. The evening of the fourth day he became calm.

They marched side by side, at the right of the army on the flank of a hill; the plain below stretched away until lost in the evening mists. The lines of soldiers, defiling below them, made undulations through the darkness. From time to time, when passing over eminences lighted by the moon, a star would quiver on the shining points of the moving spears afterwards for an instant mirror itself on the helmets, then disappear, to be continually succeeded by others. In the distance, the awakened flocks bleated, and an infinite sweetness seemed at this hour to fall over the earth.

Spendius, with uplifted head, and eyes half-closed, breathed in the fresh breeze with deep inhalations, threw out his arms, and moved them about restlessly, to better feel the caresses of the air wafted over his body. Hope of vengeance returned, transporting him. He pressed his hand over his mouth to prevent sobs escaping his lips, and thus, half swooning in a delirium, he dropped the dromedary's halter; but the animal continued to move forward with long, regular strides Mâtho relapsed into his state of sadness ; his long legs hung down to the ground, and the grasses, rubbing against his cothurnes, made a constant rustling.

Seemingly the road was without end, for at the extremity of a plain it came to a round plateau, then descended into a valley; and the mountains, that appeared in the distance to close in the horizon, as they were approached seemed to be displaced, and slip away farther into the perspective. Now and then a river appeared, flowing through the verdure of tamarisks. only to lose itself at a turn of the hills. Occasionally an enormous rock stood boldly up like the prow of a vessel, or like the pedestal of a colossal statue which had disappeared. At regular intervals they encountered little quadrangular temples, serving as shelters for

D

the faithful who made pilgrimages to Sicca, but now as firmly closed as tombs. The Libyans knocked loudly against the doors for admission; no one ever responded from within.

At this point cultivation became rare; suddenly they came upon strips of sand bristling with clumps of thorns; flocks of sheep browsed among the stones, herded by a woman about whose waist was a blue fleece-girdle. When she saw the soldiers' spears between the rocks, she fled screaming.

They were marching through a wide defile, hedged in by two chains of reddish hillocks, when a nauseous odour struck their nostrils, and they believed that they saw something extraordinary at the top of a carob tree; a lion's head stood up above the foliage.

Running towards it, they found a lion attached to a cross by its four limbs, like a criminal; his enormous muzzle hung to his breast, and his fore-paws, half concealed beneath the abundance of his mane, were widely spread apart, like a bird's wings in flight; under the tightly drawn skin, his ribs severally protruded and his hind legs were nailed together, but were slightly drawn up; black blood had trickled through the hairs, and collected in stalactites at the end of his tail, which hung straight down the length of the cross. The soldiers crowded around the beast, diverting themselves by calling him:—"Consul!" and "Citizen of Rome!" and threw pebbles into his eyes, to scatter the swarming gnats.

A hundred steps farther on they came upon two other lions; then at once appeared a long row of

AT SICCA.

crosses supporting yet other lions. Some evidently had been dead a long time, as nothing remained against the wooden crosses save the débris of their skeletons; and their half-corroded jaws were distorted in horrible grimaces. Others were of such enormous size that the trees of the crosses bent beneath their great weight and swayed in the wind, so that flocks of ravenous vultures circled in the air without ever daring to alight.

Thus was it that the Carthaginian peasantry revenged themselves when they captured ferocious beasts, hoping by such examples to terrify others. The Barbarians ceased their laughter, relapsing into a profound amazement. "What people is this," thought they, "which amuses itself by crucifying lions?"

The men from the north were vaguely disquieted, anxious, and already ill. They tore their hands on the aloe thorns, large mosquitoes buzzed in their ears, and dysentery had begun to attack the army. All were discouraged because they could not yet see Sicca, and fearful lest they should be lost and perish in the desert—the region of sands and terrors. Many would not advance further; others turned back and retook the road to Carthage.

Finally, on the seventh day, after having followed for a long time the base of a mountain, the road abruptly turned to the right, and beyond loomed up a line of walls, resting upon and blending with white rocks. Suddenly the entire city rose before them. Blue, yellow, and white veils fluttered along on the walls in the blush of the evening, as the priestesses of Tanit ran to receive the soldiers; there they waited, ranged the length of the rampart, striking tambourines, playing lyres, clattering castanets, and the sun's rays, as it set behind the Numidian mountains, gleamed between the harp-strings and their bare, outstretched arms. At intervals the instruments were suddenly silenced: then a strident cry rung out furious and continuous, a species of barking produced by clacking their tongues against the corners of their mouths. Those who were not playing remained leaning on their elbows with their chins pressed in the palms of their hands, more immobile than sphinxes—darting their large, black eyes at the advancing army.

As Sicca was a sacred city, and the temple and its dependencies occupied half of its area, it could not contain such a multitude: therefore the Barbarians camped on the plain, at their ease. Those who were disciplined took up regular quarters: others arranged themselves by nationalities or according to their own fancies.

Greeks pitched their skin-tents in parallel rows; Iberians disposed their canvas canopies in a circle; Gauls constructed wooden huts: Libyans made cabins of dry stones: and the Negroes dug with their nails holes in the sand to sleep in: and many, not knowing what to do with themselves, wandered about amongst the baggage, and at night lay on the ground rolled up in their torn mantles

The plain developed around them, bounded on all sides by mountains; here and there a palm-tree bowed on the top of a sand-hill: firs and oaks dotted the sides of precipices. Sometimes a rain cloud would hang in one part of the sky, and stream like a long scarf, while elsewhere the country would remain imbued with azure and serenity; then a warm wind would chase whirlwinds of sand. A stream descended in cascades from the heights of Sicca, where rose upon brazen columns the golden-roofed temple of the Carthaginian Venus, ruler of that country, which the Goddess seemed to fill with her soul. By the convulsions of the earth, by the variations of temperature and the play of lights, she manifested the extravagance of her power with the beauty of her eternal smile. The summit of some of the mountains formed a crescent; others resembled the bosom of a woman offering her distended breasts. Above their fatigues the Barbarians felt the overwhelming sense of this reigning influence, full of delights.

Spendius had bought a slave with the money received from the sale of the stolen dromedary. He slept before Mâtho's tent all day long; believing in his dreams that he heard the whirr of the lash, he would wake and pass his hands over the cicatrices on his legs, caused by having so long worn irons; reassured of his safety, he would sleep again.

Mâtho accepted the companionship of Spendius, who, wearing a long blade at his side, escorted him like a lictor. Sometimes he would even rest his arm on the shoulder of Spendius, who was a small man.

One evening, as they were together traversing the camp streets, they saw a number of men wearing white mantles, and in their midst they discerned Narr' Havas, the Numidian prince. Mâtho trembled. "Your sword!" cried he. "I want to kill him!"

"Not yet," protested Spendius, checking him. Narr' Havas was already advancing towards them.

He kissed his thumbs as a sign of alliance, attributing the anger he had shown at the feast to drunkenness; then he spoke at length against Carthage, but he did not say what had brought him to the Barbarians.

"Was this to betray them or the Republic?" Spendius queried to himself; and as he calculated to profit by all disturbances, he felt grateful to Narr' Havas for the future treacheries of which he suspected the Numidians.

The Numidian chief remained among the Mercenaries; he seemed desirous to attach Mâtho to himself, and sent to him fattened goats, gold-dust, and ostrich-plumes. The Libyan, amazed by these favours, hesitated whether to respond amicably, or to be exasperated; but Spendius appeased him. Mâtho seemed always irresolute and in an invincible torpor, like one who had partaken of some deadly potion, and allowed himself to be governed by his slave.

One morning, when the three started off on a lion-hunt, Narr' Havas hid a poniard under his mantle. Spendius, who observed the act, walked continually behind him; hence they returned without the Numidian having had an opportunity to draw the weapon. Upon another occasion Narr' Havas conducted them a very long distance, in fact, to the very boundaries of his own kingdom; they entered a narrow gorge, when Narr' Havas smiled while declaring to them that he no longer knew the road; however, Spendius found it again.

Mâtho more frequently than ever was melancholy as an augur; starting at sunrise he would wander into the country, throw himself on the ground, and there remain motionless till evening.

He consulted, one after another, all the diviners in the army: those who observed the movements of serpents, those who read the stars, and those who blew on the ashes of the dead. He swallowed galbanum, meadow-saxifrage, and the venom of vipers, reputed to freeze the heart. He summoned the negro women, who chanting barbaric words by moonlight pricked the skin of his forehead with golden stilettos. He covered himself with collars and amulets; invoked one after another Baal-Khamoûn, Moloch, the seven Cabiri, Tanit, and the Grecian Venus; he engraved a name on a copper plate, and buried it at the entrance of his tent. Spendius heard him constantly moaning and talking to himself. One night he ventured to enter Mâtho's tent. Mâtho, naked as a corpse, was lying flat on a lion's skin, his face buried in his hands; a suspended lamp lit up his weapons, as they hung against the tent-pole.

"You suffer?" said the slave to him. "What is the matter? Tell me!" and he shook him by the shoulders, calling him several times "Master! Master!"

Mâtho raised his large, troubled eyes towards him.

"Listen!" he said, in a deep voice, with one finger on his lips; "it is the wrath of the Gods! The daughter of Hamilcar pursues me! I have fear, Spendius!" then he pressed his hands against his breast, like a child terrified by a phantom.

"Speak to me! I am ill! I wish to recover! I have vainly tried everything: but perhaps you know stronger Gods, or some irresistible invocation?"

"What for?" asked Spendius.

Mâtho responded, striking his head with his fists: "To liberate me from this!" Then, at long intervals, he said, talking to himself: "I am doubtless the victim of a holocaust she has promised to the Gods.... She holds me bound by an unseen chain.... If I walk, then she advances; when I pause, she stops.... Her eyes burn me.... I hear her voice.... She encompasses, she penetrates me.... It seems that she has become my soul! And yet, for all that, between us flow the invisible waves of an ocean without bounds! She is remote and inaccessible! The splendour of her beauty diffuses around her a nebula of light, and I believe at moments I never saw her—that she does not exist—and that it is all a dream!"

Mâtho wept as in despair. Outside, the Barbarians slept.

Spendius, in looking at this man, recalled to view young men who, with golden vases in their hands, had formerly supplicated him, when he paraded his troops of courtesans through the cities. A pity touched him, and he said:

"Be strong, my master! Call upon your own will, and do not longer implore the Gods; they do not heed the cries of men! See, you cry out like a coward! Are you not humiliated that a woman makes you suffer thus?"

"Am I a child?" said Mâtho. "Do you believe that I yet weaken at the sight of women's faces, and at the sound of their songs? We kept them in Drepanum to sweep out our stables... I have possessed them during sieges under the crumbling ceilings, while the catapults yet vibrated!.... But that woman! Spendius, that woman!"....

The slave interrupted him:

"If she were not the daughter of Hamilcar!"

"No!" exclaimed Mâtho. "She is nothing like any other daughter of man! Have you not seen her glorious eyes under her great curved eyebrows, like suns under triumphal arches? Can you not recall, when she appeared how all the flambeaux paled, and that between the diamonds of her collar glimpses of her bosom shone resplendently—how behind her floated an odour like the perfumes from a temple, and something emanated from her entire being more fragrant than wine, and more terrible than death!.... She moves..... She stops." He remained open-mouthed, his head lowered, eyes fixed.

"But I want her! I must have her! I am dying of her! The idea of holding her in my arms brings to me a fury of rapture; and yet, withal, I hate her! Spendius, I want to overcome her! How can I do it? I long to sell myself to become her slave. You were her slave: you could see her. Tell me of her,—does she not go out on the terrace of her palace every night? Ah! the stones must thrill under her sandals, and the stars bend down to see her!"

He fell back in an access of passion, like a wounded bull. Presently he chanted: "He pursued in the forest the female monster, whose tail undulated over the dead leaves like a rivulet of silver," modulating his voice in imitation of Salammbô's, and with his hands extended, feigned to touch lightly the strings of a lyre.

To all the consolations offered by Spendius, he kept repeating the same manner of discourse. The subsequent nights were passed in the same lamentations, and the same exhortations. Mâtho endeavoured to blunt his senses by heavy drinking, but after his drunkenness had passed, he would become even sadder. Then he tried to distract his thoughts by playing knuckle-bone, losing in his unlucky wagers, one after another the gold plaques of his collar. He even visited the handmaidens of the Goddess, but afterwards descended the hillside in sobs, like one returning from a funeral.

Spendius, on the contrary, became more daring and gayer; he might be seen in the leaf-thatched drinking-booths, discoursing with the soldiers. He repaired the old cuirasses. He juggled with poniards. He gathered herbs in the fields to make decoctions for the sick. He was facetious, subtle, full of inventions and words; and the Barbarians became accustomed to his services, as they also grew to like him.

Meanwhile they eagerly awaited the promised ambassador from Carthage, whom they expected to bring for them, on the backs of mules, baskets filled with gold; and they always kept making the same calculations, figuring on the sand with their fingers. Each man in advance arranged his future course of life; one planned to have concubines, another slaves, or lands, and others thought that they would bury their treasures, or risk them on a vessel. But during this protracted season of idleness, the many diverse dispositions chafed, there continually arose disputes between the cavalry and infantry, the Barbarians and the Greeks, and above the wrangles of the men could be heard unceasingly the shrill voices of the women.

Day after day troops of men came into camp, nearly naked, wearing grasses on their heads to protect them from the sun; they were debtors of rich Carthaginians, heretofore forced to till the lands for them, who had escaped. Libyans arrived in numbers, and peasants ruined by taxes, exiles and also malefactors. Then came crowds of merchants, and vendors of oil and wine, all furious because they had not received their money, denouncing the Republic. Spendius added his voice in declaiming against her. Soon the provisions diminished; then they talked of moving in a body on to Carthage, and even entertained an idea of appealing to the Romans.

One evening, during the supper hour, heavy creaking sounds drew near, and in the distance appeared something red moving over the undulations of the ground. It was a grand purple litter, ornamented at the corners with bunches of ostrich plumes, and crystal chains, interwoven with garlands of pearls, beat against the closed hangings. Each stride made by the camels following rung large bells suspended from their breast-plates, and on all sides of them was to be seen an escort of cavalry, wearing armour of golden scales that reached from head to foot.

This cavalcade halted three hundred paces from the

encampment, to draw from the sheaths which they carried behind them, their round bucklers, Bœotian helmets, and broadswords. Some of the men remained with the camels, the others resumed their march Finally appeared the ensigns of the Republic, which were blue wooden poles, terminated by horses' heads or pine-cones. The Barbarians all arose cheering, and the women rushed towards the Guards of the Legion, to kiss their feet.

The litter advanced on the shoulders of a dozen Negroes, who marched together in a short, rapid step, going at hazard from right to left, much embarrassed by the tent-ropes and animals moving about, and by the tripods where meats were cooking. Occasionally a fat hand laden with rings would half open the curtain, and a harsh voice cry out abuse; then the porters would halt, turn about, and take another road to traverse the camp.

The purple curtains finally were lifted, disclosing on a large pillow an impassive, bloated human head. The eyebrows, joining over the nose, formed two ebony arches; gold spangles glittered in the crimped hair; and the face was so ghastly, that it seemed powdered over with marble-dust: the remainder of the body was hidden under the fleeces that filled the litter. In this man the soldiers recognised the Suffete Hanno, the one who had contributed by his delay to lose the battle of the Ægatian islands. In his victory at Hecatompylus over the Libyans, he had behaved with seeming clemency, although he was thought by the Barbarians to have been actuated by cupidity, as he had sold to his own profit all the captives, subsequently declaring to the Republic that they were dead.

After searching for some time for a commodious place from which to harangue the soldiers, Hanno made a signal, at which the litter halted, and assisted by two slaves he alighted and totteringly placed his feet on the ground. His feet were clad in black felt boots, studded with silver moons; bands like those that encase a mummy enwrapped his legs, the flesh protruding where the linen strips crossed. His abdomen outburst the scarlet jacket that covered his thighs; and the folds of his neck fell down on his breast like the dewlaps of an ox: his tunic, over which flowers were painted, was rent at the armpits; he also wore a scarf, a girdle, and a great black mantle with double lace sleeves. The amplitude of his vestments, his large collar of blue gems, his gold agrafes and his heavy earrings rendered even more hideous, if possible, his physical deformities. He appeared like a gross idol, roughly hewn out of a block of stone, as a pale leprosy covered his entire body, imparting to him the aspect of something inert. However, his nose, hooked like a vulture's beak, dilated violently, as he inhaled the air and his small eyes, with their gummed lashes, flashed with a hard, metallic glitter. He held in one hand an aloe spatula, wherewith to scratch his diseased skin.

Two heralds sounded their silver horns; the tumult ceased, and Hanno began to speak.

He commenced by eulogising the Gods and the Republic, saying that the Barbarians ought to congratulate themselves on having served Carthage; but that they should also be more reasonable, for the times were hard:—"and if a master had only three olives, was it not just that he kept two for himself?"

Thus the old Suffete interpolated throughout his discourse proverbs and apologues, nodding his head all the time to solicit approbation. He spoke in the Punic language, but those who surrounded him consisted of the most alert, who had run thither without their weapons, and were Campanians, Gauls, and Greeks, so that no one in the adjacent crowd understood him. Perceiving this, Hanno paused to reflect, meanwhile rocking himself heavily from one leg to the other. The idea came to him to convoke the captains, and his heralds cried out the order in Greek, the language which had served for word of command in the Carthaginian armies since the time of Xanthippus.

The guards with blows of their whips dispersed the mob of soldiers, and soon the captains of the phalanxes, drilled like the Spartans and the chiefs of the Barbaric cohorts, came forward wearing the insignia of their respective rank, and the armour of their nations.

Night fell; here and there blazed the fires; a great rumour stirred the encampment; and they went from one to another, asking, "What has he brought?" and "Why does not the Suffete distribute the money?"

Hanno explained to the convened captains and chiefs the infinite obligations of the Republic: her treasury was empty; the Roman tribute overwhelmed her; in fact:—"We do not know what to do! The Republic is much to be pitied!"

From time to time he rubbed his limbs with his aloe spatula, or even paused to drink, from a silver cup held to his lips by a slave, a decoction of ashes of weasels and asparagus boiled in vinegar; then, after drying his mouth with a scarlet napkin, he continued:

"That which was worth only one shekel of silver costs to-day three shekels of gold, and the farms abandoned during the war yield nothing. Our purple fisheries are nearly lost; pearls even have become exorbitant; and it is with difficulty that we can obtain sufficient unguents for service to the Gods! and, as for articles for table consumption—this subject is a calamity on which I shall not dwell. For lack of galleys the spices fail, and it will be troublesome to procure silphium, in consequence of the rebellion on the frontier of Cyrene. Sicily, from whence we get our slaves, is now closed to us! For instance, yesterday I gave more money for a bath-man and four kitchen-varlets than formerly I should have paid for a pair of elephants!"

He unrolled a long strip of papyrus, and read, without omitting a single figure, all the outlays that the Government had made, for reparations of the temples, paving streets, constructing vessels, coral-fisheries, the aggrandisement of the Syssites, and construction of engines for the mines in Cantabria. But, the captains did not understand the Punic language any better than did the soldiers, even though the Mercenaries saluted in this language. Ordinarily numerous Carthaginian officers were interspersed through the Barbaric armies to serve as interpreters, but after the recent war they had hidden, abandoning their posts, fearful of vengeance; and Hanno had not the forethought to provide himself with interpreters before setting out on the present mission. His voice was so low, it became lost on the wind.

The Greeks, girding on their iron sword-belts, listened attentively, striving to divine his meaning; the mountaineers, covered with skins like bears, looked defiantly at him, or yawned, leaning on their heavy clubs studded with brass nails. The Gauls inattentively chuckled, shaking their tall towers of hair; and the men of the desert, completely muffled up in grey woollen clothing, listened motionless. Men pushed forward from behind, till the Guards, crowded by the surging mob, actually swayed on their horses. Negroes held at arm's length lighted torches of fir-branches; and the gross Carthaginian continued his harangue, standing in full view on a knoll of turf.

Meanwhile the Barbarians grew impatient, and gave vent to murmurs. Each one apostrophised Hanno, who gesticulated with his spatula; those who wished to silence others yelled louder, vastly increasing the hubbub. Suddenly a man of stunted appearance bounded to Hanno's feet, snatched a trumpet from one of the heralds, blew it, and Spendius —for it was he—announced that he came to tell them something of importance. He rapidly reiterated this declaration in five different languages, namely, Greek, Latin, Gallic, Libyan, and Balearic: the captains, half surprised, half laughing, responded, "Speak! Speak!"

Spendius, tremblingly hesitating a moment, at last commenced by addressing the Libyans, as they were the most numerous·

"You have all heard the horrible menaces of that man!"

Hanno offered no remonstrance, as he did not comprehend Libyan; and to continue the experiment, Spendius repeated the same phrase in all the other Barbaric idioms. The soldiers looked at each other in astonishment; when all, as by tacit consent, or perhaps believing that they understood, bowed their heads to signify approval.

Then Spendius began in a vehement voice:

"In the first place, that man has said that all the Gods of other nations were but myths compared with the Carthaginian Gods! He has called you all cowards, thieves, liars, dogs and sons of bitches! He has said, that but for you the Republic would not be constrained to pay the Romans tribute, and that by your outrages you have drained Carthage of perfumes, aromatics, slaves, and silphium, as you are in league with the Nomads, on the frontiers of Cyrene. As you yourselves have heard! Then he has said that the culpable shall be punished, and read the enumeration of their punishments, such as paving the roads, fitting up the vessels, embellishing the Syssites, and being sent to dig in the mines of Cantabria."

Spendius reiterated all this to the Greeks, Gauls, Campanians, and Balearics. In recognising many of the proper names that struck their ears as the same that Hanno had used, the Mercenaries were convinced that he was giving an exact report of the Suffete's discourse. Some yelled out to him:

"You lie!"

Their voices were lost in the tumult of others, and Spendius added:

"Do you not see that he has left a reserve force

of cavalry outside the camp? At a signal from him, they are prepared to rush upon and slay you."

At this the Barbarians turned in the direction indicated; and as the crowd dispersed, there appeared in their midst, moving slowly as a phantom, a human being, bent over, thin, entirely naked, and hidden almost to his thighs by his long hair, bristling with dry leaves, dust, and thorns. He had about his loins and knees wisps of straw and shreds of cloth; his cadaverous skin hung to his fleshless limbs like rags on dry branches; his hands trembled continually, and he walked leaning on an olive staff. He came near the Negro torch-bearers. An idiotic grin revealed his pale gums, and his great frightened eyes examined the Barbarians who pressed around him.

Uttering a cry of fright, he sprang behind the Negroes, sheltering himself with their bodies, and stammered out, "Look at them! look at them!" pointing at the Suffete's guards sitting motionless in their glistening armour, their horses pawing the ground, dazzled by the torch-lights that crackled in the darkness. The human spectre struggled and yelled, "They killed them!"

At these words, which he screamed in Balearic, the Balearics drew nearer, and recognised him; but without responding to their queries, he repeated:

"Yes, killed all! all! Crushed like grapes! The fine young men! The slingers! My comrades and yours!"

They gave him wine to drink, and overcome by his emotion and weakness, he wept. Then again he launched forth a volley of words.

AT SICCA.

With difficulty Spendius managed to conceal his delight; even while explaining to the Greeks and Libyans all the horrible events recounted by Zarxas, he could scarcely credit such an apropos and unlooked-for coincidence. The Balearic soldiers paled on learning the manner in which their companions had perished. A troop of three hundred slingers had landed at Carthage in the evening and overslept themselves, so that when they arrived the next morning at the square of Khamoûn, the Barbarians had already gone, and they found themselves without defence, as their clay balls had been packed upon the camels with the other army baggage. They were allowed to enter the street of Satheb, and to proceed till they reached the oaken gate lined with brass plates, when the people, by a single movement, threw themselves upon the helpless troop.

Many of the soldiers recalled the great outcry they had heard; but Spendius, who had left the city at the head of the columns, had not heard it.

After this the corpses of the slingers were placed in the arms of the *Du-Pataci*—which surrounded the temple of Khamoûn. Then they were reproached for all the crimes committed by the Mercenaries— their gluttonies, thefts, impieties, insults, and the ruthless slaughter of the fishes in Salammbô's garden. The bodies were infamously mutilated; the priests burned the hair to torture their souls; pieces of their flesh were hung up in the butchers' shops: some of the torturers even buried their teeth in the flesh; and at night, to complete the outrages, the remains were burned on pyres at the street-crossings.

These, then, were the fires that had flashed so

long in the distance over the lake. Some of the mansions took fire, and the remaining bodies and the dying were forthwith hurriedly pitched over the walls to prevent a general conflagration. Zarxas was one of this number, and until the next day stayed in the reeds on the lake shore; then he wandered out in the country, searching for the army by its trail through the dust. During the daytime he hid in caverns, taking up his march in the night time. His wounds unstaunched, famishing and ill, he subsisted on roots and carrion. At length one day he saw on the horizon the lances, and followed them. His reason was disturbed by the force and continuance of his terrors and miseries.

While he spoke, the soldiers suppressed their ire with difficulty; when he had finished, however, it raged forth like a storm; they wanted then and there to massacre the Guards and the Suffete. Some less violent interposed, saying that at least he should be heard and let them know if they were to be paid.

All yelled "Our money!" Hanno responded that he had brought it.

They made a rush to the advance posts, dragging the Suffete's baggage to the centre of the camp. Without waiting for the porters, they unknotted the baskets. In those they opened first they found hyacinth-robes, sponges, scratchers, brushes, perfumes, and bodkins of antimony for painting the eyes,—all belonging to the Guards, rich men accustomed to these luxuries.

Afterwards they discovered on one of the camels a large bronze bath-tub, in which the Suffete indulged his ablutions during his march; for he took all sorts of precautions, even bringing in cages weasels from Hecatompylus, to be burned alive for his decoction. And as his malady imparted to him an enormous appetite, he had brought a plentiful supply of comestibles,—wines, pickles, meats and fish preserved in honey, and little Commagene-pots of goose-grease packed in snow and chopped straw. When the baskets were opened and the contents were displayed, the provisions appeared in such considerable quantities, as to provoke a laughter that swept over the Barbarians like interclashing waves.

But the wages of the Mercenaries hardly filled two esparto coffers; and even in one of these they saw the leather tokens used by the Republic to save their specie. The Barbarians seeming much surprised, Hanno declared that their accounts were very difficult, and that the Elders had not yet found leisure to examine them. In the meantime they had sent this supply. Everything was emptied recklessly out and overturned —mules, valets, litter, provisions, and baggage.

The soldiers seized upon the money in the sacks to pelt Hanno. With great difficulty he was hoisted upon an ass, and fled, clutching its mane; howling, crying, jolted, bruised, he hurled back upon the army the maledictions of all the Gods. His broad, jewelled collar rebounded to his ears; he held his long, trailing mantle between his teeth, and the Barbarians yelled after him from afar:

"Go, coward! Swine! Sewer of Moloch! Sweat out now your gold, your pestilence! Faster! Faster!" The escort in disorder galloped at his side.

The fury of the Barbarians could not be appeased: they recalled the fact that many of their numbers who had set out for Carthage had not returned: doubtless they had been killed. So much injustice exasperated them, and they began to pull up their tent pegs, roll up their mantles, bridle their horses, each one taking his casque and sword; and in an instant all was ready. Those who did not possess weapons dashed into the woods to cut bludgeons.

Day dawned: the people of Sicca awoke, and bestirred themselves in the streets to witness the evacuation.

"They go to Carthage!" it was said; and the rumour ran like wild-fire, spreading throughout the country.

From every pathway, from every ravine, men sprang forth. Herdsmen could be seen descending the mountains, running breathlessly. When the Barbarians had gone Spendius made the circuit of the plain to reconnoitre, mounted on a Punic stallion, accompanied by his slave, who led a third horse. A single tent remained on the field. Spendius entered it, exclaiming:

"Up, master! Awake! We go!"

"Where do we go?" demanded Mâtho.

"To Carthage!" cried Spendius.

Mâtho bounded on to the horse held by the slave at the entrance.

CHAPTER III.

SALAMMBO.

THE rising moon struck across the waves. Over the city still hung vast shadows, interspersed with points of light and glints of brilliant whiteness; the pole of a car in a courtyard, or some vagrant, fluttering tatters, the angle of a wall, or the glitter of a gold collar on the neck of a God. On the roofs of the temples, the glass globes radiated like enormous diamonds: but vague ruins, heaps of black earth, and gardens, made more sombre masses in the general obscurity.

At the foot of Malqua, fishermen's nets extended from house to house, like gigantic bats with outspread wings. The creaking of the hydraulic wheels that forced the water up to the last stories of the palaces was now silent. In the middle of the terraces camels tranquilly reposed, lying on their bellies like ostriches. The porters slept in the streets at the thresholds of the mansions. The colossi cast long shadows over the deserted squares. In the distance, sometimes the smoke of a sacrifice yet burning escaped through the bronze tiles; and the heavy breeze brought with the aromatic perfumes, the odours of the sea, mingled with exhalations from the sun-heated walls.

Around Carthage the motionless waters became resplendent, as the rising moon spread her light, at the same time, over the gulf, environed by mountains and over the lake of Tunis, where upon the banks of sand flamingoes formed long, rose-coloured lines; and further on below the catacombs the large salt lagoon shone like a sheet of burnished silver. The blue dome of heaven on the one side sank into the horizon down to the powdered plains, and on the other side faded away into the sea-mists; and on the summit of the Acropolis, the pyramidal cypresses, bordering the temple of Eschmoûn swayed, making a murmur like the swell that beat regularly and slowly along the mole at the foot of the ramparts.

Salammbô went out on the upper terrace of her palace, supported by a slave, who carried on an iron plate burning charcoal.

In the centre of the terrace was placed a small ivory couch covered with lynx-skins, upon which were laid pillows of the feathers of the prophetic parrots—birds consecrated to the Gods—and at the four corners were erected long cassolettes, filled with spikenard, incense, cinnamon, and myrrh. The slave lighted these perfumes.

Salammbô gazed at the polar star, then slowly saluted the four quarters of the heavens, and knelt on the ground amid the azure powder sown with gold stars, in imitation of the firmament. Then she pressed her elbows close against her sides, extending her forearms perfectly straight, with hands open, her head turned upwards and back under the full rays of the moon, saying:

"O RABBETNA! BAALET! TANIT!" Her tones continued plaintively, as if she called some one: "ANAITIS! ASTARTE! DERCETO! ASTORETH! MYLITTA! ATHARA! ELISSA! TIRATHA! .... By the hidden symbols. ... by the resounding timbrels. ... by the furrows of the earth. ... .by the eternal silence. ... by the everlasting fecundity. ... Ruler of the shadowy sea, and of the regions of azure, O Queen of humid things, all hail!"

She swayed her entire body two or three times, then threw herself face downwards, with outstretched arms, flat in the dust.

Her slave lifted her up quickly, as it was ordained that after such rites some one should always lift the suppliant from her prostration, as a sign that the Gods accepted such services; Salammbô's nurse never failed in this pious duty. This slave had been brought, when but a child, to Carthage by some merchants of Dara-Getulia, and after her emancipation she had no wish to leave her master; as a proof of her willing servitude, according to a recognised custom, she pierced in her right ear a large hole. She wore a multi-coloured striped skirt fitting tightly about her hips, falling straight down to her ankles, between which as she walked two tin links struck against one another; her rather flat face was as yellow as her tunic; very long silver pins made a halo at the back of her head, and in her nose was inserted a coral stud. She now stood near the couch with eyes downcast, more erect than a Hermes.

Salammbô moved to the edge of the terrace; her eyes wandered for an instant over the horizon, then she lowered her gaze to the sleeping city. A sigh escaped from the depths of her bosom, making her long white simarre undulate from end to end as it hung unconfined either by girdle or agrafe. Her pointed sandals with turned-up toes disappeared beneath a mass of emeralds: her hair was negligently caught up in a net of purple silk.

She raised her head to contemplate the moon—mingling with her words fragments of hymns as she murmured:

"How lightly dost thou turn, sustained by the impalpable ether! About thee it is luminous, and the movement of thy changes distributes the winds and the fruitful dews; as thou waxest and wanest, cats' eyes elongate or shorten, and the leopards' spots are changed. Women scream thy name in the paroxysms of childbirth! Thou increasest the shell-fish! Thou causest the wine to ferment! Thou putrefiest the dead! Thou formest the pearls at the bottom of the sea; and all germs, O Goddess! are quickened in the profoundest obscurity of thy humidity! When thou comest forth a quietude spreadeth over the earth; the flowers close; the waves are lulled; wearied men repose with their faces upturned towards thee; and the entire earth, with its oceans and its mountains, is reflected in thy face, as in a mirror. Thou art white, sweet, lustrous, auxiliary, immaculate, purifying, serene!"

The crescent moon just then hung over the Hot-Springs Mountain; just below it, in the notch of the two summits on the opposite side of the gulf, appeared a little star, and all around it a pale circle. Salammbô continued:

"But thou art a terrible mistress! . . . Likewise produced by thee are monsters, frightful phantoms, and deceitful dreams; thine eyes devour the stones of the edifices, and during the periods of thy rejuvenescence the sacred apes fall ill. Whither goest thou then? Why perpetually changest thou thy forms? Sometimes narrow and curved, thou glidest through space as a mastless galley, or, in the midst of stars thou resemblest a shepherd guarding his flock; anon shining and round, thou grazest the top of the mounts like a chariot wheel!

"O Tanit, dost thou not love me? I have watched thee so often! But, no, thou coursest in thine azure, whilst I remain on the motionless earth? . . ."

"Taanach, take your nebal and play softly on the silver cord, for my heart is sad."

The slave lifted a species of ebony harp, taller than herself, of a triangular shape like a delta, and placing the point in a crystal globe, began to play with both hands.

Tones succeeded, low, precipitous tones, like the buzzing of bees, and growing more and more sonorous, were wafted into the night, and mingled with the lament of the waves and with the soughing of the large trees on the summit of the Acropolis.

"Hush!" cried Salammbô.

"What is it mistress? If a breeze but blow, or a cloud only passes, everything now vexes and disturbs you."

"I know not," she replied.

"You have over-fatigued yourself by praying too long," urged the slave.

"Oh! Taanach! I would dissolve myself therein like a flower in wine!"

"Perhaps it is the odours of the perfumes?"

"No!" said Salammbô. "The spirit of the Gods dwells in good odours."

Then the slave talked to her of her father. It was believed that he had gone into the Amber country beyond the pillars of Melkarth.

"But mistress, if he should not return," she said, "you must choose, as he wished you, a husband from among the sons of the Elders; and your disquietude will vanish in the embrace of your husband."

"Why?" asked the young girl. All the sons of the Elders she had ever seen horrified her with their wild beast laughter, and their gross limbs.

"Taanach, sometimes a feeling emanates from the innermost depths of my being, like hot flushes, heavier than the vapours arising from a volcano:—voices call to me; a fiery globe rolls and rises in my breast; it suffocates me. I seem to be dying, when something so sweet flows from my brow, extending to my very feet,—thrills through every atom of my being—it is a caress which envelopes me—I feel crushed as if a God spread himself over and enthralled me. Oh! I long to lose myself in the night mists—in the ripples of the fountains, in the sap of the trees—leave my body to be but a breath of air —a ray of light, and glide through space to thee, oh mother!"

She raised her arms as high as possible, bending her body backwards, appearing as pale and delicate in her white robe, as the moon; then in her ecstacy she fell panting on her ivory couch. Taanach placed around her mistress's neck a collar of amber and dolphins' teeth to banish these terrors. Salammbô said, in a voice almost inaudible, "Go and find Schahabarim for me."

Salammbô's father had not wished that she should enter the college of priestesses, nor even that she should know aught concerning the popular Tanit. He reserved her for some alliance which would serve his political aims: so that Salammbô lived alone in her palace, as her mother had been dead for many years. She had grown up amid abstinences, fasts, and purifications, and was always surrounded by exquisite and solemn things—her body saturated with perfumes—her soul filled with prayers. Never had she tasted wine, or eaten meat, or touched an unclean animal, or put her foot in the house of death.

She was ignorant of the obscene simulachres; for each God was manifested in many different forms, and the various rites, often most contradictory, all demonstrated the same principles; therefore, Salammbô was taught to adore the Goddess in her sidereal figuration.

An influence had descended from the moon upon this maiden, for whenever the planet waned, Salammbô became feeble, languishing all day, only reviving at night; and once during an eclipse she nearly died.

But the jealous Rabbetna revenged herself on this chaste maiden, withheld from immolation; obsessing her with allurements all the stronger because they were vague, the outgrowth of faith, heightened by imagination.

The daughter of Hamilcar constantly troubled herself about Tanit. She had learned the Goddess's adventures, her journeys, and all her names, which she repeated, without their possessing for her a distinct significance. In order to penetrate the profundities of her dogma, she yearned to know, in the most secret place of the temple, the old idol, with the magnificent veil upon which depended the destiny of Carthage. The idea of a deity was not clearly revealed by her representation, for to possess or even behold her image was to partake a part of her power, and in some measure to dominate her.

Salammbô turned as she recognised the tinkling of the little gold bells that Schahabarim wore at the hem of his robe.

He came up the stairs, and pausing as he reached the threshold of the terrace, crossed his arms. His sunken eyes burned like lamps in a sepulchre; his long, thin body glided along in his linen robe, weighed down by bells alternating with emerald apples about his heels. His limbs were feeble, his head oblique, his chin peaked, his skin seemed cold to the touch, and his yellow face covered with deeply furrowed wrinkles, seemed as if contracted in a desire, in an eternal chagrin.

This man was the high priest of Tanit, and he had educated Salammbô.

"Speak!" said he. "What do you wish?"

"I hoped—you have as much as promised me—. . . . ." she stammered, half disconcerted; then suddenly continued: "Why do you despise me? What have I neglected in the rites? You are my teacher, and you have said to me that no person understands better than I the mysteries of the Goddess; but there are some which you do not wish to tell me; is not this true, O father?"

Schahabarim recalled the orders of Hamilcar concerning his daughter's education, and responded: "No! I have nothing more to teach you."

"A spirit," she resumed, "urges me to this adoration. I have climbed the steps of Eschmoûn,—God of the planets and intelligences; I have slept under the golden olive tree of Melkarth,—patron of all Tyrian colonies; I have pushed open the gates of Baal-Khamoûn,—source of light and fertilisation; I have sacrificed to the subterranean Cabiri;—to the Gods of the winds, the rivers, the woods, and of the mountains;—but all are too far, too high, too insensible—you understand? Whereas Tanit mingles in my life, she fills my soul, and I tremble with internal dartings, as if she struggled to escape the confines of my body. It seems to me that I shall hear her voice, behold her face; a brightness dazzles me, then I fall back again into the shadows."

Schahabarim was silent. She implored his attention with beseeching glances. At length he made a sign to dismiss the slave, who was not of Canaanite race. Taanach disappeared, and the priest raised one arm in the air, and commenced:

"Before the Gods, only darkness existed, and a breath floated, heavy and indistinct, like the consciousness of a man in a dream: it contracted itself, creating Desire and Vapour; from Desire and Vapour proceeded primitive Matter. It was a muddy water, black, icy, profound, encompassing insensible monsters, incoherent parts of forms to be born, such as are painted on the walls of the sanctuaries. Then Matter condensed and became an egg. It broke: one half formed the earth, the other half tho firmament. The sun, the moon, the winds, and clouds appeared, and a crash of thunder awakened the sentient animals. Then Eschmoûn, unrolled himself in the starry sphere! Khamoûn shone radiantly in the sun; Melkarth with his arms pushed him beyond Gades; the Cabiri descended into the volcanoes; and Rabbetna, like one who nourishes, leaned over the world, poured forth her light like milk, and her night like a mantle."

"And then?" she asked—for the priest had enumerated the secrets of origins, to distract her by the highest, the most abstract forms; but the desire of the maiden was rekindled under his last words, and Schahabarim, half yielding, resumed:

"She inspires and governs the loves of men."

"The loves of men!" repeated Salammbô, dreamily.

"She is the soul of Carthage," continued the priest. "Although she spreads over all, it is here she dwells, beneath the *Sacred Veil*."

"O father!" exclaimed Salammbô, "I shall see her, shall I not? You will conduct me to her? For a long time I have hesitated: now the curiosity to see her form devours me. Pity me! succour me! Let us go to the temple!"

He repulsed her by a vehement gesture, full of pride.

"Never! Do you not know that to look upon her is death? The hermaphrodite Baalim unveil only to us: men that we are in our intellects, women that we are through our weakness. Your desire is a sacrilege. Be satisfied with the knowledge you possess."

She fell upon her knees, placing two fingers against her ears in sign of repentance; sobbing, crushed by the priest's words, at the same time angry with him—filled equally with terror and humiliation.

Schahabarim remained standing, more insensible than the stones of the terrace. He looked down upon her trembling at his feet, and it afforded him a measure of delight to see her thus suffering for his divinity whom he, no more than she, could wholly embrace.

Already the birds sang, and a cold wind blew, and little clouds flitted across the pale sky. Suddenly the priest perceived on the horizon behind Tunis something like light mists floating over the ground; then it became a vast curtain of grey dust perpendicularly spread, and through the whirling mass, the heads of dromedaries, and the flash of lances and bucklers were defined. It was the Barbarian army advancing on Carthage.

CHAPTER IV.

UNDER THE WALLS OF CARTHAGE.

From the surrounding country the people, mounted on asses or running on foot, pale, breathless, wild with fear, came rushing into the city. They were flying before the Barbarian army, which, within three days, had traversed the road from Sicca, bent on falling upon and exterminating Carthage.

Almost as soon as the citizens closed the gates the Barbarians were descried, but they halted in the middle of the isthmus on the lake shore. At first they made no sign whatever of hostility. Many approached with palms in their hands, only to be repulsed by the arrows of the Carthaginians, so intense was the terror prevailing throughout the city.

During the early morning and at nightfall stragglers prowled along the walls. A small man, carefully enveloped in a mantle, with his face concealed under a very low visor, was specially noticeable. He tarried for hours looking at the aqueduct, and with such persistence, that he undoubtedly desired to mislead the Carthaginians as to his actual designs. He was accompanied by another man, of giant-like stature, who walked about bareheaded.

Carthage was defended throughout the entire width of the isthmus: first by a moat, succeeded by a rampart of turf; finally by a double-storied wall, thirty cubits high, built of hewn stones. It contained stables for three hundred elephants, with magazines for their caparisons, shackles, and provisions, as well as other stables for a thousand horses with their harness and fodder; also casernes for twenty thousand soldiers, arsenals for their armour, and all the materials and necessaries for war. Towers were erected on the second story, furnished with battlements, clad on the exterior by bronze bucklers suspended from cramp irons.

The first line of walls immediately sheltered Malqua, the quarter inhabited by seafaring people and dyers of purple. Poles were visible on which purple sails were drying, and beyond, on the last terraces, clay furnaces for cooking saumure. At the back the city was laid out in tiers, like an amphitheatre; its high dwellings in the form of cubes were variously built of stones, planks, shingles, reeds, shells, and pressed earth. The groves of the temples appeared like lakes of verdure in this mountain of diversely-coloured blocks. The public squares levelled it at unequal distances, and innumerable streets intercrossed from top to bottom. The boundaries of the three old quarters could be distinguished, now merged together and here and there rising up like huge rocks or spreading out in enormous flat spaces of walls—half-covered with flowers, and blackened by wide streaks caused by the throwing over of filth; and streets passed through in yawning spaces like streams under bridges.

The hill of the Acropolis, in the centre of Byrsa, disappeared under a medley of monuments;—such as temples with torsel-columns, with bronze capitals and metal chains, cones of uncemented stones banded with azure, copper cupolas, marble architraves, Babylonian buttresses, and obelisks poised on the points like reversed flambeaux. Peristyles reached to frontons; volutes unrolled between colonnades; granite walls supported tile partitions. All these were mounted one above another, half hidden, in a marvellous, incomprehensible fashion. Here one felt the succession of ages, and the memories of forgotten countries were awakened.

Behind the Acropolis, in the red earth, the Mappals road, bordered by tombs, extended in a straight line from the shore to the catacombs; then followed large dwellings in spacious gardens; and the third quarter, Megara, the new city, extended to the edge of the cliffs, on which was erected a gigantic lighthouse where nightly blazed a beacon.

Carthage thus deployed herself before the soldiers now encamped on the plains.

From the distance the soldiers could recognise the markets and the cross-roads, and disputed among themselves as to the sites of the various temples. Khamoûn faced the Syssites, and had golden tiles; Melkarth, to the left of Eschmoûn, bore on its roof coral branches; Tanit, beyond, rounded up through the palm-trees its copper cupola; and the black Moloch stood below the cisterns at the side of the lighthouse.

One could see at the angles of the frontons, on the summit of the walls, at the corners of the squares, everywhere, the various divinities with their hideous heads, colossal or dwarfish, with enormous or with immeasurably flattened bellies, open jaws, and outspread arms, holding in their hands pitchforks, chains, or javelins. And the blue sea spread out at the end of the streets, which the perspective rendered even steeper.

A tumultuous people from morning till night filled the streets: young boys rang bells, crying out before the doors of the bath-houses; shops wherein hot drinks were sold sent forth steam; the air resounded with the clangour of anvils; the white cocks, consecrated to the sun, crowed on the terraces; beeves awaiting slaughter bellowed in the temples; slaves ran hither and thither with baskets poised on their heads; and in the recesses of the porticoes now and again a priest appeared clothed in sombre mantle, bare-footed, wearing a conical cap.

This spectacle of Carthage enraged the Barbarians. They admired her; they execrated her; they desired at the same time to inhabit her and to annihilate her. But what might there not be in the military port, defended by a triple wall? Then behind the city, at the extremity of Megara, higher even than the Acropolis, loomed up Hamilcar's palace.

Mâtho's eyes constantly wandered in that direction. He climbed into the olive-trees, and bent forward, shading his eyes with one hand: but the gardens were deserted, and the red door with the black cross remained closed.

More than twenty times he made the circuit of the ramparts, searching for some breach to gain entrance. One night he threw himself into the gulf, and swam for three hours without pausing. He ultimately reached the foot of Mappals, endeavoured to cling to and climb up the cliffs, but cruelly tore his knees till they bled profusely, and crushed his nails, so that he fell into the water and swam back defeated.

His impuissance exasperated him: he was jealous of this Carthage that enclosed Salammbô, as of some one who might have possessed her. Stung by these thoughts, all enervation left him: thenceforth he plunged continuously into a frenzy of mad deeds. His cheeks blazed, his eyes became inflamed, his voice rasped; he strode at a rapid pace across the camp, or sat on the shore rubbing his large sword with the sand, or shot arrows at the passing vultures. His heart overflowed in furious speeches.

"Let your wrath go like a runaway chariot," said Spendius. "Cry out: blaspheme, ravage and kill; sorrow appeases itself with blood, and since you cannot satiate your love, gorge your hate; it will sustain you!"

Mâtho resumed command of his soldiers, making them manœuvre unmercifully. They respected him for his courage, and especially for his strength; besides, he inspired in their hearts a mystic awe, for they believed that he communed at night with phantoms.

The other captains were animated by his example: thus the army was very quickly under fine discipline. The Carthaginians heard from their dwellings the constant fanfare of trumpet calls, regulating these military exercises. At length the Barbarians advanced.

In order to crush them on the isthmus, the Carthaginians would have required two armies to attack them in the rear at the same time: the one debarking at the extremity of the Gulf of Utica, and the other at the Hot-Springs Mountain. But, what could the Carthaginians do now, with only the Sacred Legion, comprising at most but six thousand men? If the Barbarians diverged towards the east they would join the Nomads, and intercept the road to Cyrene and the commerce of the desert. If they fell back to the west the Numidians would revolt. Finally, their subsistence would fail, and soon or late they would be forced to devastate like locusts the surrounding country; the Rich trembled for their beautiful châteaux, for their vineyards, and for their farms.

Hanno proposed the most atrocious and impracticable measures, such as promising a large sum of money for every decapitated head of a Barbarian, or that with implements and war engines they should fire the enemy's camp. His colleague Gisco, on the contrary, advised that the Mercenaries should be paid. The Elders detested him on account of his popularity, as they dreaded to incur the risk of a master, and from terror of a monarchy strove to weaken whatever was subsidiary to, or could tend to re-establish, such a form of government.

Outside the fortifications were people of another race of an unknown origin, all porcupine hunters, eaters of molluscs and serpents—people who penetrated the caverns, captured live hyænas, and found amusement in racing them during the evenings on the sands of Megara between the stelas of the tombs. Their cabins of wrack and mud hung against the cliffs like swallows' nests: they lived there without government, without Gods, pell-mell, completely naked, and at once both feeble and savage —during all ages cursed by the Carthaginians because of their unclean food. One morning the sentinels perceived that these creatures had all gone.

At length the members of the Grand Council decided that they would go personally to the Barbarians' camp, without collars or girdles, and with their sandals uncovered, like their plebeian neighbours. Accordingly one day they advanced at a tranquil step, throwing salutations to the captains, or even tarrying to talk with the soldiers, saying that all war was now at an end, and that they would do justice to the demands of the Mercenaries.

Many of these patricians saw for the first time a Mercenarian camp. Instead of finding the confusion that they had imagined, over everything order ruled, and a frightful stillness prevailed. A rampart of turf enclosed the army within a high wall that could not be shaken by the shocks of catapults. The camp streets were constantly kept sprinkled with fresh water. Through holes in the tents they saw lurid eyes gleaming mid the shadows. The stacks of spears and the suspended panoplies dazzled them like mirrors. They talked in undertones among themselves, and seemed constantly in fear of overturning with their long robes some of the vast medley of objects.

The soldiers demanded provisions, and engaged to pay for them out of the money that the Republic owed them. Beeves, sheep, guinea-fowls, dried fruits, lupins, as well as smoked mackerel—those excellent mackerel which Carthage exported with large revenue to all other ports—were sent to them. But the soldiers disdainfully walked around the magnificent cattle, disparaged that which they coveted, offering for a sheep the price of a pigeon, for three goats the value of a pomegranate. The eaters-of-unclean-things set themselves up as arbitrators, affirming that they were being duped. Then they drew their swords and threatened to kill the ambassadors.

The commissioners of the Grand Council wrote down the number of years' pay due to each soldier; but it was now impossible to know how much the Mercenaries had originally been engaged for, and the Elders were frightened at the exorbitant sums that they would be obliged to pay. It would necessitate the sale of the reserve of silphium, and compel them to impose a tax on the commercial cities. The Mercenaries were impatient; already Tunis sympathised with them.

The Rich, stunned by Hanno's fury and by the reproaches of his colleague Gisco, recommended that the citizens who might perchance know any Barbarians should go and see them immediately, in order to regain their friendship by fair promises; such confidence would calm them.

Tradesmen, scribes, workers from the arsenals, and entire families went to the Barbarians. The soldiers permitted all these Carthaginians to enter their encampment, but by a single passage, so narrow that only four men abreast could elbow their way.

Spendius stood against the barrier, and caused each one to be thoroughly searched. Mâtho faced him, examining the multitude, seeking to find some one whom he might have formerly seen at the palace of Salammbô.

The encampment resembled a city, it was so filled with people and movement. Yet the two distinct crowds, military and civic, commingled without being confounded; the one dressed in linen or woollen, wearing felt-caps pointed like pine-cones, and the other vested in iron, wearing metal helmets. Amid the moving varlets and vendors strolled about women of all nations: brown as ripe dates, green as olives, yellow as oranges. These women had been sold by sailors, or chosen in the trader's closet, or stolen from caravans, or taken during the sacking of cities; that they might be wearied with lust while they were young, or might be overwhelmed with blows when they were old, and who would die neglected on the roadside, during the retreats, along with the abandoned beasts of burden, in the midst of the baggage.

The wives of the Nomads dangled over their heels their square cut, tawny coloured robes, of dromedaries, hair. The Cyrenaic musicians, with painted eyebrows, and enveloped in violet gauze, sang as they squatted on mats; old negresses, with their hanging breasts, picked up sun-dried dung for fuel. Syracusians wore gold plaques in their hair; Lusitanians were tricked out with necklaces made of shells; the Gallic women wore wolves' skins over their white breasts;

and robust children, covered with vermin, naked, uncircumcised, playfully butted the passers-by on their abdomens with their lusty heads, or crept up behind them, like young tigers, to bite their hands.

The Carthaginians promenaded through the camp, much surprised by the quantity of strange articles with which it teemed. The most miserable were melancholy, while the others strove to dissimulate their uneasiness.

Soldiers slapped them familiarly on their shoulders bidding them be gay; and as soon as they perceived some person of note, invited him to join their sports: if one perchance consented to play a game of discs, then the soldiers managed to crush his feet; or in boxing, after the first pass, broke his jaw.

The slingers terrified the Carthaginians, with their slings, the snake-charmers with their vipers, and the cavalry with their horses. These citizens of peaceful occupations lowered their heads and forced a smile at these outrages. Some, to manifest an assumed bravery, even made signs that they desired to become soldiers. They were set to cleave wood and to curry mules; or buckled in armour, and rolled about like hogsheads through the camp streets. Afterwards, when they were disposed to take leave, the Barbarians pulled out their own hair, and with grotesque contortions, demonstrated their pretended grief.

Many of the Mercenaries, from foolishness or prejudice, truly believed that all Carthaginians were very rich; they followed, begging their visitors to give them something; asked for all that they wore that seemed beautiful in their barbaric eyes—a ring, a girdle, sandals, or the fringes off their robes; after the Carthaginians were utterly despoiled, and said, "But we have nothing more; what do you want?" they would answer, "Your women! your lives!"

In due time the military accounts were given to the captains, read to the soldiers, and definitely approved. Then the soldiers demanded the tents, which were given to them;—the Greek polemarchs asked for some of the beautiful armour fabricated in Carthage; the Grand Council voted a sum of money for this acquisition. Then the cavalry-men pretended that it would be but just for the Republic to indemnify them for their horses; one would affirm to have lost three in such and such a siege, and another five on a certain march, another fourteen over precipices. They were proffered the fine stallions of Hecatompylus; but no, they preferred the payment in money.

Finally they demanded to be paid in silver, and not with leather tokens, for all the grain due to them, and that at the highest prices at which it was sold during the war, so that they even went so far as to demand for one measure of meal four hundred times more than had actually been given for a sack of wheat. This injustice and greed exasperated the Council; however, it was necessary to yield.

Then the delegates of the soldiers and the Council were reconciled, swearing amity by the genius of Carthage and by the Gods of the Barbarians. With demonstrations and Oriental verbosity they exchanged excuses and caresses. The soldiers now demanded as a proof of amity the punishment of the traitors who had estranged them from the Republic.

The Carthaginians feigned that they did not comprehend; the Barbarians, explaining more clearly, boldly declared that they must have Hanno's head. Frequently during the day they would leave their camp and sally forth to the foot of the walls, crying out for some one to throw the Suffete's head down to them, at the same time holding their robes outstretched to receive the demanded guerdon.

Perhaps the Grand Council might have yielded, had not a last exaction, more outrageous than all others followed, for now the Mercenaries demanded in marriage for their chiefs, maidens to be chosen from the noble families. This was an idea of Spendius, that many thought easy to achieve and strongly expedient. However, their audacious pretension in wanting to mix with the Punic blood filled the citizens with such indignation, that they brusquely signified to the soldiers that henceforth they had nothing more to expect or receive from Carthage. Then the soldiers exclaimed that they had been basely deceived, and that if within three days they did not receive their payment, they should go themselves and wrest it from Carthage.

The bad faith of the Mercenaries was not quite so complete as the Carthaginians supposed, for Hamilcar had made them exorbitant promises—vague, it is true, but solemn, and reiterated. They had been led to believe that, when they landed at Carthage, the city would forthwith be given up to them, and that they should share among themselves the city treasure; hence, when they came, only to find their payments were repudiated, or would be paid with great difficulty and delay, the disillusion of their pride, as well as the rebuff to their cupidity, was severe.

Dionysius, Pyrrhus, Agathocles, and the generals of Alexander, had they not furnished examples of marvellous fortunes? The ideal of Hercules, whom the Canaanites confused with the sun, illumined the horizon of the armies. It was well known that soldiers from the ranks had worn diadems, and the re-echoing fame of falling empires made the Gauls dream of glory in their oak forests, and imbued with ambition the Ethiopians on their native sands. But here was a people always ready to utilise the courageous; and the thief chased from his tribe, the parricide skulking on the highways, the sacrilegious pursued by the Gods, all the starving, and all desperados endeavoured to reach the port, where the agents of Carthage recruited soldiers. Usually the Republic kept her promises; however, in this instance the ardour of her avarice had dragged her into a perilous infamy. The Numidians, the Libyans, the whole of Africa, would now unitedly throw themselves upon Carthage. The sea only remained free to her. But there she would come into collision with Rome: so, like a man assailed by murderers, she felt death lurking all around her.

The Council concluded it would be necessary to have recourse again to Gisco, for the Barbarians would probably accept the intervention of their former general. One morning the chains of the port were lowered, and three flat boats passed through the canal of the Tænia and entered the lake.

At the prow of the first boat Gisco was perceived; behind him, and higher than a catafalque, loomed up an enormous case, ornamented with rings like pendant wreaths. Following, appeared a legion of interpreters coiffured like sphinxs, with parrots tattooed on their breasts. Friends and slaves came after, all without arms, and in such a multitude that they touched shoulder to shoulder. These three long, crowded, boats solemnly advanced amid the cheers of the expectant army that watched them from the shore.

As soon as Gisco landed, the soldiers rushed to meet him. He soon erected, with sacks piled on top of each other, a kind of tribunal, and declared that he would not leave until he had integrally paid them all.

The outburst of applause prevented his speaking for some time. Then he resumed by censuring the wrong-doings of the Republic and the wrong-doings of the Barbarians; the great fault had been with those who had mutinied, with such extreme violence, as to have frightened Carthage. The best proof of the Republic's present good intentions was the fact that they had sent him—the eternal adversary of Hanno—to treat with them. They certainly could not suppose that the people would be so inept as to anger its braves, or so ungrateful as to discount their services. Gisco prepared to pay the soldiers, commencing with the Libyans. As they declared the lists falsified, he set them aside.

They defiled before him by nations, and spread out their fingers to indicate the term of years they had served. Each man was successively marked on his left arm with green paint; scribes made with a stiletto holes on sheets of lead; while others drew out the accounts from open coffers.

Presently a man passed by who tramped heavily, like an ox.

"Come up near to me," said Gisco, suspecting some fraud. "How many years have you served?"

"Twelve," responded the Libyan.

Gisco slipped his fingers under the fellow's jaws, as the chin-piece of the helmets produced, after being worn for a long time, two callosities that were called *carroubes*, and "having *carroubes*" was synonymous to being a veteran.

"Thief!"—cried Gisco. "That which is missing on your face you must have on your shoulders!" At this he tore off the man's tunic, disclosing a back covered with bleeding sores. In truth he was a slave labourer of Hippo-Zarytus. Yells arose, and the culprit was beheaded.

As soon as night fell, Spendius went about to stir up the Libyans, saying to them:

"When the Ligurians, the Greeks, Balearics, and all the men of Italy shall be paid, they will return to their native countries, but you others must remain in Africa; scattered among the tribes without any defence! Then the Republic will revenge herself! Beware of voyages! Are you going to believe all these speeches? The two Suffetes are in accord! This one abuses your confidence! Do you recollect the island of bones, and Xanthippus, whom they sent to Sparta on a rotten galley?"

"How are we to act?" demanded they.

"Be circumspect," replied Spendius.

The two subsequent days were spent in paying the people of Magdala, Leptis and Hecatompylus. Spendius spread fresh dissensions among the Gauls, saying:

"They will pay the Libyans, afterwards the Greeks, then the Balearics, then the Asiatics, and all the others! But you, who are in the minority, will be given nothing! You will never more see your country! You have no vessels! They will kill you to save your keeping!"

The Gauls set out to seek Gisco. Autharitus, the man whom he had wounded in Hamilcar's gardens, addressed him, but was thrust back by the slaves, and disappeared, swearing to revenge himself.

Demands and complaints multiplied. The most persistent penetrated into the Suffete's tent, and, to move him to pity, they would take his fingers and make him feel their toothless mouths, their emaciated arms, and the cicatrices of their wounds. Those who were not yet paid became exasperated; those who had received their pay demanded an additional sum for their horses; and the vagabonds and outcasts, taking the soldiers' weapons, declared that they had been forgotten. Every moment men surged forward in eddies; the tents cracked under the strain, and finally toppled over; the multitude, giving vent to yells, crowded between the ramparts, swaying and surging from the entrance to the centre of the camp. When the tumult became too loud, Gisco posed his elbow on his ivory sceptre, and gazed over the sea of faces, remaining motionless, with his fingers buried in his beard.

Mâtho often went aside to interview Spendius, but ever took his place again facing the Suffete; and Gisco felt perpetually his eyes like flaming fire-lances darting towards him. Above the crowd frequently they interchanged words of abuse, but neither understood the other. Meanwhile, the distribution continued, and the Suffete for every obstacle found ready expedients.

The Greeks quibbled about the differences in the moneys; but he furnished such satisfactory explanations, that they withdrew without a murmur. The Negroes demanded their pay in the white shells used in commerce through the interior of Africa; he offered to send thither and bring a supply to Carthage; then, like the others, they accepted the silver money. The Balearics had been promised something better—women. The Suffete responded that an entire caravan of virgins was expected for them; but as the road was long, it would still require six moons. However, when they arrived at their destination, they would be fat, and well rubbed with benzoin, and they should see them on the vessels in the Balearic ports.

Suddenly Zarxas, now fine and vigorous, leaped like a mountebank upon the shoulders of his friends, and cried out, "What have you reserved for the dead?" pointing to the gate of Khamoûn.

Under the last rays of the sun the brass plates that garnished the gate from top to bottom were refulgent, and the Barbarians believed that they saw on them a track of blood. Every time Gisco vouchsafed to speak, their yells recommenced; finally he descended with a solemn step, and shut himself up in his tent.

At sunrise, when he went forth again, his interpreters, who had lain outside his tent, did not stir. They lay on their backs, eyes fixed, tongues protruding between their teeth, and their faces blueish;

UNDER THE WALLS OF CARTHAGE.

white froth oozed from their nostrils, their limbs were stiff, as though they had been frozen during the night, and around the neck of each was drawn a little leather cord.

From this time there was no cessation of the rebellion. The murder of the Balearics recalled by Zarxas confirmed the suspicions set brewing by Spendius. They imagined that the Republic always sought to deceive them. It must be ended! They could do without interpreters! Zarxas, with a sling around his head, sang war songs; Autharitus brandished his great sword; Spendius would whisper something to one, and to another furnish a poniard. The most powerful endeavoured to pay themselves; but those least enraged requested that the distribution should go on.

During this excitement no one laid down their weapons, and their wrath centred upon Gisco in a tumultuous hatred. Some went up beside him Just so long as they only vociferated their wrongs, they were patiently listened to; but the moment they uttered the slightest word in his favour they were immediately stoned, or their heads would be cut off by a sabre blow from behind. The heap of sacks soon became red as an altar during a sacrifice.

They were terrible after their repast, for they had drunk wine! This was an indulgence forbidden under pain of death in the Punic armies; but in derision of her discipline, they lifted their cups towards Carthage. Afterwards they turned on the slaves of the finances and began killing them. The word *strike*, different in each language, was understood by all.

Gisco knew perfectly well that his country had forsaken him, but he did not desire her to be dishonoured. When the soldiers recalled to him that the government had promised them vessels, he swore by Moloch to furnish them himself at his own expense, and pulling off his collar of blue stones, threw it to the crowd as a pledge to his oath.

Then the Africans made a claim for their grain, according to the arrangement with the Grand Council. Gisco spread out the accounts of the Syssites, traced with violet paint on sheep-skins, and read all that had entered into Carthage, day by day, month by month.

Suddenly he stopped; his eyes opened widely, as if he had discovered between the figures his own death sentence. In effect the Elders had made fraudulent reductions, and the grain sold during the most calamitous period of the war was rated so low in these accounts that only the blindest person could have been deceived.

"Speak!" cried they; "louder! Oh! he strives to deceive us, the coward! We distrust you!"

He hesitated for some time; at length he again took up his task.

The soldiers, without suspecting the accounts rendered by the Syssites to be inaccurate, accepted them. The abundance that they found Carthage possessed of, threw them into a jealous rage. They fell upon and broke open the sycamore coffer; it was now three-quarters empty, but having seen such enormous sums taken from it, they had deemed it inexhaustible. Had Gisco hidden some in his tent? The soldiers climbed over the sacks, led on by Mâtho, yelling:

"The money! the money!"

Gisco at last responded.

"Let your general give it to you!"

Without speaking further, he turned upon them his large yellow eyes and long pale face, whiter than his beard. An arrow whistled towards him, and was arrested by its feathered barb, and held fast by his broad gold earring; a thread of blood trickled down from his tiara upon his shoulder.

At a gesture from Mâtho all advanced upon Gisco. He threw out his arms; but Spendius with a running knot fastened his wrists together; another man pitched him over, and he disappeared in the prevailing disorder of the crowd, which tumbled over the sacks. They completely ransacked his tent, finding nothing but the necessities of life; then searching closer, found three images of Tanit, and in a monkey's hide, a black stone, which had fallen from the moon.

The numerous Carthaginians who had accompanied Gisco were all of the war party, and were men of importance. They were taken outside of the tents, and thrown into the pit of filth. They were attached by chains to stakes driven in the earth, and their food was held out to them on the points of javelins.

Over all of these captives Autharitus kept surveillance, heaping upon them invectives; but as they did not comprehend his language, they made no response, and the Gaul would, from time to time, throw stones in their faces, to make them cry out.

Next day a languor invaded the army. According as their rage subsided an inquietude possessed them. Mâtho suffered from a strange sadness. It seemed to him that he had indirectly outraged Salammbô: the Rich were like a dependence of her person. He sat at night on the edge of their pit, and in their moans fancied he heard something akin to her voice, of which his heart was full.

Meanwhile, all accused the Libyans, who alone were paid. Notwithstanding that national antipathies and personal hatreds were reviving, everyone felt the present peril in yielding to them. Reprisals after such an outrage would be formidable. They must by common adhesion ward off the vengeance of Carthage. Cabals and harangues were never ended; everyone talked; no one listened; and Spendius, ordinarily so loquacious, now to all proposals shook his head.

One evening he carelessly asked Mâtho if there were any springs in the interior of the city.

"Not one!" responded Mâtho.

The next day Spendius led him to the lake shore. "Master, if your heart is intrepid, I will conduct you to Carthage."

"How?" breathlessly asked Mâtho.

"Swear to execute my orders, and to follow me like a shadow," said Spendius.

Mâtho raised his arm toward the planet Cabira, saying:

"By Tanit I swear it!"

Spendius resumed:

"To-morrow, after sunset, wait for me at the foot of the aqueduct between the ninth and tenth arcades. Bring with you an iron pike; wear a helmet without aigrette, and leathern sandals."

The aqueduct to which he alluded traversed

obliquely the entire isthmus—a work considerably enlarged later by the Romans. Notwithstanding Carthage's disdain for other peoples, she had awkwardly taken this new invention from Rome; as Rome herself had taken the Punic galley. It was of a broad low architecture of five ranges of superposed arches, with buttresses at the base and lions' heads at the summit, which abutted on the western side of the Acropolis, where it plunged under the city, turning almost a river into the cisterns of Megara.

At the hour agreed upon, Spendius found Mâtho waiting at the rendezvous. He fastened a sort of harpoon to the end of a long rope, that he whirled rapidly like a sling; as the iron caught in the masonry, they moved one behind the other and climbed up along the wall. After reaching the first story, each time that the harpoon was thrown it fell back, hence, in order to discover some fissure, they were compelled to walk on the edge of the cornice, which on each row of arches they found became narrower. At times the rope slackened, and again it threatened to break. At length they attained the upper platform, where Spendius bent over, sounding the stones from time to time with his hands.

"It is here"—said he—"we will begin!" and pressing on the pike Mâtho had brought, he commenced to disjoint one of the stones.

They perceived, in the distance below them, a troop of cavalry galloping, without bridles on their horses, their gold bracelets bounding in the loose draperies of their ample mantles. In advance could be distinguished a man crowned with ostrich-plumes, holding a lance in each hand as he galloped.

"Narr' Havas!" exclaimed Mâtho.

"What matter?" replied Spendius, leaping into the hole he had just made by displacing a stone. Mâtho, by his orders, tried to prize out one of the blocks of stone, but from lack of space he could not move his elbows.

"We shall return,"—said Spendius;—"go before me."

Then they ventured into the water-conduit. The water reached up to their waists; soon they staggered, and were obliged to swim. Their limbs were knocked against the inner walls of the very narrow channel, and as they progressed, the water gradually rose, till it almost reached the superior stones, against which they tore their faces, as the swift current carried them resistlessly along. An atmosphere heavy as that of a sepulchre pressed upon their lungs, and with their heads under their arms, their knees together, elongating themselves as much as possible, they passed like arrows through the obscurity, stifled, gasping for breath, nearly dead. Suddenly all grew dark before them —the velocity of the water redoubled. They sank. When they arose to the surface again they remained for some minutes floating on their backs, inhaling the delicious pure air. The arcades one behind the other opened out in the middle of the wide walls separating the basins; all were full, and the water continued as one unbroken sheet the length of the cisterns. Through the air-holes in the cupola of the ceiling, a pale clearness spread over the water like discs of light: the darkness thickened towards the walls as they retreated indefinitely—here the slightest noise made a tremendous echo.

Spendius and Mâtho resumed swimming, and passing the openings of the arches, crossed many chambers in succession : two similar but much smaller ranges of basins extended parallel on each side. They lost themselves, and were compelled to turn and swim back for some distance. Something resisted under their feet: it was the pavement of the gallery running the length of the cistern. With great precaution they proceeded to feel the walls, striving to detect an issue; but their feet slipped, and they fell into the deep basin; they struggled up, but again fell back. As they struck out again they experienced a frightful fatigue in swimming —their limbs seemed about to dissolve in the water—their eyes closed—they seemed in death-throes.

Spendius struck his hand against the bar of a grating; both men shook it vigorously; it yielded, and they found themselves on the steps of a stairway closed at the top by a bronze door. With the point of a poniard they wrested open the bolt fastening this door from the outside, and at once gained access to pure, fresh air.

The night was full of silence, and the sky swelled above to an immeasurable height; clumps of trees projected beyond the long lines of walls; the entire city slept; and the fires of the advance posts shone through the night like lost stars.

Spendius, who had spent three years confined in the *ergastulum*, knew the quarters of the city but imperfectly. Mâtho, however, conjectured that in order to reach Hamilcar's palace, they must go to the left by crossing Mappals.

"No!" said Spendius; "conduct me to the temple of Tanit."

Matho essayed to speak.

"Remember!" said the former slave, as he lifted his right arm, and pointed to the resplendent planet of Cabira.

Mâtho silently turned towards the Acropolis. They crept cautiously along the enclosures of fig-trees bordering the pathways. The water trickled from their limbs upon the dust; their wet sandals made no sound. Spendius, with eyes more gleaming than torches, at each step peered into the bushes, as he groped behind Mâtho, constantly clutching in his hands, ready for immediate action, the two poniards he wore attached to his arms, that were held in place below the armpits by a leather band.

CHAPTER V.

TANIT.

AFTER leaving the gardens, they found the enclosure of Megara an obstacle; however, they soon detected a breach in the high wall, through which they passed. The ground descended, forming a very broad valley. It was an excellent point for a reconnaissance.

"Listen," said Spendius; "and above all, fear nothing: I will execute my promise;" and with an air of reflection he paused, as if to weigh his words. "You remember that time, just at sunrise, as we stood on the terrace of Salammbô's palace, when I pointed out Carthage to you? We were strong that day, but you would not heed me." Then in a graver voice he pursued: "Master, there is, in the sanctuary of Tanit, a mysterious veil, fallen from Heaven, that conceals the Goddess."

"I know that," replied Mâtho.

Spendius resumed: "It is divine, as it is a part of Tanit. ... The Gods reside where their simulachres dwell. It is because Carthage possesses it, that Carthage is powerful." Then leaning forward he whispered, "I have brought you with me, to ravish this veil!"

Mâtho recoiled with horror. "Go! seek some one else! I do not wish to aid in such an execrable crime."

"But Tanit is your enemy," replied Spendius. "She persecutes you, and is destroying you with her wrath. You can thus revenge yourself. She will obey you. You will become almost immortal and invincible!"

Mâtho bowed his head.

Spendius continued: "If we succumb, the army will become self-annihilated. We have neither escape, succour, nor pardon to hope for! What chastisement of the Gods can you fear when once you possess, in your own hands, their strength? Do you prefer to perish miserably the night of a defeat under the shelter of a bush, or be burned at the stake amid the outrages heaped upon you by the populace? Master, at some future day you will enter Carthage between the colleges of pontiffs, who will kiss your sandals; and if the veil of Tanit then weighs upon you, re-establish it in her temple. Follow me! Come, take it!"

A terrible desire devoured Mâtho: he would like to abstain from the sacrilege, and yet possess the veil He thought, perhaps he did not desire to take it merely to monopolise its virtues. However, he did not probe to the bottom of his intentions, but paused at the limit where his thoughts frightened him.

"We will go on," he said; and they moved forward at a rapid pace, side by side, without speaking.

The ground ascended, and the habitations drew

closer together; they turned aside in the narrow streets, walking in the midst of shadows. The esparto-hangings closing the doorways beat against the walls; camels ruminated before heaps of cut grass in a square; then their path led them under a gallery covered over with foliage, where a pack of dogs barked at them. The space suddenly enlarged, and they recognised the western façade of the Acropolis. At the foot of Byrsa spread out a long, black mass; it was the temple of Tanit, a collection of monuments and gardens, courts and fore-courts, hemmed in by a little wall of uncemented stones, over which Spendius and Mâtho vaulted.

This first enclosure shut in a grove of plane-trees, planted as a precaution against the pest and infections of the atmosphere. Here and there were scattered tents in which, during the day, were sold depilatory pastes, perfumes, clothing, crescent-shaped cakes, images of the Goddess, and representations of the temple carved in blocks of alabaster. They had now nothing to apprehend, as, during the nights that the planet did not appear, all rites were suspended; however, Mâtho slackened his pace; he stopped before the three ebony steps leading to the second enclosure.

"Go on!" urged Spendius.

Pomegranates, almonds, cypresses, and myrtles, alternated regularly, and were as motionless as bronze foliage; the path, paved with blue stones, creaked under their feet; and roses in full bloom embowered the long alley. They soon came to an oval opening, protected by a grating. Then Mâtho, who was terrified by the silence, said to Spendius:

"It is here that the Sweet Waters and Bitter Waters are mixed."

"I have seen all that," replied the former slave, "in the city of Maphug, at Syria."

By a stair of six silver steps, they proceeded up to the third enclosure. An enormous cedar occupied the centre; its lowest branches disappeared under loops of fabrics and necklaces appended by the faithful. They advanced a few steps more, and the façade of the temple deployed before them.

Two long porticoes, with architraves reposing on dwarfish pillars, flanked a quadrangular tower, ornamented on the platform by a crescent moon. At the angles of the porticoes, and at the four corners of the tower, were erected vases full of burning aromatics. Pomegranates and colocynths loaded the capitals: interlacements and lozenges alternated regularly with garlands of pearls, festooning the walls, and a hedge of silver filigree formed a wide semicircle before a brass stairway descending from the vestibule.

There was at the entrance, between a stela of gold and a stela of emerald, a stone cone; in passing, Mâtho kissed his right hand.

The first room was very lofty; innumerable openings pierced the vaulted ceiling, through which the stars were visible. All around the wall, in reed-baskets, were heaped beards and hair, first indications of adolescence; and in the centre of the circular apartment the body of a woman rose from a pedestal covered with breasts. Fat, bearded, with eyelids lowered, she had the air of smiling; her hands crossed the lower part of her gross abdomen—polished by the kisses of her votaries.

Then they found themselves in the open air in a transverse corridor, where an altar of scanty proportions was placed against an ivory gate, barring the passage. Beyond this the priests alone were privileged to pass—as a temple was not a place for the congregation of the people, but the particular abode of its divinity.

"The undertaking is impossible," exclaimed Mâtho. "You did not dream of this obstacle; we must go back."

Spendius carefully examined the walls. He coveted the veil: not that he reposed confidence in its virtues, for Spendius believed only in the Oracle; but he was persuaded that, if the Carthaginians discovered themselves deprived of the veil they would fall into great consternation.

To find some outlet, they made a tour at the back. Under the turpentine thickets could be seen little buildings of various forms. Here and there a stone phallus stood up; and large stags tranquilly wandered about, crushing under their cloven hoofs the fallen pine-cones.

They retraced their steps between two long parallel galleries. Tiny cells opened out on these. Tambourines and cymbals hung on the cedar columns. Extended on mats outside, women slept, whose bodies were so greased with unguents that they exhaled an odour of aromatics, and extinguished cassolettes; and they were so covered with tattooing, collars, bracelets, vermilion, and antimony, that they might easily have been mistaken for idols—thus lying about on the ground—but for the movement of their breasts.

Lotuses surrounded a fountain, where swam fish like Salammbô's; then in the background, against the wall of the temple, clung a spreading vine, with tendrils of glass bearing clusters of emerald grapes; rays from the precious stones made a play of light beween the painted columns over the visages of the sleeping women.

Mâtho felt suffocated in the warm atmosphere that pressed upon him from the cedar compartments. All the symbols of fecundation, the lights, the perfumes, and the exhalations overcame him. Through this mystic bewilderment he dreamed of Salammbô; she was in his imagination confused with the Goddess, and his passion grew stronger, liberating and spreading itself from the depths of his being, as the great lotuses blossoming on the surface of the fountain were rooted in the waters' depth.

Spendius calculated what sums of money he formerly could have gained by the sale of these sleeping women, and with a rapid glance in passing, he computed the value of the gold necklaces.

The temple, on this side as on the other, was impenetrable. They retraced their steps behind the first chamber. While Spendius sought to ferret out an ingress, Mâtho, prone before the ivory gate, implored Tanit, supplicating her not to permit their contemplated sacrilege. He endeavoured to appease her by caressing words such as one might address to an angry being. Meanwhile Spendius descried above the door a narrow aperture.

"Stand up!" said Spendius.

Mâtho complied, putting his back against the wall, standing erect. Then Spendius, placing one foot in his hands and the other on his head, was enabled to reach the top of the opening, through which he crawled and disappeared. Then Mâtho felt strike his shoulders the knotted rope that Spendius had wound about his body before entering the cisterns. Clutching it with both hands, he drew himself up until he attained the opening, through which he crawled, and on the other side found himself beside Spendius, in a large hall full of shadow.

An attempt like this was most extraordinary. The inadequacy of the means to prevent it showed that it was deemed impossible. The inspired terrors, more than the walls, defend such sanctuaries. Mâtho at every step expected to meet his death.

A light twinkled in the extremity of the darkness; they drew nearer. It was a lamp burning in a shell placed on the pedestal of a statue wearing the cap of the Cabiri. Diamond discs studded her long blue robe, and chains, passing under the pavement stones, attached her heels to the ground. At the sight of this idol Mâtho suppressed a scream, stammering, "Ah! behold her! behold her!" ... Spendius took up the lamp, moving it about to better light himself.

"How impious you are!" murmured Mâtho; and yet he followed him.

They entered an apartment containing nothing except a black painting representing another woman. Her legs reached to the top of one of the walls; her body occupied the entire ceiling; from her navel hung suspended by a thread an enormous egg, and the remainder of her body, her head downward, descended the other wall to the level of the pavement, where her finger-ends touched.

H

To pass beyond they drew aside a tapestry; a puff of wind extinguished the light, and they were compelled to grope about, bewildered by the complications of the architecture. Suddenly they felt under their feet something singularly soft. The sparks of light flashed and sprang; they seemed to tread on unconsuming fire. Spendius stooped down, patted the floor with his hands, and detected that it was carefully carpeted with lynx-skins. Then it seemed to them that a thick, moist rope, cold and clammy, slid between their legs. Through the fissures cut in the wall, narrow rays of whiteness entered; they continued to move on by these uncertain streaks of light; presently they were able to distinguish a large black serpent, as it darted quickly away and disappeared.

"Let us fly!" exclaimed Mâtho. "It is she! I feel her! She comes!"

"Ah! no," responded Spendius, "the temple is empty."

A dazzling light made them lower their eyes; however, once accustomed to the glare, they saw all about innumerable beasts, emaciated, panting, extending their claws; those above were confused with those beneath in a mysterious disorder, most frightful to behold. Serpents had feet; bulls had wings; fishes with human heads devoured fruits; flowers blossomed in crocodiles' jaws; and elephants, with their trunks elevated, floated through the air as freely and proudly as eagles. A terrible effort distended their imperfect or manifold members. They seemed as they thrust out their tongues to long to exhale their souls with their breath. All forms were found here, as if the receptacle of germs had burst in a sudden development, and emptied itself over the walls of the hall.

Twelve blue crystal globes encircled the margin of the room, supported on monsters resembling tigers. Their eyeballs protruded like the eyes of snails, and menacingly curving their thick-set backs, they turned towards the farther part of the hall, where, refulgent on an ivory chariot, was enthroned the supreme Rabbet, the Omniparient, the last-imagined.

Tortoise shells, plumes, flowers, and birds were profusely heaped up about the idol, reaching to her waist. Silver cymbals, hitting against her cheeks, pended from her ears. Her large fixed eyes stared upon the intruders; a luminous gem set in an obscene symbol on her forehead flashed all over the hall, and was reflected above the entrance in the red copper mirrors.

Mâtho took a step, a stone receded under the pressure of his heels, and behold! all the spheres revolved, the monsters roared, music burst melodiously swelling forth like the harmony of the planets; the tumultuous soul of Tanit gushed and expanded. She was about to rise, and with outstretched arms she seemed to fill the sanctuary. Suddenly the monsters closed their jaws, and the crystal globes revolved no more.

Then a lugubrious modulation coursed through the air, lasting for some time, and finally died away.

"The veil!" exclaimed Spendius. Nowhere could it be seen. Where then to find it? How discover it? And if the priests had hidden it! Mâtho experienced a rending of his heart, like a deception in his faith.

"Come this way!" whispered Spendius. Guided by an inspiration, he led Mâtho behind Tanit's chariot, where a slit a cubit wide was cut in the wall from the top to the bottom. Through this they penetrated into a small, round room, so lofty that it resembled the interior of a column. In the centre was a large black stone, half-spherical, like a tambourine; flames burned above, and an ebony cone was erected at the back, upholding a head and two arms. Beyond, appeared a cloud wherein stars scintillated; in the depths of its folds were figures representing Eschmoûn, the Cabiri, many of the monsters already seen, the sacred beasts of the Babylonians, and numerous other unknown creatures. This passed like a mantle under the visage of the idol, and ascending it spread out over the wall, hanging to the corners; it was at the same time bluish—like night; yellow—like dawn; and purple—like the sun; harmonious, diaphanous, glittering, and light.

This was the mantle of the Goddess, the sacred Zaïmph, which no one had the power to behold! They both grew pale.

"Take it!" at last said Mâtho. Spendius did not hesitate, but supporting himself on the idol, unfastened the veil, which sank upon the ground. Mâtho placed one hand beneath it, and put his head through the opening in the middle; then he completely enveloped himself in the Zaïmph, and threw out his arms to better contemplate its splendour.

"Let us go!" said Spendius.

Mâtho stood panting, with his eyes riveted on the pavement. Suddenly he exclaimed:

"But, if I now go to her palace, I no longer need fear her beauty! What can she do against me? Behold, I am more than a man now! I can traverse flames! I can walk on the sea! Transport possesses me! Salammbô! Salammbô! I am thy master!"

His voice thundered. He appeared to Spendius of superior height, and transfigured.

Footsteps drew near; a door opened and a man appeared; a priest with a tall cap peered about with wide-open eyes. Before he had made a sign, Spendius rushed upon him, grappled him and buried the two poniards in his sides. His head rang out upon the pavement.

They paused for some time, as motionless as the body, listening. They heard nothing but the soughing of the wind through the half-open door, that led into a narrow passage. Spendius entered, followed by Mâtho. They almost immediately found themselves in the third enclosure, between the lateral porticoes among the habitations occupied by the priests. They hastened, fancying there must be some short way out behind the cells.

Spendius, crouching on the edge of the fountain, washed his blood-stained hands. The women still slept; the emerald vine shone with vitreous lustre. They resumed their way.

Something ran behind them under the trees, and Mâtho, who wore the veil, frequently felt something tug very gently at the fringe; it was a large cynocephalus, one of those that lived at liberty in the precincts of the temple. This creature clung to the veil as if it was conscious of the theft; nevertheless they dare not strike it, fearful that it might increase its cries. Suddenly its anger seemed appeased, and it trotted beside them, swinging its body and its long hanging arms.

On reaching the barrier it gave a bound, and sprang into a palm-tree.

Quitting the last enclosure, they diverged towards Hamilcar's palace, as Spendius comprehended that it would be useless to endeavour to dissuade Mâtho from his course.

They went on by the Tanners' street, through the square of Muthumbal, and the vegetable-market, and the cross-roads of Cynasyn. At the corner of a wall a man recoiled, frightened by this sparkling object that crossed through the darkness.

"Hide the Zaïmph," whispered Spendius.

Other people passed, but they continued unobserved.

At length they perceived the mansions of Megara. The lighthouse, built at the back on the summit of the cliff, illumined the sky with a large, clear, red light; and the shadow of the palace, with its terraces rising one above the other, projected over the gardens like a monstrous pyramid. They entered the gardens through a hedge of jujube trees, cutting off obstructing branches with their poniards. Everything bore traces of the Mercenaries' recent feast and depredations: the paddocks were broken down; the watercourses were dried up; the doors of the *ergastulum* stood open; no one was visible about the kitchens or cellars. They were astonished by the prevailing silence, broken only by the hoarse breathing of the elephants moving about in their paddocks, and the crepitations from the lighthouse, where a beacon of aloe wood burned.

Mâtho meanwhile repeated : "Where is she ? I want to see her ; take me to her."

"It is a madness,"—replied Spendius ;—"she will summon her slaves to her succour, and, in spite of your power, you will be killed !"

They attained the stairway of the galleys. Mâtho raised his head, and believed he could see on high a dim light softly radiating. Spendius endeavoured to detain him, but he sprang swiftly up the steps.

In returning to these places where he had previously seen her, the interval that had elapsed was instantly effaced from his memory. Just now, she was chanting between the tables—she had disappeared—and ever since he seemed to have been climbing that stairway. The sky overhead was covered with fire ; the sea filled the horizon ; and at every step an increasing immensity surrounded him ; he continued to climb with that strange facility that one experiences in dreams.

The rustling of the veil grazing against the stones recalled his new power, but, in the excess of his hope, he no longer knew what he ought to do ; this incertitude intimidated him. From time to time he pressed his face against the quadrangular openings in the closed apartments, and in many he fancied he could faintly see those sleeping within.

The last story was narrower, and formed like a thimble on the top of the terraces. Mâtho slowly made the circuit. A milky light filled the talc-sheets which closed the little openings in the wall, and, in their symmetrical arrangement through the dark, resembled rows of fine pearls. Mâtho's heartbeat quickened as he recognised the red door with the black cross. He was inclined to fly, but he pushed the door, and it swung open.

A suspended lamp, fashioned like a galley, burned at the extremity of the room, and three rays escaping from its silver keel, trembled over the high red wainscoting decorated with black bands. An assemblage of small gilded beams formed the ceiling with amethysts and topazes set in the knots of the wood. Stretched against the wall of the long sides of the room were very low couches made of white straps; and shell-like arches opened in the depth of the wall, from which many garments in disorder, hung down to the floor.

An onyx step surrounded an oval basin, on the edge of which rested a pair of dainty serpent-skin slippers close beside an alabaster pitcher. Humid footprints were clearly defined on the pavement beyond, and the vapours of exquisite perfumes floated everywhere.

Mâtho glided over the pavement, encrusted with gold, mother-of-pearl, and glass; and, despite the highly polished surface, it seemed to him that his feet sank, as if he walked in sand. Behind the silver lamp he noticed a large azure square, suspended in the air by four cords; he drew towards it, with back bent and mouth open. Strewn about the room among purple cushions were flamingoes' wings, with handles of black coral branches, tortoise shell combs, cedar caskets, and ivory spatulas. Slipped over antelopes' horns were rows of rings, and bracelets; and in a chink in the walls, on a reed lattice, were placed clay vases, filled with water cooled by the incoming breezes. Frequently Mâtho struck his toes, as the floor was of unequal heights, making the chamber like a succession of apartments. At the end a silver balustrade surrounded a carpet, painted with beautiful flowers. He reached the suspended couch, beside which stood an ebony stool, serving as a step.

The light was arrested at the edge of the couch, and shadow, like a large curtain, completely hid all objects, save a little bare foot peering from under a white robe, resting on the corner of a red mattress. Mâtho very softly drew down the lamp to make a closer inspection. The occupant of the couch slept, resting her cheek on one hand, and with the other arm thrown out and exposed. The rings of her wavy black hair tumbled about her in such abundance, that she appeared actually to lie on a mass of black plumes; her white, wide tunic was crushed in soft draperies to her feet, indistinctly defining the outlines of her form; and her eyes were partially revealed between the half-opened lids. The perpendicular couch-hangings enshrouded her in a bluish atmosphere, and the swaying movement, imparted to the cords by her respiration, rocked her suspended couch mid-air. An enormous mosquito buzzed.

Mâtho stood motionless, holding the silver galley at arm's-length. Suddenly the airy mosquito hangings ignited and disappeared. Salammbô awoke. The fire had become self-extinguished. She did not speak. The lamp flickered over the wainscoting great moire splashes of light.

"What is it?" she exclaimed.

He responded: "It is the veil of Tanit."

"The veil of Tanit?" cried Salammbô, as, supporting herself on her hands, she leaned tremblingly over the side of her couch.

He continued: "I have sought it for you in the depths of the sanctuary! Behold!" The Zaïmph glittered, covered with rays.

"You remember, then?"—queried Mâtho.—"In the night you appeared in my dreams; but I could not divine the mute command in your eyes."

She placed one foot on the ebony stool to descend.

"If I had understood, I should have hastened, I would have abandoned the army, I would not have left Carthage. To obey you I would descend by the cavern of Hadrumetum into the realms of the Shades! Forgive me! Mountains have seemed to weigh upon my days, and yet something drew me on. I strove to reach you; but, without the aid of the Gods I should never have dared! Let us depart; you must follow me, or if you do not desire to go, I will remain. To me it makes no difference!! Drown my soul in the vapour of your breath! let my lips be crushed in kissing your hands!"

"Let me see it!" she exclaimed. "Nearer! nearer!"

As the dawn broke, a wine-coloured hue spread over the talc-sheets in the walls. Salammbô leaned back falteringly on the pillows.

"I love you!" cried Mâtho.

She stammered, "Give it to me!" and they drew nearer together.

She moved steadily forward, robed in her white trailing simarre, her large eyes riveted on the veil. Mâtho contemplated her, dazzled by the splendour of her head. Holding towards her the Zaïmph, he attempted to envelope her in an embrace. She threw out her arms to repulse him. She suddenly paused; and they remained, silently regarding one another with open mouths.

Without knowing what he solicited, a horror seized her. She raised her narrow eyebrows, her lips parted, and she trembled in consternation; at length recovering, she struck in one of the brass pateras hanging at the corner of the red mattress and screamed out:

"Help! Help! Back! Sacrilegious! Infamous! Accursed! Come to me, Taanach, Kroûm, Ewa, Micipsa, Schaoûl!"

Spendius's frightened face appeared in the wall between the argil ewers, as he uttered with alarm, "Fly! they are coming!"

A great uproar ascended, shaking the stairway, and a host of women, valets, and slaves burst into the apartment, carrying spears, maces, cutlasses, and poniards. They were paralysed with indignation at finding a man in Salammbô's room. The women servants uttered funereal wails, and the eunuchs fairly paled under their black skins.

Mâtho remained behind the balustrade, the Zaïmph enveloping him; thus he resembled a sidereal God, environed by the firmament. The slaves were about to throw themselves upon him, but Salammbô hindered them.

"Do not touch that! It is the mantle of the Goddess!"

She had retreated into a corner, but now she stepped towards Mâtho, and extending her bare arm towards him, cursed him:

"Malediction on you, who have robbed Tanit! Hate, vengeance, massacre, and sorrow! May Gurzil, God of battles, rend you! May Mastiman, God of death, strangle you! and may the other—whom I dare not name—burn you!"

Mâtho uttered a cry, like one wounded by a spear.

Frequently she repeated, "Go! Go!"

The throng of servants scattered as Mâtho with downcast eyes slowly passed out through their midst. At the door he was retarded by the fringe of the Zaïmph becoming entangled on one of the golden stars adorning the pavement, but by a brusque movement of his shoulders he detached it, and descended the stairs.

Spendius, bounding from terrace to terrace, overleaping the hedges and ditches, escaped from the gardens and reached the foot of the lighthouse; here the wall was abandoned, as the cliff was inaccessible. He advanced to the edge, then lying down on his back, slid to the bottom; then swimming, he reached the Cape of the Tombs, from whence he made a wide circuit by the salt lagoon, re-entering the Barbarians' camp at evening.

The sun had risen as Mâtho descended the roads, glaring about him with terrible eyes, like an escaping lion. An indistinct murmur, emanating from the palace, and recommencing in the distance from the direction of the Acropolis, struck his ears. It was rumoured that some one had taken from the temple of Moloch the treasure of Carthage; others spoke of the assassination of a priest; elsewhere it was imagined that the Barbarians had entered the city.

Mâtho, not knowing how to leave the precincts, pursued a straight path; as soon as he was seen a clamour was raised. The people understood; consternation ensued; then an immense rage possessed them. From the back part of Mappals, from the heights of the Acropolis, from the catacombs, from the lake shore, multitudes ran. The patricians left their palaces, tradesmen their shops, women abandoned their children; some seized swords, axes, and clubs; but the same superstitious obstacle which had hindered Salammbô likewise checked this mob.

How could they retake the veil? Only to look upon it was deemed a crime; it was of the nature of the Gods, and mere contact was fatal.

On the peristyles of the temples the priests wrung their hands in sheer desperation. The guards of the Legion galloped at hazard; people went up on the house-tops, thronged the terraces, and climbed upon the shoulders of the colossi and into the ships' riggings. Still Mâtho advanced, and at every step the rage and terror of the people augmented. The streets emptied at his approach, and the human torrent receded on both sides to the top of the walls. Mâtho saw everywhere only glaring eyes, strained wide-open as if to devour him, and the defiant, closely clenched fists, and heard the gnashing teeth between threatening lips; but above all Salammbô's imprecations resounded in his ears, in multiplied echoes.

Suddenly a long arrow directed at Mâtho whirred past, then another, and still another; stones also flew by, only to rebound about him on the ground;

but the missiles, all indifferently directed, passed over his head; for they feared to strike the Zaimph. Recognising this fact, Mâtho made the veil serve as a shield, holding it first to the right, then to the left; then before, then behind him: thus thwarted, they could imagine no expedient. He walked faster and faster; finding the street openings all impassable, barred by ropes, chariots, and snares, his attempts to effect egress were balked, and he had ever and anon to retrace his steps; at length he entered the Square of Khamoûn, where the Balearic slingers had perished. Mâtho stopped, and grew as pallid as death. This time he believed himself lost. The multitude, witnessing his dilemma, clapped their hands with joy.

He ran up to the huge, very high closed gate, which was most formidably constructed of heart of oak sheathed with brass, and studded with iron nails. Mâtho sprang with all his might against it; the people stamped their feet, wild with delight at witnessing the impotence of his fury. Then he pulled off his sandal, spat upon it, and struck the immovable panels with it; again the entire concourse of people yelled, forgetting in their transport the veil.

They were about to rush forward to crush him. Mâtho moved his large vague eyes over the crowd. His temples throbbed giddily; he felt invaded by such enervation as besets a drunken man. All at once he saw dangling the long chain that served to work the lever of the gate. With a fierce bound he grasped, and forcibly pulled the chain, at the same time using his feet as a buttress; the enormous valves, yielding to his mad strength, half-opened.

Once outside, he took the sublime Zaïmph from his neck, and lifted it over his head as high as possible. Distended and borne up by the sea breeze, the relucent material became resplendent in the sunshine, displaying its wondrous medley of inshot colours and precious stones; and over all its sheen could be descried the faint images of its Gods.

Thus Mâtho bore his trophy as he traversed the entire plain until he reached the encampment, and from the walls the irate, dismayed people watched the fortune of Carthage pass into the enemy's camp.

CHAPTER VI.

HANNO.

"I OUGHT to have carried her away!" Mâtho said to Spendius during that evening. "I should have seized and abducted her from her palace! No one would have dared resist me!"

Spendius did not heed this as he lay on his back refreshing himself with delight beside a large jar of honey-water, wherein he would from time to time plunge his head, in order to drink more copiously.

Mâtho resumed: "What is to be done.... How can we re-enter Carthage?"

"I do not know," answered Spendius.

This impassibility exasperated Mâtho, who exclaimed:

"What! The blame is yours! You led me; then you desert me, coward that you are! Why then should I obey you? Do you believe yourself my master? Oh! panderer, slave, son of slaves!" He ground his teeth in wrath, and lifted his large hand over Spendius.

The Greek did not respond. A clay sconce burned

softly against the tent-pole, where the Zaïmph glittered in the suspended panoply.

All at once Mâtho drew on his cothurnes, buckled on his jacket of plates of brass, and put on his helmet.

"Where are you going?" asked Spendius.

"I shall return to the palace! Leave me! I shall carry her off! And if they offer me opposition I shall crush them like vipers! I shall put her to death, Spendius! Yes," he repeated, "I shall kill her! You will see, I shall kill her!"

Spendius, who was listening attentively, brusquely pulled down the Zaïmph and threw it into a corner, and covered it with fleeces.

A murmur of voices became audible; torches blazed; and Narr' Havas entered, followed by about twenty men. They wore white woollen mantles, leather collars, wooden earrings, and hyena-skin shoes, and were armed with poniards. Pausing at the threshold, they leaned upon their lances, like shepherds resting.

Narr' Havas was the finest of the group. The leather straps encircling his thin arms were ornamented with pearls. His wide mantle was fastened round his head by a gold band, from which an ostrich plume fell drooping on his shoulders. A continual smile revealed his teeth; his eyes were sharp as arrows; his entire bearing was somewhat attentive, and yet indifferent.

He declared that he came to join the Mercenaries, as the Republic had for a long time menaced his kingdom; consequently, he was interested in aiding the Barbarians, and he possessed the power to be useful to them.

"I will furnish you with elephants, for my forests are full; with wine, oil, barley, dates, pitch, and sulphur for sieges; with twenty thousand foot soldiers, and ten thousand horses. If I now address you, Mâtho, it is because the possession of the Zaimph has rendered you the first in the army; we were also friends formerly," he added.

Meanwhile Mâtho contemplated Spendius, who listened intently, sitting on a heap of sheep-skins, all the time making little signs of assent with his head.

Narr' Havas talked on, calling upon the Gods to witness his sincerity. Then he cursed Carthage. To attest the violence of his imprecations, he broke a javelin, and all his men uttered in unison a deafening howl.

Mâtho, carried away by this avowed rage, cried out that he accepted the proffered alliance.

Then they brought a white bull and a black sheep —symbolical of day and night—which they slaughtered on the edge of a pit, into which, when it became full of blood, they plunged their arms. Afterwards Narr' Havas placed his outspread hand on Mâtho's breast, and Mâtho placed his hand on Narr' Havas's breast; then they repeated the stigmata on their tent-cloths. Subsequently the night was spent in eating. The remnants of meat, with all the skins, bones, horns, and hoofs, were burned.

Mâtho, at the time he returned to the camp wearing the veil of the Goddess, had been hailed with tremendous acclamation. Even those who were not of the Canaanite religion felt in their vague enthusiasm the advent of a Genius. As for seeking to capture the Zaimph, no one dreamed of such a thing; the mysterious manner whereby he had acquired it, sufficed in the minds of the Barbarians, to make his possession of it legitimate. Thus thought the soldiers of African race; but others, whose hatred against the Republic was of more recent origin, knew not how to decide. If they had only possessed vessels, they would have immediately set sail for their own countries.

Spendius, Narr' Havas, and Mâtho expedited envoys to all the tribes of the Punic territory. Carthage had exhausted these peoples by exorbitant taxes; punishing delinquents, and even those who murmured, by chains, the executioner's axe, or the cross. They were compelled to cultivate that which pleased the Republic, and furnish that which she demanded. No one had the right to possess a weapon. Whenever villages revolted, the inhabitants were sold as slaves; the governors were estimated like wine-presses, according to the quantity they were able to produce.

Outside of the region immediately subject to Carthage, were their allies, who contributed only a moderate tribute; beyond these allies wandered the Nomads, who could be let loose upon them. By this system the harvests were always abundant, the breeding studs skilfully conducted, the plantations superb. Old Cato, a master in agriculture and slave-raising, ninety-two years later was thereby amazed, and his cry, "*Delenda est Carthago,*" repeated in Rome, was but an exclamation of jealous cupidity.

During the last war the exactions had been

doubled, so that nearly all the cities of Libya had surrendered to Regulus. As punishment, the Republic compelled them to give one thousand talents, twenty thousand head of cattle, three hundred sacks of gold-dust, and considerable advances of grain; and the chiefs of tribes had been crucified or thrown to the lions.

Carthage was especially execrated by Tunis, an older city than the metropolis, she could not forgive the grandeur of the Republic, as she lay facing its walls, crouching in the mud on the water's edge, like a malignant beast watching its prey. The transportations, the massacres, the epidemics, had not enfeebled her; moreover, she had supported Archagathus, son of Agathocles. The eaters-of-unclean-things soon found arms there.

The couriers had not as yet set out on their mission; but a universal joy spread abroad throughout the provinces. Without waiting for cause, the stewards of the houses and the functionaries of the Republic were strangled in the baths; old weapons were now brought forth from caverns, where they had formerly been hidden, and the iron of ploughs was forged into swords; children deftly whetted javelins on the door-steps; and the women contributed their necklaces, rings, earrings, and, in fact, everything that could be transposed or converted in any manner to serve for the desired destruction of Carthage. Each one wished to give something. Stacks of lances accumulated in the towns like sheaves of maize. Cattle and money were sent to Mâtho, who without delay paid all arrears to the Mercenaries, and this, which was the suggestion of

Spendius, resulted in Mathô's being named Schalischim of the Barbarians.

Meanwhile men flowed in from all quarters. First came the autochthons, who were followed by the slaves from the fields. Caravans of negroes were seized and armed, and the merchants who were going to Carthage, in the hope of a more certain and speedy profit, united with the Barbarians. Incessantly numerous bands arrived, and from the heights of the Acropolis the Carthaginians could see the army rapidly swelling.

On the platform of the aqueduct the Guards of the Legion were posted as sentinels, and near them, at certain distances, were erected huge brazen vats, in which boiled quantities of asphalt. Below, on the plain, the vast concourse stirred about tumultuously. They were uncertain, experiencing that embarrassment always inspired in Barbarians whenever they encountered walls.

Utica and Hippo-Zarytus withheld their alliance. Phœnician colonies, like Carthage, they were self-governed, and in the treaties which the Republic concluded had always caused to be subjoined clauses to distinguish them from it. Yet they respected this strongest sister, who protected them, and they did not believe that a mass of Barbarians was capable of vanquishing her, but on the contrary, that Carthage could annihilate the enemy. They desired to remain neutral, and live peacefully.

But the position of these two colonies rendered them indispensable. Utica, at the end of a gulf, was convenient to bring outside assistance into Carthage. If Utica should alone be captured, then

Hippo-Zarytus, six hours further distant on the coast, could replace the loss, and the metropolis could thus be revictualled, and would be found impregnable.

Spendius wanted the siege to be undertaken immediately. Narr' Havas strongly opposed such action, as it was necessary he should first return to the frontier. This was the opinion of the veterans called in council, and approved by Mâtho; and it was decided that Spendius should attack Utica; Mâtho, Hippo-Zarytus; that the third army corps, commanded by Autharitus, resting upon Tunis, should occupy the plain of Carthage, and that Narr' Havas should return to his own kingdom to procure elephants, and with his cavalry hold the roads.

The women clamoured violently at this decision; they coveted the jewels of the Punic dames. The Libyans also protested, declaring that they had been summoned to engage in a siege against Carthage, and now they were ordered away. The soldiers departed almost alone.

Mâtho commanded his companions with the Iberians and Lusitanians, the men from the West and from the islands; while those who spoke Greek requested that they might be placed under Spendius's command, because of his astuteness.

The Carthaginians experienced great stupefaction when they saw this army all at once in motion, stretching away under the mountain of Ariana, by the road to Utica on the sea-coast. A section remained before Tunis; the rest disappeared, to reappear on the other shore of the gulf, on the outskirts of the woods, in which it was again lost to view.

Possibly this army numbered eighty thousand men. The two Tyrian cities would offer no resistance, and they would return against Carthage. Already a considerable army cut her off, occupying the base of the isthmus, and soon Carthage must perish from hunger, as the people could not subsist without the aid of the provinces, since the citizens paid no contributions, as at Rome.

Carthage was lacking in political genius. Her eternal strife for gain had prevented her from exercising that prudence which promotes the highest ambition. She was like a galley anchored on the Libyan sands, maintained there by force of toil. The nations, like billows, roared about her, and the least storm shook this formidable machine to the foundation.

Her treasury had been drained by the Roman war, and all that had been squandered and lost during the bargaining with the Barbarians. However, she must have soldiers, and no Government now reposed trust in the Republic! Ptolemy, not long before, had refused to loan Carthage two thousand talents. And yet another not insignificant cause of discouragement was the rape of the Veil. Spendius had indeed wisely foreseen this.

But this people, who felt itself detested, clasped to its heart its money and its Gods, and its patriotism was maintained by the constitution of its government.

In the first place, the power belonged to all, without anyone being able to monopolise it. Personal debts were considered as public debts. The men of Canaanite race had the monopoly of commerce. In multiplying the profits of piracy by the practice of usury, and by rigorously making the most of the slaves and lands and the poor, men sometimes became wealthy. Wealth alone opened all her magistracies, and even though the power and money were perpetuated in the same families, the oligarchy was tolerated because each had the hope of attaining to it.

The societies of commerce, wherein the laws were elaborated, elected the inspectors of finance, to whose discretion it was left, on quitting office, to nominate the hundred members of the Council of Elders who belonged to the Grand Assembly, a general convention of all the Rich.

As for the two Suffetes, these relics of kingship, inferior to Consuls, they were elected on the same day, from two distinct families, in order that they might be divided by various animosities, and mutually enfeebled. They were not empowered to deliberate on the war, and when they were conquered, the Grand Council crucified them.

Hence the strength of Carthage emanated from the Syssites, who were established in a grand court in the centre of Malqua, the spot where, it is said, the first bark manned by Phœnician sailors had landed. Since that period the sea had greatly retired. It was a group of small chambers of an archaic architecture, built from the trunks of palm-trees, with stone corner-pieces, separated one from another, affording to each chamber complete isolation for the various companies in their conferences. The

Rich gathered therein daily to discuss their own interests, as well as those of the Government, from the search for pepper to the conquest of Rome.

Three times every moon they had their couches carried up on the high terrace bordering the wall of the court; and from below they could be observed sitting at table in the open air, without cothurnes or mantles; their diamonds flashing on their fingers as they handled their food, and their large ear-rings dangling between the flagons, glittered. They were all strong and fat, half-naked, happy, and laughing, eating in the open blue, like huge sharks disporting in the sea.

At the present time, however, they could not dissemble their anxiety; they were too pale. The crowd below awaited their adjournment, to escort them to their palaces and to ascertain the news. As during times of the plague, all the houses were closed; occasionally the streets would suddenly swarm with people, and just as suddenly empty and become deserted. Some ascended the Acropolis, others ran towards the port. Every night the Grand Council deliberated in session. At last the people were convened on the square of Khamoûn, and it was officially announced that they had decided to reinstate in command Hanno, the conqueror of Hecatompylus.

He was a pious, artful man, merciless to the Africans — a true Carthaginian. His revenues equalled those of the Barca family, and no other man had such experience in administrative affairs.

Hanno decreed the enrolment of all able-bodied citizens, placed catapults upon the towers, demanded exorbitant supplies of weapons, even ordered the construction of fourteen galleys, which were not required; and ordered everything to be registered and accurately inscribed. He was borne by his slaves to the lighthouse, the arsenal, and into the treasury of the temples; and could always be seen in his large litter, as it rocked from step to step, ascending or descending the stairways of the Acropolis. At night, in his palace, as he could not sleep, he prepared himself for the coming battle by shouting in a terrible voice military manœuvres.

Everyone, by excess of terror, became brave. The Rich at cock-crow would aligne the length of Mappals, turning up their robes as they practised the use of the pike. But having no instructor, they disputed among themselves as to methods. When out of breath, they would sit panting on the tombs, only to recommence their exercises after resting. Many even imposed on themselves a regimen. Some imagined that to acquire strength it was necessary to eat large quantities, and gorged themselves; others, incommoded by corpulence, endeavoured to reduce themselves by long fastings.

Utica had already frequently invoked the assistance of Carthage; but Hanno would not move until the last screw was set in every war machine. He lost three more moons of time in the equipment of the hundred and twelve elephants, stabled in the ramparts. These vanquishers of Regulus, so cherished by the people, certainly could not be treated too well. Hanno ordered their brazen breastplates to be recast, their tusks gilded, their towers enlarged, and had made for them most beautiful purple caparisons, bordered with very heavy fringes. Inasmuch as their conductors were called Indians, as the first doubtless came from the Indies, he ordered that they should wear Indian costumes, consisting of a white turban round the head, and little breeches of byssus, which, with their transverse pleats, looked like two valves of a shell, fastened on their hips.

During all these preparations, Autharitus's army remained stationed before Tunis, concealed behind a wall, constructed of mud taken from the lake, and protected on the top by thorn-bushes. The Negroes planted, in various places, on large stakes, frightful images, human masks composed out of birds' feathers, heads of jackals and serpents, which gaped towards the enemy to frighten them; and by such measures the Barbarians considered themselves to be utterly invincible, and danced, wrestled, and juggled, convinced that Carthage before long would perish.

Any other general than Hanno could have crushed with facility this multitude, so embarrassed by herds and women, and who, furthermore, were not versed in any military tactics: and Autharitus, being discouraged, no longer required his men to drill.

They scattered before him, as he passed by, rolling his large blue eyes. Then when he arrived at the lake shore, he removed his seal-skin tunic, unknotted the cord holding back his long red locks, and soaked them in the water. He regretted that he had not deserted, and gone over to the Romans with the two thousand Gauls of the temple of Eryx.

Frequently during the middle of the day the sun's

rays suddenly vanished, then the gulf and open sea seemed as motionless as molten lead. A cloud of brown dust rose perpendicularly, then coursed along in whirling eddies, under the force of which the palm trees bowed, the sky became obscured, stones could be heard rebounding on the backs of the animals, and the Gaul would glue his lips against the holes in his tent, gasping from exhaustion and melancholy. He fancied that he inhaled the perfumes of his native pastures on autumn mornings, that he saw the snowflakes, and again heard the lowing of the aurochs lost in the mists, and closing his eyes, he seemed to see the fires of the long cabins thatched with straw, as they quivered on the marshes at the end of the woods.

There were others who also possibly regretted their absence from their native country as much as he, though it was not so far away. For the Carthaginian captives could in fact distinguish, at the other side of the gulf, on the declivities of Byrsa, the canopies spread out in the courts of their dwellings. Sentinels patrolled around these prisoners perpetually. Each man wore an iron yoke, by which all were attached to one chain. The crowd never wearied coming to look upon these patrician captives. The women pointed out to their little children the beautiful Punic robes hanging in tatters upon their attenuated limbs.

Every time that Autharitus contemplated Gisco, a fury possessed him in memory of the old general's injury to him, and he would certainly have killed him but for the oath he had made to Narr' Havas. He then returned to his tent and drank a mixture of barley and cumin, till he became drunk to unconsciousness: at noontime the following day he awoke, consumed by a horrible thirst.

Mâtho, in the meantime, besieged Hippo-Zarytus. This city was protected by a lake communicating with the sea, and had three lines of fortifications, and on the heights which overlooked her, a wall extended, fortified by towers.

Never before had Mâtho commanded in similar undertakings. Then the thought of Salammbô beset him, and he dreamed of the pleasures of her beauty, as in the delights of a revenge that transported him with pride. His desire to see her again was bitter, furious, constant. He even thought of offering himself as a bearer of truce, in the hope that once in Carthage he might make his way to her. Often he would sound the signal for assault, and without waiting for aught, would dart on to the pier that they were endeavouring to construct in the sea. Here he tore up the stones with his hands, turned everything upside down, plunging and striking about in every direction with his broad sword. The Barbarians followed his leadership, and dashed pell-mell upon the works; the overcrowded ladders broke with a loud crash, and masses of men tumbled into the water, which leaped in reddened waves against the walls. At last the tumult abated, and the soldiers withdrew to renew the assault. Mâtho seated himself outside his tent, wiped his blood-bespattered face, and, turning towards Carthage, wistfully gazed at the horizon.

Facing him, among the olive, palm, myrtle, and plane trees, were two wide pools, which joined another lake, the contour of which was not perceptible from this point of view. Behind a mountain rose other mountains, and in the middle of the immense lake stood an island, perfectly black, of a pyramidal shape. On the left, at the extremity of the gulf, the sand heaps resembled great golden billows arrested in their course, and the sea, flat like a pavement of lapis-lazuli, ascended imperceptibly to the sky on the horizon. The verdure of the country in places disappeared under long yellow patches, the carobs shone brilliant as coral buttons, the vines hung in festoons from the top of sycamores. The faint murmur of the water was audible, the tufted skylarks hopped about, and the last fires of the sun gilded the carapaces of the tortoises as they left the rushes to inhale the sea breezes.

Mâtho, sighing deeply, lay flat on the ground, digging his nails into the sand, and wept, feeling wretched, mean, and forsaken. He could never possess Salammbô; and he could not even succeed in capturing a city. At night, alone in his tent, he contemplated the Zaïmph, querying of what service was this thing of the Gods to him? And doubts supervened in the Barbarian's thoughts. Then it seemed to him, on the contrary, that the vestment of the Goddess belonged to Salammbô, and that a part of her soul floated in it, more subtle than a breath, and he caressingly patted it, breathed with his face buried in its folds, kissed it with sobs. He drew it about his shoulders to intensify the illusion, and believed he embraced her.

Sometimes, by the light of the stars, he would

suddenly start out, stepping over the sleeping soldiers wrapped in their mantles; then at the gates of the camp he leaped upon a horse, galloped away, and two hours afterwards was at Utica in the tent of Spendius. At first he talked of the siege, but his real motive was to assuage his sadness by talking about Salammbô.

Spendius exhorted him to wisdom.

"Repulse from your soul these miseries that degrade it! You formerly obeyed others, but now you command an army; and if Carthage is not conquered, at least we shall have provinces granted to us, and we will become kings!"

But why had not the possession of the Zaïmph given them victory?

According to Spendius it was necessary to wait. Mâtho imagined that the veil concerned exclusively those of the Canaanite race, and with barbarian subtilty, said to himself:

"The Zaïmph will avail me nothing; but, because they have lost it, it avails them nothing."

Then succeeded a scruple of pertubation; he feared in adoring the Libyan God Aptouknos to offend Moloch, and timidly asked Spendius to which of these Gods it would be well to sacrifice a man.

"Always sacrifice!" said Spendius, laughing.

Mâtho did not comprehend this indifference, and suspected that the Greek had a genius of whom he did not wish to speak.

All religions, as all races, met together in these Barbarian armies, and they were ever considerate of the Gods of others, as they all inspired terrors. Many mingled in their native religion foreign practices. It was very well not to adore the stars, but this or that constellation being fatal or helpful, they made sacrifices to it. An unknown amulet, found by chance in a moment of peril, became a deity. Or perhaps it was a name—nothing but a name—which they repeated without ever striving to understand its meaning.

But to many the result of having pillaged numerous temples, and seen many nations and massacres, was that they ended by believing only in destiny and death, and every night they slept with the placidity of wild beasts.

Spendius would have spat upon the images of Jupiter Olympus; notwithstanding, even he dreaded to speak aloud in the dark, and he never failed to put on his right sandal first.

He erected a long quadrangular terrace fronting Utica, but in proportion as it was built up the ramparts were also raised higher. That which was beaten down by one army, was almost immediately found re-erected by the other.

Spendius looked carefully to his troops, and constantly devised plans, endeavouring to recall the stratagems he had heard recounted in his travels.

Why did not Narr' Havas return? The delay filled them with inquietude.

Hanno had completed his preparations.

During one moonless night he transported his elephants and soldiers across the Gulf of Carthage on rafts. They then turned the Hot-Springs Mountain, to evade Autharitus, and proceeded so slowly that, instead of surprising the Barbarians the next morning, as the Suffete had calculated, they only arrived at noon on the third day.

On the eastern side of Utica a plain extended as far as the great lagoon of Carthage; behind it debouched at a right angle a valley, cutting between two low mountains, suddenly closing in. Further off, to the left, the Barbarians were encamped in such a manner as to blockade the port. They were sleeping in their tents—as on this day besieged and besiegers were too much fatigued to enter into combat, and had sought repose—when at the curve of the hills the Carthaginian army appeared.

The camp followers, armed with slings, were stationed on the wings. The Guards of the Legion, wearing armour of golden scales, formed the first line: their large horses, denuded of manes, hair, and ears, wore a silver horn in the centre of their foreheads, making them resemble rhinoceroses. Between their squadrons, young men, wearing on their heads small helmets, balanced in both hands ash-wood javelins; the heavy infantry, armed with long pikes, moved in the rear. All the vendors were laden with as many weapons as they could possibly carry: some bore a lance, an axe, a mace, and two swords: others, like porcupines, bristled with darts, and their arms stood out from their cuirasses of sheets of horn, or plaques of metal. Finally appeared the scaffoldings of the lofty war engines: *carrobalistas*, onagers, catapults, and *scorpions*, oscillating on cars, drawn by mules and quadrigas of oxen.

As the army unfolded itself, the captains ran breathlessly from right and from left, delivering

K

orders, closing up the lines, and maintaining proper spaces.

The Elders in command had come decked in purple casques, with magnificent fringes, that became entangled in the straps of their cothurnes. Their faces, daubed over with vermilion, glistened under enormous helmets, surmounted by images of Gods. They carried shields bordered with ivory, and studded with jewels; as they passed in glittering array, it was as though suns traversed brass walls.

The Carthaginians manœuvred so awkwardly, that the Barbarians, in derision, invited them to be seated; and screamed out to them that they would soon empty their huge bellies, dust the gilding from their skins, and make them drink iron.

At the top of a pole planted before Spendius's tent, a strip of green cloth fluttered as a signal. The Carthaginians responded by a great bluster of trumpets, cymbals, drums, and flutes made of asses' bones.

Already the Barbarians had leaped outside the palisades, and now were face to face with their enemies, and within javelin's length of them.

A Balearic slinger advanced a step, placed in his sling one of his clay balls, and twirled his arm; an ivory shield was shattered, and the two armies mingled in conflict.

The Greeks with their long lances pricked the horses' nostrils, making them fall back on their riders; the slaves whose duty it was to sling stones had chosen those which were too large, and they fell close to them. The Punic foot soldiers, in striking out to cut down the enemy with their long swords, exposed their right sides; the Barbarians plunged into their lines, thrusting them through and through with their broad swords: they madly stumbled over the dying and dead, blinded by the blood that spurted into their faces. This confused mass of pikes, helmets, cuirasses, swords, and human limbs swirled and writhed, widening and narrowing in elastic contractions.

The Carthaginian cohorts became more and more broken; their heavy war engines could not be extricated from the sands: at length the Suffete Hanno's litter—his grand litter, with the crystal pendulums, that had been seen since the very commencement of the attack swaying among the soldiers like a barque on the billows—suddenly foundered. He doubtless was killed! The Barbarians found themselves alone. They burst forth into song.

Presently the dust began to settle, when Hanno reappeared on the back of an elephant. He was bare-headed; a negro carried over him an umbrella of byssus. His collar of blue plaques struck on the painted flowers of his black tunic, circles of diamonds enclasped his enormous arms; he advanced, mouth wide open, brandishing an enormous spear expanding at the end like a lotus, and more brilliant than a mirror.

Soon the earth trembled, and the Barbarians saw, bearing down upon them in one straight line, all the Carthaginian elephants, with their tusks gilded, ears painted blue, sheathed in bronze, shaking above their purple caparisons the leather towers, in each of which were three archers holding large, drawn bows.

The soldiers scarcely had time to seize their arms,

they were ranged at hazard, frozen with terror, and struck with indecision.

Already from the tops of the towers volleys of arrows and javelins, fire-lances and masses of lead, were being hurled at them. Some to climb up clung on to the fringes of the caparisons, but their hands were hewn off with cutlasses, and they fell backwards on the drawn swords of their own comrades.

Their frail pikes were soon broken, and the elephants plunged into the phalanxes like wild boars through clumps of grasses, uprooting, as they went along, the palisades with their trunks, and traversed the camp from end to end, overturning the tents under their chests.

Panic-stricken, the Barbarians had taken flight, hiding themselves in the hills that bordered the valley from whence the Carthaginians had issued.

Hanno, presented himself before the gates of Utica as conqueror, and sounded his trumpet. The three judges of the city appeared, in the opening of the battlements, on the summit of a tower. The people of Utica did not desire to receive as guests so many well-armed men. Hanno lost his temper. Finally they consented to admit him with a small escort.

The streets were too narrow for the passage of the elephants, and it was necessary to leave them outside the city gates.

As soon as the Suffete entered the city, the principal men came to salute him. He demanded to be immediately conducted to the bath-house, and there summoned his cooks.

Three hours later, he was still deeply immersed in the oil of cinnamon with which the bath-tub was filled, and while bathing he ate from off a cow-hide stretched across the tub flamingoes' tongues and poppy-seeds, seasoned with honey. His Greek doctor, in a long, yellow robe, stood beside him, immobile, from time to time having the temperature of the bath increased; and two young boys leaned on the steps of the bath rubbing the leper's legs. But the care of his body did not arrest his love for public affairs, for he occupied himself with the dictation of a letter to the Grand Council; and, as some prisoners had been taken, he queried with himself as to what terrible chastisement he could possibly invent.

"Stop!" said he to the slave who stood near, writing on the palm of his hand. "Let them be brought to me! I wish to see them."

And from the extremity of the hall, which was now filled with the whitish vapour from the steam, through which the torches cast red spots, some one pushed forward three Barbarians: a Samnite, a Spartan, and a Cappadocian.

"Proceed!" said Hanno. "Rejoice, light of the Baals! your Suffete has exterminated the voracious dogs! Benedictions on the Republic! Ordain prayers!" He perceived the captives, and then burst into laughter. "Ha! ha! ha! my braves of Sicca. You do not shout so loud to-day. It is I! Do you recognise me? Where then are your swords? What terrible men truly!" —and he feigned to hide as though he experienced great fear.—"You asked for horses, for women, for lands, for magistracies, and doubtless also for priesthoods! Why not? Ah well, I will furnish you the lands, and you shall never leave them. You shall be married to new gallows! For your payment, ingots of lead shall be cast in your mouths, and I will put you in the very best places, very exalted, among the clouds, to be near the eagles!"

The three Barbarians, long-haired, covered with tatters, looked at him without comprehending what he said. Wounded on their knees, they had been lassoed and captured, the ends of the heavy chains on their hands dragged on the stones. Hanno was indignant at their impassibility.

"On your knees! On your knees! Jackals! Dirt! Vermin! Excrement! And they do not respond? Enough! Silence! Let them be flayed alive! No! not now, presently!"

He snorted like a hippopotamus, and rolled his eyes about. The perfumed oil trickled down his gross body, sticking to the scales on his skin; and the torchlights threw over him a pink hue.

He resumed his official letter: "During four days we have suffered intensely from the sun. In the passage of the Macar some mules were lost. Despite the enemies' position, the extraordinary courage . . . Oh! Demonades, how I suffer! Let the bricks be reheated till they are red."

A raking noise was then heard in the furnaces. The incense fumed yet stronger in the large perfume-pans, and the shampooers, entirely naked, dripping like sponges, rubbed over his joints a paste composed of wheat, sulphur, black-wine, bitches'-milk, myrrh, galban, and storax.

An incessant thirst consumed him. The man

dressed in the yellow robe, however, did not yield to his patient's desire; but held to him a gold cup in which smoked a broth of vipers.

"Drink this!" urged he, "in order that the strength of the serpents, born of the sun, may penetrate the marrow of your bones. And take courage! O reflection of the Gods! You know, moreover, that a priest of Eschmoûn observes around the Dog the cruel stars from whence you derive your malady. They pale like the spots on your skin; therefore you ought not to die of it."

"Ah, yes! That is true!" repeated the Suffete— "I ought not to die of it!" And from his violet purple lips escaped a breath more nauseous than the exhalations of a corpse.

His eyes, denuded of lashes, resembled two burning coals; heavy folds of skin hung on his forehead; his ears stood out from his head, and began to enlarge; and the deep wrinkles that formed semicircles around his nostrils gave him a strange, frightful aspect, the air of a savage brute.

His unnatural voice resembled a roar as he said: "Perhaps you are right, Demonades. In fact, look even now, some of the ulcers are closed; I feel robust! See how I eat!"

And, less from a desire to gormandise than actuated by ostentation—and to convince himself that he was actually improving—he first ate of the minced cheese and marjoram, then the boned-fish, pumpkin, oysters with eggs, horse radish, truffles and brochettes of little birds.

In looking at the prisoners whilst he ate, he delighted in the imagination of their tortures.

In the meanwhile he also recalled Sicca: and his rage for all his sufferings burst forth in a volley of insults against these three men.

"Ah, traitors! Wretches! Infamous! Accursed! And you outraged me! Me!—the Suffete Hanno! Their services, the price of their blood, as they have said. Ah! yes! their blood! their blood!" Then he talked to himself: "All shall perish! Not one shall be sold! It would be best to conduct them to Carthage. No, let me see. . . . without doubt I have not brought enough chains . . . Write: 'Send to me.' . . . How many prisoners are there? Let some one go and ask Muthumbal. Go! No pity! And have all their hands cut off, and brought to me in baskets!"

But strange cries, at once hoarse and shrill, penetrated the hall, above Hanno's voice and the clatter of the dishes which were being placed around him. The cries redoubled; and in an instant a furious trumpeting of elephants burst forth, as if the battle had broken out anew. A tremendous tumult encompassed the city.

The Carthaginians had not endeavoured to pursue the Barbarians. They had established themselves at the foot of the walls with their baggage, valets, and all their satraps' train, and had given themselves up to rejoicing under their beautiful pearl-embroidered tents. The Mercenaries' recent camp was merely a heap of ruins on the plain.

Spendius had regained his courage. He dispatched Zarxas towards Mâtho, and hastened through the woods to rally his men. Their losses were not great, and enraged at having been thus conquered without combat, they were re-forming their lines, when a vat of petroleum, doubtless abandoned by the enemy, was discovered. Spendius had swine brought from the neighbouring farm-houses, besmeared them with the bitumen, and setting fire to them, turned them loose towards Utica.

The elephants, terrified by these running flames, stampeded over the rising ground. A volley of javelins was hurled upon the infuriated creatures; they turned back upon the Carthaginians, disembowelling them with strokes of their tusks, and trampling them beneath their massive feet, suffocating and crushing them. The Barbarians descended the hill behind them; the Punic camp, being without entrenchments, was sacked at the first charge, and the Carthaginians found themselves crushed against the city gates, which were kept closed from the fear of the possible invasion of the Mercenaries.

At daybreak Mâtho's foot soldiers were seen advancing from the west, and at the same time the Numidian cavalry of Narr' Havas appeared, bounding over the ravines and underbrush, driving before them the fugitives like hounds chasing hares.

This change of fortune interrupted the Suffete, and he screamed for some one to assist him to leave the sweating bath.

Before him yet stood the three captives. A negro, the same who had carried his umbrella during the battle, leaned towards him and whispered something in his ear.

"What then?" slowly asked the Suffete. "Ah, kill them!" he added, in a brusque tone.

The Ethiopian drew from his belt a long poniard,

and the three heads fell. One bounded in the midst of the scraps of the Suffete's recent feast, then rolled into the tub of oil, and floated for some time with open mouth and fixed eyes.

The morning light entered the slits in the walls, and the three bodies could be seen lying on their breasts. Great streams gurgled from the headless trunks like fountains, and a sheet of blood flowed over the mosaics, which were sanded with blue powder. The Suffete paused to dip his hands in the warm pool, rubbing the blood over his knees, this being esteemed a remedy for his malady.

Evening came. He escaped from Utica with his escort, taking to the mountains to rejoin his army. He found only the remnants of it. Four days later he was at Gorza, on the top of a defile, when Spendius's troops showed themselves below them. Had twenty good lancers attacked the front of their advancing column, they could easily have arrested them; however, the paralysed Carthaginians watched them pass by. Hanno recognised in the rear guard the Numidian king. Narr' Havas bowed his head to salute him, making a sign that he could not interpret.

Hanno's forces returned towards Carthage in terror, only venturing to march at night, and hiding by day in the olive woods. During every stage some of the men died. They frequently believed themselves to be lost. Finally they attained the Cape of Hermæum, where vessels came to transport them. Hanno was so fatigued, so desperate, and especially so overwhelmed by the loss of the elephants, that he vainly besought Demonades to administer poison to him, and thereby put an end to his existence.

Besides, he already imagined himself extended on his cross.

Carthage did not possess the energy to be indignant with him. They had lost four hundred thousand nine hundred and seventy-two shekels of silver, fifteen thousand six hundred and twenty-three shekels of gold, eighteen elephants, fourteen members of the Grand Council, three hundred patricians, eight thousand citizens, corn for three moons, considerable baggage, and all their war engines.

The defection of Narr' Havas was absolute. The two sieges recommenced, and now Autharitus's army extended from Tunis to Rhades. From the top of the Acropolis could be seen, in the surrounding country, wide columns of smoke ascending to the sky from the burning châteaux of the patricians.

One man only had the power to save the Republic. The Carthaginians repented that they had misunderstood him, and even the peace faction voted holocausts for Hamilcar's return.

The sight of the Zaimph had utterly overcome Salammbô. At night she believed she could hear the footsteps of the Goddess, and would awake in a fright and scream out. Every day she sent nourishment into the temples. Taanach wearied herself executing her orders, and Schahabarim quitted her no more.

CHAPTER VII.

HAMILCAR BARCA.

The Annunciator-of-the-Moons watched nightly, from the top of the temple of Eschmoûn, to proclaim through his trumpet the movements of the planet. One morning he perceived in the west something, resembling a bird, skimming its long wings over the surface of the sea. It was a ship of three banks of oars, the prow terminating in a sculptured horse.

The sun rose; the Annunciator-of-the-Moons shaded his eyes, and seizing his clarion at arm's length, sent a ringing blast over Carthage.

The people, unable to believe the announcement, disputing amongst themselves the probability of its truth, issued from every house. The pier was soon crowded with curious people. Finally, Hamilcar's trireme was recognised by all.

The vessel advanced in a proud, wild fashion, her yard perfectly straight, her sail bulging the entire length of the mast. Cleaving the foam about her, her gigantic oars struck the water in cadence. From time to time the extremity of her keel, fashioned like a plough-share, was seen as she plunged; and under the beak at the end of the prow, the sculptured horse with ivory head, rearing its two forefeet, seemed to course over the plains of the sea.

As she rounded the promontory her sail fell; the wind had ceased; and now, near the pilot, could be discerned a man standing bare-headed. It was the Suffete Hamilcar! About his sides he wore shining plates of iron; a red mantle, attached to his shoulders, allowed his arms to be freely seen; two very long pearls pended from his ears, and his black bushy beard fell down upon his breast.

The approaching galley, tossed between the rocks, coasted the mole, and the excited crowd followed her along on the stones, shouting:

"Hail! Benediction! Eye of Khamoûn! Oh, deliver us! It is the fault of the Rich! They desire your death! Guard yourself, Barca!"

He made no response, as if the clamour of the oceans and the din of battles had completely deafened him. But as the vessel came under the stairway which descended from the Acropolis, Hamilcar lifted his head, crossed his arms, and looked at the temple of Eschmoûn. He gazed still higher, into the dome of the pure sky, and in a sharp tone cried out an order to his sailors. The trireme bounded through the water. She grazed the idol set up at the corner of the pier to ward off tempests; and in the commercial port, full of filth, splinters of wood, and fruit-rinds, she crowded back in her passage, and ripped open the sides of vessels moored to piles ending in crocodiles' jaws.

The people continued to run, following the vessel. Some excitedly plunged into the water and swam alongside of her. Soon the vessel reached the head of the port, before the formidable gate, bristling with spikes. The gate lifted, to allow the trireme to pass, and it vanished under the profound vault.

The Military Port was completely separated from the city, and when ambassadors came, they were obliged to enter between two walls into a passage emerging to the left before the temple of Khamoûn. This large basin of water was round, like a cup, and surrounded by quays, where docks were built to harbour vessels. In front of each dock were two columns, carrying on their capitals the horns of Ammon, which formed a continuous portico all around the basin. In the centre, on an isle, was built a house for the Suffete of the sea. The water was so limpid that the bottom of the basin, paved with white shells, was apparent.

The noise from the streets did not penetrate thus far, and Hamilcar, in passing, recognised the triremes which he had formerly commanded. Of the old fleet there now scarcely remained twenty vessels in shelter on the shore—leaning over on their sides, or straight on their keels, with their poops high in the air, displaying their bulging prows covered with gilding and mystic symbols. The chimeras had lost their wings, the Patæcian Gods their arms, the bulls their silver horns; yet all, though half defaced, inert, and rotten, were full of romance, and yet exhaled the aroma of past voyages; now, like disabled soldiers who again meet their old commander, these dilapidated vessels seemed to say to him:

"Here we are! Here we are! And you also—you are vanquished!"

No one except the Suffete of the sea had the right to enter the admiralty. Until proof of his death should be established, he was always considered to be in existence. By this observance the Elders avoided an additional master. Hence, despite their disaffection towards Hamilcar, they had not failed to respect the custom.

The Suffete entered the deserted apartments, at every step finding armour, furniture, and familiar objects, all of which, however, astonished him; even in the vestibule there yet remained in a cassolette the ashes of the perfumes burned at the time of his departure, as an offering to conjure Melkarth. It was not thus that he had hoped to return!

All that he had done, all that he had seen—the assaults, the incendiary fires, the legions, the tempests—unrolled before his mind: Drepanum, Syracuse, Lilybreum, Mount Etna, the plateau of Eryx, his five years of battle, till the fatal day when, laying down their arms, they had lost Sicily. He resaw the citron-woods, the herdsmen tending their goats on the grey mountains, and his heart leaped wildly as another Carthage established away there came before his imagination. His projects and his memories buzzed in his brain, yet dizzy from the pitching of the vessel. An overwhelming pang seized him, and suddenly becoming weak, he felt the need of drawing nearer to the Gods. He ascended to the last story of his mansion; then, after withdrawing, from a gold shell suspended on his arm, a spatula studded with nails, he opened a small oval room. The narrow black rondels, encased in the walls, were as transparent as glass, and admitted a soft light. Between these regular rows of discs, hollows were made like the niches used for urns in a *columbarium*. Each one of these hollows contained a round, dark-coloured stone, apparently very heavy. Only superior souls honoured these *abaddirs*, fallen from the moon. By their fall these stones signified the planets, the sky, the fire; by their colour, the darkness of night; and by their density, the cohesion of terrestrial things.

A stifling atmosphere filled this mystic place. These round stones placed in the niches were slightly whitened by the sea-sand, which had been driven by the wind through the door. Hamilcar counted them, one after another, touching each with the tip of his finger; then hiding his face under a saffron-coloured veil, fell upon his knees, and, with outstretched arms, threw himself prone on the ground.

Outside, the daylight struck against the laths of the black lattices; in their diaphanous thickness shrubberies, hillocks, whirlwinds, and indistinct outlines of animals were discerned. Within, the light entered, frightful and yet pacific, as it should be from behind the sun in the gloomy regions of of future creations.

Hamilcar struggled to banish from his thoughts all the forms, all the symbols, and all appellations of the Gods, in order to better grasp the immutable spirit which these appearances concealed. Something of the planetary vitality penetrated his being, hence he felt for death, and all hazards, a disdain, most erudite and most personal.

When he arose he experienced a serene intrepidity, invulnerable alike to mercy or fear; and feeling half-suffocated, he ascended to the top of the tower that overlooked Carthage.

The city descended in a sweeping curve, with her cupolas, temples, golden-roofs, mansions, clumps of palms, and here and there glass globes, from which refracted lights sparkled; and surrounding this horn of plenty opening out towards him, were the ramparts, built like a gigantic border. Below, he perceived the ports, the squares, the interior of the courts, and the outlines of the streets, and from this height men appeared as mites, and almost level with the pavement-stones.

"Ah! if Hanno had not arrived too late on the morning of the battle of the Ægatian islands!" Thus thinking, he turned his eyes to the extreme horizon, extending his arms tremblingly towards Rome.

A multitude occupied the steps of the Acropolis. In the square of Khamoûn, people jostled each other to see the Suffete appear; the terraces gradually became thronged with eager gazers, some of whom recognised and saluted him. In order, however, to more effectually incite their impatience, he immediately withdrew from sight.

Hamilcar found awaiting him below in the hall the most important men of his faction—Istatten, Subeldia, Hictamon, Yeoubas, and others. They

L

recounted to him all that had occurred since the conclusion of the peace—the avarice of the Elders; the departure and subsequent return of the soldiers; their demands; the capture of Gisco, the rape of the Zaimph; the succour, and subsequent desertion, of Utica; but not one dared tell him of the events which concerned him personally. Finally they separated, to meet again at night with the Assembly of Elders in the temple of Moloch.

This deputation had but just gone, when a tumult broke forth outside the gate. Some one attempted to enter, in spite of the servants' protests; and as the uproar redoubled, Hamilcar ordered that the unknown person should be shown in.

An old negress appeared, evidently much broken, wrinkled, trembling in a stupid manner, and enveloped to her heels in wide blue veils. She came forward, facing the Suffete. They looked at one another for some moments. Suddenly Hamilcar quivered; at a gesture of his hand his slaves withdrew; and he signed to the negress to move with caution, drawing her by the arm to a remote room.

The negress threw herself on the floor to kiss Hamilcar's feet; roughly lifting her up, he asked:

"Where have you left him, Iddibal?"

"Away, there, master!"

Throwing aside the veils, she rubbed the black from her face with one of the sleeves of her tunic: the senile, trembling, stooping figure was transformed, revealing a robust old man, whose skin seemed somewhat tanned by exposure to sand, wind, and sea. A tuft of white hair stood up on the crown of his head, like a bird's aigrette. With an ironical glance he pointed to the discarded disguise, which had fallen on the floor.

"You have done well, Iddibal. It is well!" Then, with a piercing look of scrutiny, Hamilcar added, "Does anyone yet suspect?"

The old man swore by the Cabiri that the secret was perfectly guarded. They never quitted their cabin, which was three days from Hadrumetum; the shores were peopled with tortoises, and the dunes were covered with palm trees. "And, obedient to your orders, master, I am teaching him to lance javelins, and to manage the teams."

"He is strong, is he not?"

"Yes, master, and intrepid also; he fears neither serpents, nor thunder, nor phantoms. He runs barefooted, like a herdsman, on the very edge of the precipices."

"Speak! Speak!"

"He invents snares to capture wild beasts. The other moon—would you believe it?—he surprised an eagle. He clutched it; and the blood of both child and struggling bird spattered through the air in large drops, like wind-blown roses. The furious bird enveloped him with the beating of its strong wings; but the dauntless boy seized it more firmly, and pressed it against his chest; and, in proportion as its death agony increased, his laughter redoubled, till it rung out superb, like the clash of swords."

Hamilcar lowered his head, evidently dazzled by these presages of greatness.

"But, for some days he has been restless and agitated. He watches the far-off sails passing by at sea; he is sad, and refuses his food; he asks questions about the Gods, and he desires to know Carthage."

"No! no! not yet!" exclaimed the Suffete.

The old slave seemed to understand the peril that frightened Hamilcar, and resumed:

"But how restrain him? Already he has made me promise; and I should not have come to Carthage except to buy for him a poniard with a silver handle encircled with pearls."

Then the slave recounted how, having espied the Suffete on the terrace, he had managed to pass the guards of the Port in the guise of one of Salammbô's women, in order to attain his master's presence.

Hamilcar remained a long time lost in meditation. At last he said:

"To-morrow, at sunset, present yourself at Megara, behind the purple factory, and imitate the cry of a jackal three times. If you do not then see me, the first day of each moon return to Carthage. Forget nothing! Cherish him! Now you may speak to him of Hamilcar."

The slave resumed his disguise, and they left the house and the Port together. Hamilcar continued alone on foot without an escort, as the conferences of the Elders were, on all extraordinary occasions, secret, and each one attended mysteriously.

At first he skirted the eastern face of the Acropolis, then passed by, in successive order, the vegetable-market, the galleries of Kinisdo, and the suburb of the perfumers. The scattered lights were dying out; silence settled on the wider streets, and shadowy forms gliding through the darkness followed him: others came up—all, like him, directing their steps along the Mappals.

The Temple of Moloch was built at the foot of a steep gorge, in a sinister spot. From the bottom only the high walls could be perceived rising indefinitely, like the sides of a monstrous tomb. The night was sombre; a grey fog seemed to press upon the sea waves, as they beat against the cliffs, sobbing and sounding like a death gurgle; and the human shadows gradually vanished, as if they had glided through the walls like spirits.

Just beyond the entrance of these walls was a vast quadrangular court, bordered by arcades; in the centre rose a massive structure, with eight uniform sides. Cupolas surmounted it, ranged around the second story, which supported a form of rotunda, from which sprang a cone with a returning curve, terminating on the summit in a ball.

Fires burned in filigree cylinders fastened on standards, borne by men. These lights flickered in the gusts of wind, and reddened the golden combs holding the braided tresses at the nape of the necks of the servitors. These torch-bearers ran forward, calling each other to receive the Elders. Here and there on the pavement enormous lions crouched like sphinxes—the living symbols of the Sun, the Devourer. They dozed with half-closed eyes; but, awakened by the tramp of feet and sound of voices, they slowly rose and approached the Elders, whom they recognised by their costumes; they rubbed against their thighs, curving their backs, and yawning sonorously, and the vapour of their breaths floated like mist across the flames of the torches.

The agitation increased; the gates were closed; all the priests took flight, and the Elders disappeared under the columns, which formed a deep vestibule around the temple. These columns were disposed in a fashion to reproduce in circular ranges, comprised one within another, the Saturnian period, containing the years, the months within the years, and the days within the months—finally, they touched the wall of the sanctuary.

In this vestibule the Elders deposited their narwhal-tusk staves—as a law, which was always observed, punished with death anyone who should enter a session with any weapon.

At the bottom of their robes many displayed a rent stayed by a purple braid, to manifest that they were too preoccupied mourning their relatives to bestow time in the arrangement of their clothing, and this evidence of their bereavement prevented the rent from destructively enlarging. Others, as a sign of mourning, enclosed their beards in a small pouch of violet-coloured skin, attached by two cords to their ears.

Their first act on assembling was to embrace one another, breast to breast. They surrounded Hamilcar to offer congratulations; they truly seemed like brothers meeting a brother again.

The majority of these men were thick-set, with hooked noses, resembling the Assyrian Colossi; some, nevertheless, by their projecting cheek-bones, their great height, and narrow feet, betrayed an African origin from Nomad ancestors. Those who lived constantly in the depth of their counting-houses had pale faces; others maintained about them the severity of the desert, and strange jewels sparkled on all their fingers, tanned by unknown suns. The navigators were recognisable by their rolling gait, and the agriculturists retained about their persons the odours of wine-presses, dried grasses, and the sweat of their mules. These old pirates tilled farms; these money-makers equipped vessels: and these proprietors of plantations kept slaves who exercised the various trades. All were learned in the religious disciplines, expert in stratagems, unmerciful and wealthy. Protracted cares had imparted to them an air of weariness; their flaming eyes were full of defiance, and the habit of travel, and of lying, and of traffic, and of command, gave to their persons an aspect of cunning and violence—a sort of brutality, circumspect and passionate. Besides, the influence of Moloch made them solemn.

At first they walked through a long, vaulted hall, oval, like an egg. Seven doors, corresponding to the seven planets, spread against the wall seven squares of different colours. After a long room, they entered another similar hall, in which, at the far end, was a lighted candelabrum, covered with chased flowers, and each one of its eight golden branches bore in a chalice of diamonds a wick of byssus. This candelabrum was placed on the last of the long steps leading to a grand altar, terminating at the corners in brazen horns. Two lateral stairways led up to its flat top, where the stones were covered under a mountain of accumulated ashes, and something indistinct smouldered slowly upon it. Then beyond, higher than the candelabrum, and even higher than man's breast, in which yawned seven apertures; his open wings spread out over the walls; his elongated hands reached to the floor; three black stones, encircled in yellow, represented three eyeballs in his forehead; and his bull's head was raised by a terrible effort, as if to bellow.

Around the hall were ranged ebony benches; behind each was erected a bronze standard, resting on three paws, and supporting a torch. All these lights were reflected over the polished surface of the mother-of-pearl lozenges paving the hall. The room was so lofty that the red walls, as they neared the dome, appeared black, and on high the three eyes of the idol seemed like stars half lost in the night.

The Elders sat on the ebony benches, having thrown over their heads the ends of their long robes. They remained motionless, with their hands crossed in their wide sleeves; and the mother-of-pearl pavement resembled a luminous stream that ran under their bare feet from the altar towards the door.

In the centre the four pontiffs sat back to back on four ivory chairs, forming a cross. The pontiff of Eschmoûn robed in hyacinth, the pontiff of Tanit in a white linen robe, the pontiff of Khamoûn in a reddish woollen garment, and the pontiff of Moloch in purple.

Hamilcar moved forward to the candelabrum, and making a circuit of it, examined the burning wicks, then threw upon them a perfume powder. Instantly violet flames sprang up at the extremities of the branches.

Now a shrill voice broke forth, another responded,

and the hundred Elders, the four pontiffs, and Hamilcar, all at the same time rose to their feet, intoning a hymn, always repeating the same syllables and re-swelling the sounds; their voices continued to rise until they became terrible, when, with a single stroke, all were silent.

They paused some minutes. At last Hamilcar drew from his breast a small statuette with three heads, blue like a sapphire, and placed it before him. It was the image of Truth, the very genius of his speech. Afterwards he replaced it in his breast, and all, as though seized by a sudden rage, screamed out:

"These Barbarians are your good friends! Traitor! Wretch! You have come to see us perish, have you not? . . . Let him speak! . . . No! No! . . ."

They revenged themselves for the constraint which had been imposed on them by the official ceremony; and though they had longed for the return of Hamilcar, they were now indignant that he had not prevented their disasters, or, rather, that he also had not undergone them like themselves.

As soon as the tumult was calmed, the pontiff of Moloch arose, saying:

"We demand that you explain why you have not returned to Carthage before."

"What does that matter to you?" disdainfully responded the Suffete.

Their outcries redoubled.

"Of what do you accuse me? Perhaps, that I have conducted the war badly? You have seen the ordinances of my battles, you others conveniently leave to the Barbarians. . . ."

"Enough! Enough!" they yelled

He resumed in a deep voice, to make himself better heard:

"Oh, that is true! I deceive myself! Lights of the Baal. Here in your midst are braves! Gisco, rise up!" And, moving along the altar step, half-closing his eyes, seemingly in search of some one, he repeated: "Rise up, Gisco! You can accuse me; they will defend you! But where is he?" Then, pausing as though to correct himself: "Ah! in his dwelling, without doubt. Surrounded by his sons, commanding his slaves, happy, and enumerating on the walls the collars of honour that the country has conferred upon him!"

They writhed about, shrugging their shoulders, as if lashed with whip-thongs.

"You do not even know whether he is dead or alive!" And, without heeding their clamour, he told them that in abandoning the Suffete they had forsaken the Republic. Likewise that the Roman treaty of peace, advantageous though they thought it, was more calamitous than twenty battles.

Some—the least wealthy of the Council, who were always suspected to incline towards the people or towards tyranny—applauded.

Their adversaries, the chiefs of the Syssites and administrators, triumphed over them by force of numbers; the most important were ranged near Hanno, who sat at the other end of the hall before the high door closed by a hyacinth tapestry.

The ulcers on Hanno's face were covered with paint; the gold-powder from his hair had fallen upon his shoulders, where it made two brilliant patches; and the hair appeared white, fine, and crinkled, like lamb's wool. His hands were swathed with linen bandages saturated with perfumed grease, that trickled down and dropped on the pavement; and his malady seemed considerably augmented, for his eyes were so covered by the folds of his eyelids that, in order to see, he was compelled to tip his head backwards.

His partisans urged him to speak. At length he said, in a harsh, hideous voice:

"Less arrogance, Barca! We have all been conquered! Each one must bear his misfortune; therefore resign yourself!"

"Inform us, rather," Hamilcar smilingly said,—"how you steered your galleys into the Roman fleet?"

"I was driven by the wind out of my course," responded Hanno.

"You are like the rhinoceros, who treads in his own dung; you expose your own folly! Be silent!" and they began mutual recriminations respecting the battle of the islands of Ægates. Hanno accused Hamilcar of not having come to join forces with him.

"But that would have entailed leaving Eryx. It was necessary to take to the open. What prevented you? Oh! I forgot—the elephants are afraid of the sea!"

Hamilcar's partisans found his pleasantry so good that they laughed heartily, till the dome of the temple re-echoed like the beating of drums.

Hanno denounced the indignity of such an outrage, protesting that his malady had attacked him as the result of a chill during the siege of Hecatompylus; and the tears coursed down his face as a winter rain over a ruined wall.

Hamilcar continued: "If you had loved me as much as you do that man, there would to-day be great joy throughout Carthage! How many times have I not implored you for aid, and you have always refused me money!"

"We needed it here," said the chief of the Syssites.

"And when my affairs were desperate—for we have been compelled to drink the urine of our mules cooled in our helmets, and have eaten the thongs of our sandals; when I fairly longed that the blades of grass were soldiers, or that I could form battalions with our rotting dead—you recalled the vessels yet remaining with me!"

"We could not risk all," interrupted Baat-Baal, owner of gold mines in Darytian-Gaetulia.

"In the meantime, what have you done here in Carthage, in your dwellings, behind your walls? There were the Gauls on the Eridanus that should have been set in motion; the Canaanites at Cyrene, who would have come to our aid; and while the Romans were sending ambassadors to Ptolemy...."

"He praises the Romans to us now!" some one cried out. "How much have they paid you to defend them?"

"Ask that of the plains of Bruttium, of the ruins of Locri, Metapontum, and Heraclea! I have burned all their trees, have pillaged all their temples, and even to the death of the grandsons of their grandsons...."

"Truly, you declaim like an orator!" interrupted

Kapouras, an illustrious merchant. "What then do you want?"

"I say that you must be more ingenious, or more formidable! If the entire of Africa rejects your yoke, it will be because you do not know how to adjust it to her shoulders—enfeebled masters that you are! Agathocles, Regulus, Cœpio, any of the brave men, have only to land in order to subjugate the Republic; and when the Libyans in the east combine with the Numidians in the west, and the Nomads shall have come from the south, and the Romans from the north....."

A cry of horror rang out.

"Oh! you will strike your breasts, roll yourselves in the dust, and tear your mantles! What matter? You will be obliged to turn the millstones in Suburra, and gather the vintage on the hills of Latium."

They struck their right thighs to demonstrate their offence at such a suggestion, lifting the sleeves of their robes like the large wings of frightened birds.

Hamilcar, carried away by an inspiration, continued in the same strain as he stood apart on the highest step of the altar, quivering with terrible emotion. He lifted his arms, and the rays from the candelabrum burning behind him, passed in streaks between his fingers, like golden javelins.

"You will lose your vessels, your fields, your chariots, your suspended couches, and your slaves who now shampoo your feet! The jackals will make their lairs in your palaces, the plough turn over your tombs; there will only remain the cry of the eagles and heaps of ruins! Thou shalt fall, Carthage!"

The four pontiffs threw out their hands to ward

off this anathema. All had risen to their feet; but the Suffete of the sea, a sacerdotal magistrate under the protection of the sun, was inviolable, so long as the assembly of the Rich had not judged him. A terror dwelt in the altar on which he stood. They recoiled.

Hamilcar said no more. With eyes fixed and face as pale as the pearls in his tiara, he panted, almost terrified at himself, and his spirit lost in lugubrious visions. From the height where he stood, the flambeaux on the bronze standards appeared to him to be a vast crown of fire laid flat on the pavement; the black smoke that escaped rolled up through the darkness of the dome. The intensity of the silence reigning for some moments was such that the distant sea-roar could be heard.

After a time the Elders counselled among themselves. Their interests, their very existence, were attacked by the Barbarians. But they could not conquer them without the Suffete's aid; and, despite their pride, this fact made them unmindful of all minor considerations. They took his friends aside, and in a parley made interested reconciliations, understandings, and promises.

Hamilcar protested that he no longer desired to be involved in the details of any command. All besought and implored him to reconsider his decision. When the word treason escaped their lips, he lost temper, retorting that the only traitor to Carthage was the Grand Council, as the engagements with the soldiers expired with the war, hence they became free as soon as the war ended. He even extolled their bravery, and depicted all the advantages that would accrue if the soldiers could be permanently attached to the Republic by donations and privileges.

At this, Magdassan, an old governor of provinces, rolling his yellow eyes about, said:

"Truly, Barca, from force of travel, you have become a Greek, a Latin, and I know not what! Why do you talk of recompense for these men? Let ten thousand Barbarians perish rather than one of us."

The Elders nodded their heads approvingly, and murmured: "Yes; why have so much trouble on this score? We can always procure Mercenaries when needed."

"Yes, and you can conveniently get rid of them, is it not so? Abandon them, as you did in Sardinia. Warn the enemy the road they must take, as was done for those Gauls in Sicily, or else debark them in the open sea. While returning, I saw the rocks whitened with their bones!" retorted Hamilcar.

"What a pity!" impudently ejaculated Kapouras.

"Have they not turned a hundred times to the enemy?" exclaimed others.

"Why, then," answered Hamilcar, "in spite of your laws, have you recalled them to Carthage? And why, when once here in your city, poor and numerous amidst your wealth, did the idea not occur to you to weaken them by some division? Afterwards you dismissed them with their women and children—without keeping a single hostage! Did you imagine that they would assassinate each other and spare you the pain of fulfilling your pledges? You hate them because they are strong! You hate me even more, because I am their master!

Ah! I just now felt, when you kissed my hands, that you all restrained yourselves with difficulty from biting them!"

If the sleeping lions had entered at this moment from the outer court, howling wildly, the uproar could not have been more terrible. But the pontiff of Eschmoûn rose, and with his knees tightly pressed together, his elbows straight, and hands half open, said:

"Barca, Carthage desires you to take the general command of the Punic forces against the Barbarians!"

"I refuse!" responded Hamilcar.

"We will give you full authority," screamed out the chiefs of the Syssites.

"No!"

"Without any control! Without division! All the money that you want! All the captives, all the booty, fifty zerets of land for each dead enemy."

"No! no! Because with you it is impossible to vanquish them!"

"He is afraid!"

"Because you are cowards, avaricious, ungrateful, pusillanimous, and fools!"

"He treats with the enemies! To put himself at their head," cried out some.

"And return on us," screamed others.

And from the extremity of the hall Hanno yelled, "He aspires to be king!"

Then they all bounded up, overturning the benches and flambeaux, and darted in a crowd towards the altar, brandishing their poniards.

Hamilcar, searching under his sleeves, drew forth

two large cutlasses. Advancing his left foot, he confronted and defied them all, as, with flashing eyes, bending forward, he stood immovable under the golden candelabrum.

Thus, as a precaution, every member of the conference had carried concealed weapons into the temple: it was a crime; they looked at one another terrified. As all were culpable, each quickly reassured himself, and gradually turned his back to the Suffete, retreating to the body of the hall, enraged and humiliated. For the second time they had recoiled before Hamilcar.

They remained for some moments standing. Some, who had carelessly wounded their fingers, held them in their mouths, or rolled them up gently in the ends of their mantles, and, as they were dispersing, Hamilcar heard their remarks:

"Ah! it is a point of delicacy. He does not wish to afflict his daughter!"

A voice, in a very loud tone, answered: "Doubtless, since she takes her lovers from amongst the Mercenaries!"

At first he staggered; then his eyes searched rapidly over the throng for Schahabarim. The pontiff of Tanit had alone remained seated. Hamilcar could only perceive in the distance his tall cap. All sneered at the Suffete to his very face, and, as his agony augmented, their joy increased, while amid the confused yells he could hear those who were last to depart, screaming back at him:

"He was seen leaving her bed-chamber!"

"One morning in the month of Tammouz!"

"He is the thief of the Zaïmph!"

M

"A very fine man!"

"Taller than Hamilcar!"

At this he jerked off his tiara the badge of his dignity—his tiara of eight mystic rows, in the centre of which was an emerald shell—and with both hands dashed it fiercely to the ground. The gold circles broke and rebounded, and the pearls rang out on the pavement.

On his pale forehead now appeared a long cicatrix that moved like a serpent between his eyebrows; his limbs trembled; he went up by one of the lateral stairways leading to the altar, and stepped on the top. It was to consecrate himself to the Gods by offering himself as a holocaust. The movement of his flowing mantle agitated the lights of the candelabrum, which was lower than his sandals, and a fine powder was raised by his steps, and floated about him like a cloud, as high up as his girth. He paused between the legs of the brass colossus, took up two handfuls of those ashes, the sight of which alone made all the Carthaginians tremble with terror, and said:

"By the hundred flambeaux of your Intelligences! By the eight fires of the Cabiri! By the stars! By the meteors! And by the volcanoes! By all that which burns! By the thirst of the desert! By the saltness of the Ocean! By the cavern of Hadrumetum the realm of Souls! By the extermination! By the ashes of your sons, and the ashes of the brothers of your ancestors, with which I now commingle those of mine! You, the hundred Councillors of Carthage, you have lied in accusing my daughter! And I, Hamilcar-Barca, Suffete of the

sea, Chief of the Rich and Ruler of the people, before Moloch with the bull's head, I swear. . . . . ."
They waited for something awful; but he resumed in a much louder and calmer voice—" That I will not even speak of it to her!"

The sacred servitors, wearing gold combs, entered, some carrying sponges of purple, and others palm branches. They drew aside the hyacinth curtain spread before the doorway, and through the opening could be perceived at the end of the other halls the vast rose-coloured sky, which seemed to be but a continuation of the temple's vault, resting on the horizon of the blue sea.

The sun, just leaving the billows, rose, striking in full effulgence against the breast of the brazen idol, which was divided into seven compartments, closed by gratings. Moloch's jaws, revealing his red teeth, opened in a terrible yawn; his enormous nostrils were dilated; the broad daylight seemed to animate and impart to him a terrible air of impatience, as though he would like to bound outside to mix with the sun, with the God, and course with him through the immensities of space.

Meanwhile the flambeaux, still burning, scattered on the mother-of-pearl pavement, appeared like splashes of blood.

The Elders reeled from exhaustion, and filled their lungs by long inhalations of fresh air; the perspiration ran down their livid faces; their fierce outcries had robbed them of their voices; but their wrath against the Suffete had not subsided, and their adieux were parting threats, to which Hamilcar responded.

"To-morrow night, Barca, in the temple of Eschmoûn!"

"I shall be there——!"

"We will have you condemned by the Rich!"

"And, I you by the people!"

"Take heed, lest you end on a cross!"

"And you, torn in the streets!"

As soon as they reached the threshold of the court they resumed a calm deportment.

Their runners and charioteers awaited them at the gate. The majority departed on white she-mules. The Suffete sprang into his chariot, grasping the reins himself; the two horses arched their necks, struck in cadence the stones, which rebounded under their hoofs, and ascended the entire distance to Mappals, at such a fleet gallop, that the silver vulture ornamenting the end of the pole seemed to fly as the chariot swept quickly past.

The road crossed a field set with long stones with pointed pyramidal tops; on each was sculptured an open hand, as though the dead lying beneath had reached out of their tombs towards heaven to claim something. Further along were scattered cone-shaped cabins, built of clay, branches, and reed wattles. Little stone walls, runnels of water, esparto ropes, and hedges of Indian figs irregularly separated these habitations, which became closer and closer together in approaching the Suffete's gardens.

But Hamilcar kept his eyes fixed on a large tower of three stories, forming three enormous cylinders, the first built of stone, the second of brick, and the third entirely of cedar, supporting a copper cupola on twenty-four juniper columns, over which fell like garlands the interlacings of brass chainlets. This lofty edifice dominated the buildings that extended to the right, consisting of the warehouses and counting house, while the palace of the women loomed up at the end of the avenue of cypresses, which alligned like two bronze walls.

When the rumbling chariot had entered through the narrow gate, it halted under a wide hangar, where the horses were immediately hoppled and fed with heaps of chopped grass.

All the servants ran forward. They were indeed a host; for those who worked in the adjacent country, in terror of the soldiers had betaken themselves to Carthage. The farm labourers, clothed in animals' skins, dragged behind them chains riveted to their ankles; the workers in the purple factories had their arms stained red, like executioners; the sailors wore green caps; the fishermen coral necklaces; the hunters bore a net across their shoulders, and the people of Megara wore white or black tunics, leather breeches, and skull-caps of straw, felt, or linen, according to their different employments or industries.

In the rear pressed a populace in rags, who lived without employment, far from the dwelling houses, sleeping on the ground, sheltered only by the trees in the gardens, eating the scraps from the kitchens—human excrescences which vegetated in the shadow of the palace.

Hamilcar tolerated them from prudential reasons, even more than from disdain. Many of their number had never before seen the Suffete, but all, to manifest their joy, wore flowers in their ears.

Men, coiffed like sphinxes, armed with large clubs, brandished them about in the crowd, striking right and left to keep back the slaves over-curious to see their master, so that he might not be pressed upon by their numbers or incommoded by their odours.

They all threw themselves flat on the ground, crying out:—"Eye of Baal! May your mansion flourish for ever!" and between the men thus prostrated in the avenue of cypresses, the intendant of the intendants, Abdalonim, coiffed in a white mitre, advanced towards Hamilcar, carrying a censer in his hand.

Salammbô descended the stairway of the galleys. All her women followed behind her, and at each step she advanced they also descended.

The heads of the negresses in contrast made large black spots amid the line of bandeaux of golden plaques which bound the foreheads of the Roman women. Others wore in their hair silver arrows, emerald butterflies, or long pins spreading like the sun's rays. Over the medley of their white, yellow, and blue garments, their fringes, agraffes, necklaces, rings, and bracelets glittered. The robes rustled, and the clattering of sandals, accompanied by the dull sound of the naked feet upon the wood, was audible. Here and there a tall eunuch, whose shoulders overtopped the women, smiled with his face aloft in the air.

As soon as the acclamations of the men were quieted, the women, with faces hidden by the sleeves of their dresses, uttered in unison a strange cry, like the howl of a she-wolf, and so furious and strident that it seemed to make the grand ebony stairway, now covered with women, vibrate like a lyre from top to bottom.

The wind fluttered their long veils and gently waved the slender papyrus stems.

It was the month of *Schebaz*, in the middle of winter; the pomegranate trees, at this season in flower, stood out in relief against the azure sky; through the branches the sea appeared, with an island in the distance, half lost in the mist.

Hamilcar paused when he perceived Salammbô.

Born after the death of several male children, she had not been welcomed, for the birth of a daughter was considered a calamity in the religions of the sun. However, at a later period, the Gods had given him a son; but he ever retained some memory of his blighted hopes, and as it were the shock of the malediction he had pronounced against her.

Meanwhile, Salammbô continued to advance towards him. Pearls of various colours fell in long clusters from her ears over her shoulders, dangling down as far as her elbows; her hair was crimped in a mode to simulate a cloud. Around her neck she wore small quadrangular gold plaques representing a woman between two lions rampant, and her costume reproduced completely the accoutrements of the Goddess Tanit. Her hyacinth robe, with flowing sleeves, drawn tightly in at the waist, widened out at the bottom. The vermilion of her lips made her pearly teeth appear even whiter than they actually were; the antimony on her eyelids caused her eyes to assume an almond shape. Her sandals of a bird's plumage, with very high heels, gave her a more imposing height. She was extraordinarily pale, doubtless in consequence of the cold.

At length she arrived before Hamilcar, and, without looking up, or raising her head, she addressed him, saying:

"All hail, Eye of Baalim! Eternal glory! Triumph! Contentment! Rest! Wealth! There was a long period when my heart was sad, and the household languished, but the master who returns is like Tammuz restored to life; and under thy care, O father, a joy, a new existence, will expand over all!"

And taking from Taanach's hand a little oblong vase, in which fumed a mixture of farina, butter, cardamon, and wine, she continued: "Drink a full draught of the welcome cup prepared by thy servant."

"Benediction on thee!" he replied, mechanically seizing the golden vase she proffered to him.

All the while he examined her with a scrutiny so keen that Salammbô, troubled thereat, stammered out:

"Some one has told thee, O master! . . . ."

"Yes! I know!" answered Hamilcar, in a low voice. Was this a confession? Or did she merely allude to the Barbarians? And he added a few vague words concerning the public embarrassment that he himself hoped now to dispel.

"O father!" exclaimed Salammbô, "thou canst never efface that which is irreparable!"

At this he started back, and Salammbô was astonished by his amazement, as she did not dream of

Carthage, but of the sacrilege of which she felt herself an accomplice. This man, who made the legions tremble, whom she scarcely knew, frightened her like a God. He had divined it; he knew all; something terrible was about to befall her; she cried out—"Mercy!"

Hamilcar lowered his head slowly. Disposed as Salammbô was to accuse herself, she dared not now open her lips; notwithstanding she was almost suffocated with the desire to complain to, and be comforted by her father. Hamilcar combated his inclination to break his oath. However, he kept it from pride, or through fear of putting an end to his uncertainty, and scanned her full in the face, trying with all his power to discover what she hid at the bottom of her heart.

Salammbô, panting, buried her head gradually in her bosom, crushed by his too austere scrutiny. He was now sure that she had yielded to the embrace of a Barbarian. He shuddered, lifting both his fists over her. She uttered a scream, and fell down among her women, who eagerly pressed about her.

Hamilcar turned on his heels, followed by all of his attendants. The door of the warehouses was thrown open, and he entered into a vast, round hall, whence long passages radiated like the spokes of a wheel from its hub, leading into other halls. A stone disc was erected in the centre, surrounded by a railing for holding the cushions that were heaped upon the carpets. The Suffete at first walked with long, rapid strides, breathing heavily, striking the ground sharply with his heels. He passed his hand across his forehead like one tormented by flies; then, shaking his head, he perceived the accumulation of his wealth, and became calmer. His thoughts were attracted to the perspective of the passages and to the adjoining halls filled with the rarest treasures. Therein were amassed bronze plates, ingots of silver, and pigs of iron alternating with blocks of tin brought from the Cassiterides, by way of the Darksome sea; gums from the countries of the Blacks overflowed their sacks, made from the bark of palm-trees; and gold dust, heaped in leather bottles, imperceptibly filtered through the worn seams; delicate filaments, drawn from marine plants, hung between the flax from Egypt, Greece, Taprobane, and Judea. Madrepores, as broad as bushes, bristled at the base of the walls, and an indefinable odour floated about, evidently emanating from the abundant store of perfumes, spices, hides, and ostrich plumes, tied in large bunches at the very top of the roof. Before each passage elephants' tusks stood up, joined at the points, forming an arch above the doorway.

Finally, he mounted the stone disc. All the intendants stood with their arms crossed and heads bowed, while Abdalonim, in a proud manner, lifted his pointed mitre.

Hamilcar interrogated the Chief of the Ships. He was an old pilot, with eyelids inflamed by the wind; his white locks fell to his hips, as though the foam of tempestuous waves had lingered in his beard.

He answered that he had sent a fleet by Gades and Thymiamata, endeavouring to reach Eziongeber by rounding the South Horn and the promontory of Aromata.

Other vessels had continued to the west during

four moons, without making land; but the prows of the vessels became entangled in the grasses: the horizon resounded continually with the noise of cataracts; blood-coloured fogs obscured the sun, and a breeze, freighted with perfumes, put all of the crews to sleep, and their memories had been thereby so much disturbed that at present they could recount naught concerning this region. Meantime, other vessels had ascended the streams of Scythia, penetrating Colchis to the Jugrians and the Estians; had carried away from the archipelago fifteen hundred virgins;* and sent to the bottom all foreign vessels navigating beyond the cape of Æstrymon, in order that the secret of the routes might not be known. King Ptolemy had kept back the incense from Schesbar, Syracuse, and Elatea. Corsica and the islands had furnished nothing. Then the old pilot dropped his voice to announce that one trireme had been taken at Rusicada by the Numidians — "For they are with them, master."

Hamilcar knitted his eyebrows, then signed to the Chief of the Journeys to speak. This man was wrapped in a brown robe without girdle, and his head was bound round by a long scarf of white material, which passed over his mouth and fell back on his shoulders.

The caravans had been regularly despatched at the winter equinox. But out of fifteen hundred men bound to the further Ethiopia with excellent camels, new leather bottles, and stocks of painted linen, one only had returned to Carthage; all the others had perished from fatigue, or had become dazed by the terrors of the desert. He said that he had been far beyond the Black Harosch, afterwards to the Atarantes, and the country of the big apes, and thence to immense kingdoms where even the ordinary utensils were made of gold: in this region were seen a stream the colour of milk, spreading out like a sea, forests of blue trees, aromatic hills, monsters with human faces, vegetating on rocks, whose eyes to behold you expanded like flowers; then behind, the lakes covered with dragons, to the mountains of crystal that supported the sun. Other caravans had returned from the Indies, bringing back peacocks, pepper, and some new tissues. As for those who went to purchase chalcedonies, by the road of the Syrtis and the temple of Ammon, they had doubtless perished in the sands. The caravans of Gaetulia and Phazzana had furnished their usual supplies, but the Chief did not at present dare to equip any other expeditions.

Hamilcar, comprehending by this that the Mercenaries occupied the country, gave vent to a dull moan, as he leaned on his other elbow.

The Chief of Farms, who was summoned next in order, experienced such fear that he trembled violently, in spite of his thick-set shoulders and great red eyes; his flat-nosed face resembled a mastiff's, and was surmounted by a network of bark-fibres; he wore a girdle of leopard skin with all the hair intact, in which shone two formidable cutlasses.

As soon as Hamilcar turned towards him, he uttered a cry to invoke all the Baals, protesting it was not his fault! He could do nothing! He had observed the temperature, the land, the stars; had made the plantations at the solstice of winter; had pruned during the wane of the moon; and had inspected the slaves, and provided them with clothing.

Hamilcar, becoming irritated by such loquacity, clacked his tongue, and the man with the cutlasses continued in a rapid voice:

"Ah, master! They have plundered all! Sacked all! destroyed all! Three thousand feet of timber were cut down at Maschala, and at Ubada the granaries were broken open and the cisterns were filled up! At Tedes they took away fifteen hundred gomors of wheat; at Marazzana they killed the herdsmen and ate the herds, and burned your house, your beautiful house of cedar beams, where you spend the summers. The slaves of Tuburbo, who reaped the barley, took flight to the mountains; and of the asses, riding and working mules, the cattle of Taormina, and the Oringis-horses, not one remains; all were taken away. It is a curse. I cannot survive it!"

He commenced to cry, adding: "Ah! if you only knew how full the cellars were, and how the ploughs shone! Ah, the fine rams! Ah, the fine bulls!"

Hamilcar's rage suffocated him; he burst forth: "Be quiet! Am I then a pauper? No lies! Speak the truth! I wish to know all that I have lost, to the last shekel, to the last cab! Abdalonim, bring me the accounts of the vessels, of the farms, of the caravans, and those of my household! And if any of your consciences be troubled, sorrow on your heads! . . . . . . Leave!"

All the intendants walking backwards, touching their fingers to the ground, left the Suffete's presence.

Abdalonim took from the middle of a nest of

pigeon-holes in the wall the accounts kept on knotted cords, bands of linen or of papyrus, and shoulder-blades of sheep covered with fine writing. He laid them all at Hamilcar's feet, and placed in his hands a wooden frame, strung with three interior wires on which slipped gold, silver, and horn balls, and began:

"One hundred and ninety-two houses in the Mappals, rented to the new Carthaginians at the rate of one beka per moon."

"Hold! That is too much! Provide for the poor. Write the names of those whom you believe to be the most courageous, and endeavour to ascertain if they are attached to the Republic. What next?"

Abdalonim hesitated, surprised by such generosity.

Hamilcar impatiently wrested from his hands the linen bands, saying, as he looked:

"What, then, is this? Three palaces around Khamoûn at twelve kesitath per month! Put it twenty. I do not wish to be devoured by the Rich."

Abdalonim after a long salute resumed: "Loaned to Tigilas, until the end of the season, two kikars at thirty-three and a third per cent. maritime interest; advanced to Bar-Malkarth fifteen hundred shekels on the security of thirty slaves, but twelve died in the salt marshes."

"In other words, they were not robust," laughingly said the Suffete. "No matter! if he needs money, satisfy his requirements! One must always lend, and at different interest, according to the wealth of the people."

Then the servitor hastened to read all the reports: on the iron mines of Annaba, the farming of the coral fisheries, the purple factories, the yield of the tax on the resident Greeks, and the exportation of silver to Arabia, where it was valued ten times more than gold; then on the captures of vessels, allowing for the tithes for the temple of Tanit, saying about the last item, "Each time I have declared one-fourth less, master."

Hamilcar kept account, rattling the balls under his fingers.

"Enough! What have you paid?"

"To Stratonicles of Corinth, and three merchants of Alexandria, on the letters, which behold have been cashed, ten thousand Athenian drachmas and twelve Syrian talents of gold. The provisions for the crews rising to twenty minæ per month for a trireme. . . ."

"I know it! How much are the losses?"

"Here, see the account on these sheets of lead," said the intendant. "With reference to the vessels chartered in common, as they were frequently compelled to throw the cargoes overboard, the unequal losses were divided according to the number of partners. For cordage borrowed from the arsenals that it has been impossible to return, the Syssites have exacted eight hundred kesitath before the expedition to Utica."

"The Syssites again!" said Hamilcar, lowering his head, and remaining as if crushed under the weight of all the hatreds he felt levelled at him. "But, I do not see here the expenses of Megara."

Abdalonim became pale, and turned to bring from

another case the sycamore-wood tablets filed in bundles, and tied together with leather straps.

Hamilcar listened, curious as to the domestic details, calmed by the monotony of the man's voice in enumerating the accounts, while Abdalonim read slower and slower, and suddenly letting the wooden tablets fall to the ground, threw himself flat on his face with arms extended, in the position of one condemned.

Hamilcar, without evincing any emotion, picked up the tablets; his lips parted and his eyes opened widely when he saw charged for the expenses of one day an exorbitant consumption of meats, fish, birds, wines, and aromatics, vases broken, slaves killed, and napery destroyed.

Abdalonim, remaining prostrate, told him of the Barbarians' feast and that he had not the power to escape from executing the commands of the Elders. Salammbô, too, had commanded that money should be prodigally expended to receive the soldiers.

At the name of his daughter Hamilcar bounded up; then compressing his lips, he sank back amid the cushions, tearing the fringes with his nails, his eyes fixed, panting.

"Get up!" said the Suffete.

Then he descended from the dais, followed by Abdalonim, whose knees trembled. But seizing an iron bar, he went to work like a fury to unseal the pavement. A disc of wood flew out and revealed under the entire length of the passage, numerous broad coverlids that concealed pits where grain was stored.

"Eye of Baal! You see by this," said the servant,

timorously, "they have not taken all! For these pits are deep, each one fifty cubits, and full to the top! During your absence I have had similar pits dug in the arsenals and in the gardens, so that your mansion is as full of grain as your heart is of wisdom."

A smile passed over Hamilcar's face.

"It is well, Abdalonim." Afterwards he whispered: "You must obtain grain from Etruria and Bruttium, and from whatever place you can; it makes no difference at what price! Amass and keep it stored. It is necessary that I alone possess all the grain in Carthage."

Then, when they reached the extremity of the passage, Abdalonim, with one of the keys hanging from his girdle, opened a large quadrangular room, divided in the centre by cedar pillars. Gold, silver, and brass coins were piled on tables, or stowed in niches that extended the length of the four walls, reaching up to the beams of the roof; enormous coffers of hippopotamus hide leaned in the corners, supporting rows of smaller bags; and bullion heaped up, made hillocks on the pavement, while from place to place piles too high had toppled over, appearing like columns in ruins. The large pieces of Carthaginian money, stamped on the face with a representation of Tanit and a horse under a palm tree, were mixed with those of the colonies on which were impressed the figure of a bull, a star, a globe, or a crescent. Then, disposed about in unequal sums, were pieces of all values, and dimensions, and ages, from the ancient ones of Assyria, that were thin as a finger-nail, to the old ones of Latium, that were thicker than a hand ; there were also the buttons of Ægina, the tablets of Bactria, and the short cylinders of ancient Lacædemonina. The coins were rusty, greasy with dirt, and many were covered with verdigris caused by water, having been fished up in nets, or blackened by fire, as found after sieges in the midst of the ruins of cities.

The Suffete had very quickly calculated if the present sums corresponded to the gains and to the losses that had just been submitted to him, and he was about proceeding when he discovered three brass jars completely empty. Abdalonim averted his head with a sign of horror, and Hamilcar resigned himself in silence.

They crossed other passages and through other halls, coming at last before a door where, to guard it better, a man was fastened about the body by a long chain, rivetted in the masonry of the wall—a Roman custom but recently introduced into Carthage. His beard and nails had grown excessively long, and he swayed from right to left, with a continued oscillation, like that of captive animals.

As soon as he recognised Hamilcar, he dashed towards him, crying out : " Mercy, Eye of Baal ! Pity ! Kill me ! It is now ten years since I have seen the sun ! In the name of your father, mercy !"

Without answering him, Hamilcar clapped his hands. At this signal three men appeared, who, with the assistance of Abdalonim, set at once to work, straining their arms in the effort to retire from its rings the enormous bar securing the door. When accomplished, Hamilcar took a torch, and disappeared in the darkness beyond.

This was believed to be the passage leading to the sepulchre of the family; but only a wide pit would have been found, excavated to throw thieves off the track, and it concealed nothing.

Hamilcar passed by it, then, leaning down, turned aside on its rollers a very heavy millstone, which revealed an opening, through which he entered an apartment built in the form of a cone. The walls were covered with brass scales. In the centre, on a granite pedestal, was erected a statue of a Cabirus, bearing the name of Aletes, the discoverer of the mines in Celtiberia. Against the base of this statue, on the ground, were placed crosswise, broad golden bucklers, and monstrous silver vases with closed necks, all of such an extravagant form as to make them useless, it being the custom to cast such quantities of metal in these objects as to render it next to impossible to embezzle or even move them.

With the torch he carried he lighted a small miner's lamp fixed in the idol's cap. Suddenly the hall was illuminated with green, yellow, blue, violet, wine and blood coloured lights; for it was filled with precious stones placed in golden calabashes hanging like sconces to brass plates, or in their native blocks ranged along at the base of the walls. Here were to be found in abundance turquoises torn from the mountains by the swirl of a sling; carbuncles formed by lynxes' urine, tongue-like stones fallen from the moon, *tyanos*, diamonds, *sandastrum*, beryls, the three varieties of rubies, the four species of sapphires, and the twelve species of emeralds. These precious stones flashed variously like splashes of milk, like blue icicles, or like silver dust, and threw their rays in sheets, in beams, or twinkled like stars. The thunder-stones engendered by the thunder scintillated near the chalcedonies, which antidoted poisons. The light also disclosed topazes from Mount Zabarca, subtle in warding off terrors; opals from Bactria, employed to prevent abortions; as well as horns of Ammon, that were placed under beds to invite dreams.

The fantastic fires from these gems and the flame of the lamp were mirrored in the broad, gold shields. Hamilcar stood with folded arms, smiling—and he revelled less in the spectacle than in the consciousness of his riches. They were inaccessible, inexhaustible, infinite. The thought of his ancestors sleeping beneath his feet sent thrilling to his heart some measure of their eternity: he felt at this moment drawn very near to the subterranean spirits. He experienced an emotion akin to the joy of a Cabirus, and the large luminous rays striking his face, resembled the end of an invisible network that crossed abysses, and attached him to the centre of the world.

An invading idea made Hamilcar shiver: he went behind the idol, and walked straight to the wall: then searched on his arm amid numerous tattooings: examined a horizontal line with two perpendicular lines, which in Canaanite figures expressed thirteen; then he counted to the thirteenth brass plate on the wall, when he again lifted his sleeve, and with his right hand traced on another part of his arm other lines more complicated, delicately moving his fingers as though he played on a lyre. Finally, he struck seven blows with his thumb, at which one entire section of the wall turned around as a single block. This masked a sort of cellar, in which were enclosed mysterious things that possessed no names, but of an incalculable value. Hamilcar descended the three steps, took from a silver vat an antelope's skin that floated in a black liquid, and then reascended.

Abdalonim then walked before him. At each step he struck the pavement with his tall staff ornamented on the handle with bells, and before the door of each room cried Hamilcar's name, accompanied with praises and benedictions.

In the circular gallery, from which radiated all the lobbies, were small beams of algum-trees; piled along the walls were sacks of henna, cakes of Lemnos-earth, and tortoise-shells filled with pearls. The Suffete in passing grazed with his robe, without even glancing at them, gigantic pieces of amber, formed by the sun's rays, and almost divine.

A mist of odorous vapour escaped from one of the closed rooms.

"Open that door!" the Suffete commanded.

They entered. Naked men were laboriously engaged kneading pulp, pounding herbs, stirring the fires, pouring oil into jars, opening and closing little oval cells excavated all around in the walls, which were so numerous that the room resembled the interior of a bee-hive. Myrobalans, bdellium, saffron, and violets overflowed the place, and scattered about were gums, powders, roots, glass phials, branches of dropwort and rose petals; the scents were stifling, in spite of the clouds from the storax that crackled in the centre on a brass tripod.

The Chief of Perfumes, pale and very tall, like a

long wax flambeau, came forward to greet Hamilcar, by crushing over his hands a roll of aromatic ointment, whilst two slaves rubbed his heels with harewort leaves. The Suffete repulsed them, for they were Cyrenians of infamous customs, but tolerated because of their secret knowledge in compounding perfumes.

In order to make a display of his vigilance, the Chief of Perfumes offered to the Suffete, in an electrum spoon, a little malobalthrum to taste ; then with an awl pierced three Indian bezoars. Hamilcar, who comprehended the artifices of the craft, took a hornful of balm, and approached the fire, spilling it on his robe, when a brown stain appeared, which proved it was adulterated. At this revelation he looked fixedly at the Chief, and, without saying a word, threw the gazelle-horn in his face.

Indignant as he was that these adulterations should be committed to his detriment, yet upon perceiving some packages of spikenard that were being packed for exportation to the countries beyond the seas, he ordered antimony to be added to make them heavier. Then he demanded where were the three boxes of *psagas* destined for his own personal use.

The Chief of Perfumes avowed that he knew nothing about them, as the soldiers had invaded the distillery with drawn knives, and coerced him by threats to open the three boxes.

"You, then, fear their wrath more than mine?" cried the Suffete, and through the fumes his eyeballs flashed like torches upon the tall, pale man, who began to comprehend the situation. "Abdalonim, before sunset have him flogged, and torture him!"

This damage, though less than the others, had exasperated him. In spite of his efforts to banish the Barbarians from his thoughts, he was continually reminded of them. Their excesses were confused with his daughter's shame, and he wished that all those of his household who knew, might not mention it to him. But something impelled him to plunge deeper in his misfortune, and, taken with an inquisitorial rage, he paid visits of inspection to the hangars, behind the house of commerce, examining the stores and supplies of bitumen, wood, anchors, cordage, honey, and wax; then the magazines of fabrics, the reserves of provisions, not forgetting the marble yards and the granary of silphium.

Then he crossed to the opposite side of the gardens, inspecting with keen scrutiny in their cabins the domestic artisans whose products were sold; watched the tailors as they embroidered mantles, some as they knotted the nets, others who combed the wool for cushions or cut out sandals, and viewed the Egyptian workers polishing papyrus with a shell. The shuttles of the weavers clacked, and the armourers' anvils clanged. To these last craftsmen he said:

"Forge swords! Always forge! I shall need them." And he pulled from his breast the antelope skin, macerated in poisons, he had but recently taken out of the silver vat, and ordered them to cut and fashion from it a breastplate for him, that would be more solid than brass, and invulnerable alike to weapons or flames.

As soon as he had reached the various workers,

Abdalonim, in order to divert the Suffete's anger from himself, sought to irritate him against them by disparaging their work, murmuring:

"What a task! It is a shame! Truly the master is too good!"

Hamilcar, without heeding, proceeded on his way. He slackened his pace, as the path was barred by large, noble trees, completely charred, as one finds them in the woods where herdsmen have camped. The roads were barricaded, the palisades were broken, the water was lost in the ditches; fragments of glass and bones of apes appeared in the midst of muddy puddles. On the bushes tatters of cloth hung, and under the citrons decaying flowers emitted a yellow, noisome fume. In truth, the servants had abandoned everything, believing that Hamilcar would never return.

At each step he discovered some new disaster, ever more proofs of the very thing he had forbidden himself to learn aught about. Lo! even now, as he walked about, he soiled his purple brodequins, crushing under foot the very filth of the Barbarians; and yet he did not now possess the power to make these wretches fly to atoms at the end of a catapult. He experienced a sense of humiliation for having so recently defended them in the Assembly: it was treachery and treason; but as he could not avenge himself on the soldiers, or on the Elders, or on Salammbô, or on any person, and his wrath sought some victim, he condemned to the mines all the garden slaves by a single decree.

Each time that Abdalonim saw his master approach the parks he shook in terror. But Hamilcar took the road first to the mill, from whence issued a lugubrious melopœia.

In the midst of clouds of flour-dust turned the heavy mills, constructed of two porphyry-cones, placed one upon the other; the uppermost one was of funnel-shape, and revolved as it ground the grain on the second cone by the aid of strong bars pushed by men, holding their chests and arms firmly against them, or pulling with all their might, harnessed to the bars. The friction of the breast-strap had formed around their armpits purulent sores, such as might be seen on asses' withers; and black, filthy rags, hardly covering their loins, flapped over their thighs like long tails. Their eyes were red, and the shackles on their feet clattered while they panted and heaved and tugged in accord. On their mouths were muzzles, fastened by little bronze chains, rendering it impossible for them to eat the meal, and gauntlets, made without separated fingers, muffled their hands, preventing them from pilfering.

At the entrance of the Suffete, the wooden bars creaked more loudly, the grain grated in grinding. Many of these slaves, upon seeing him, fell down on their knees, while the others continued their drudgery, treading heedlessly over their kneeling companions.

The Suffete asked for Giddenem, the governor of the slaves, who appeared, displaying the dignity of his office by the richness of his costume: his tunic, slit at the sides, was of fine purple; heavy rings dragged down his ear-lobes; and to join the bands of material enveloping his legs was a gold lacing, like a serpent coiling around a tree, reaching from his ankles to his hips. In his hands, covered with rings, he held a string of jet beads, to identify the men subject to the accursed malady.

Hamilcar signed him to detach the slaves' muzzles, when they all, with cries like famished animals, rushed upon the meal, burying their faces in the heaps to devour it.

"See, you starve them, and exhaust their forces!" said the Suffete.

Giddenem replied that he was obliged to do so in order to subdue them.

"According to this, it was scarcely worth the while to send you to the training-school for slaves at Syracuse. Bid all the other slaves come before me."

And the cooks, butlers, grooms, runners, porters of the litters, men from the sweating-baths, and the women with their children, all ranged themselves in the gardens in a single file, from the house of commerce as far as the park for wild animals. These creatures all held their breaths, terror-stricken, and a vast silence reigned over Megara. The sun lengthened its rays over the Lagoon below the catacombs. The peacocks began to squawk. Hamilcar moved step by step, before this array of slaves.

"Of what use are these old slaves?" said he. "Sell them; there are too many Gauls; they are drunkards! and too many Cretans, they are liars! Buy for me instead Cappadocians, Asiatics, and Negroes."

He was astonished at the small number of children, saying, "Every year, Giddenem, the establishment should have some births. You must leave the huts open every night, so that they may mix at liberty."

In succession, the governor pointed out to him the thieves, the lazy, and the mutinous, and he distributed the manner of chastisements, with reproaches to Giddenem, who, like a bull, drooped his low forehead, with his thick intercrossed eyebrows.

"Look, Eye of Baal," said the governor, designating a robust Libyan, "there; behold one who was discovered with a rope around his neck."

"Ah! so you want to die?" disdainfully said the Suffete.

And the slave, in an intrepid tone, answered "Yes!"

Without caring either for the example or pecuniary loss, Hamilcar ordered—"Away with him!"

Perhaps he had in his mind the idea of a sacrifice. It was a misfortune that he himself inflicted in order possibly to ward off more terrible ones.

Giddenem had hidden the mutilated slaves behind the others, but Hamilcar perceived them, and demanded of one:

"Who cut your arm?"

"The soldiers, Eye of Baal."

Then addressing himself to a Samnite, who hobbled like a wounded heron, he said:

"And you—who did that to you?"

The governor had broken this slave's leg with an iron bar. Such atrocious imbecility exasperated the Suffete, and he jerked away from Giddenem the string of jet.

"Curses be upon the dog who wounds the herds! Crippler of slaves—the bounty of Tanit! Ah, thus would you ruin your master! Let him be smothered in a dung-heap! But those who are missing, where are they? Have you allowed the soldiers to assassinate them?"

Hamilcar's face became so terrible that all the women fled, and the slaves drew back, making a wide circle; meantime Giddenem frantically kissed Hamilcar's feet, who stood with his hands lifted over him.

But his mind, now lucid as during the most critical moment of battle, recalled a thousand odious things, the ignominies from which he had turned, and by the light of his anger, as by the fulgurations of a terrible storm, he instantly resaw all his disasters. The governors of the fields had fled from terror, possibly by connivance with the soldiers; all were deceiving him. For a long time he had restrained himself; but now he cried out:

"Let them be brought! and branded on their foreheads with hot iron, as cowards!"

The fetters, pillories, knives, and chains for those condemned to the mines, the *cippes* to grip their legs, the *numella* to confine their shoulders, and the scorpions, or whips of three thongs terminating in brazen chains, all were brought and spread out through the middle of the gardens.

The slaves were placed facing the sun, towards Moloch the Devourer, extended on the ground flat on their faces, or on their backs; and those condemned to flagellation were fastened against trees with two men beside them, the one who struck the blows, and the other who counted the stripes. The former wielded the whip with both arms, the thongs whistled sharply through the air at each blow, making the bark fly off the plane-trees, and the blood spurt from the culprit's body like rain over the foliage; and red masses writhed, howling, at the foot of the trees.

Those who were branded tore their faces with their nails. The wooden vices creaked, dull thuds were heard, and at times, above all, a sharp scream from the victim suddenly pierced the air.

In the direction of the kitchens could be seen, amid ragged clothing and dishevelled hair, men with bellows reviving the fires, and the atmosphere was charged with the odour of burning flesh.

The whipped creatures fainted; but retained by the cords around their arms, helplessly rolled their heads on their shoulders with closed eyes. Those who watched them uttered screams of fright; and the lions, perhaps recalling the recent feast, yawned and stretched themselves against the confines of their pits.

Salammbô was now seen on the platform of her terrace: she walked rapidly from right to left in terror. Hamilcar saw her, and it seemed to him that she lifted her arms towards him to beseech mercy. With a gesture of horror he straightway passed into the elephant paddocks.

These animals were always the pride of the noble Punic families. They had borne their ancestors, had triumphed in the wars, and they were venerated as favourites of the sun. Those of Megara were the strongest in Carthage.

Before his departure on his last expedition, Hamilcar had charged Abdalonim under oath that he would ever watch over these creatures. But they had died from their mutilations, and now only three remained, lying in the middle of the court in the dust, before the remnants of their manger.

Recognising Hamilcar, the elephants came towards him. One had his ears dreadfully slit; another a large gaping wound on his knees; and the third had his trunk cut off. They looked at him with a pitiful air, like reasoning persons; and the one that had lost his trunk lowered his enormous head, and bending his knees, endeavoured to stroke his master gently with the hideous extremity of the stump. At this caress from the wounded animal tears gushed from the Suffete's eyes, and he sprang upon Abdalonim.

"Oh, wretch! to the cross! to the cross!" Abdalonim fainted, falling backward on the ground.

From behind the purple factories, whence blue smoke slowly curled up to the heavens, at this moment a jackal's yelp echoed. Hamilcar paused.

The thought of his son, like the contact with a God, calmed him at once. It was a prolongation of his strength, an indefinite continuation of his personality, which now he caught a glimpse of; and the slaves could not comprehend from what source came this sudden appeasement to their master.

He immediately diverged towards the purple factories; he passed before the *ergastulum*, a long, black stone structure built in a square pit, with a little passage around it, and a stairway at each of the corners.

To complete his signal Iddibal was doubtless waiting for nightfall. Nothing was yet pressing, Hamilcar thought. As he descended into the prison some cried out to him:

"Turn back!" The most daring followed him.

The open door swung and battered to and fro in the wind. Twilight entered through the narrow loopholes, revealing in the interior broken chains hanging to the walls. Behold, these were all that remained of the war captives! Then Hamilcar grew extraordinarily pale, and those who lingered outside in the ditch saw him support himself by his hand against the wall to keep from falling. But the jackal yelped three times in succession. Hamilcar lifted his head, he did not speak a word, he did not move. As soon as the sun had completely set he disappeared behind the fig-tree hedge; and at night, as he entered the assembly of the Rich convened in the temple of Eschmoûn, he said:

"Lights of the Baalim, I accept the command of the Punic forces against the Barbarian army!"

CHAPTER VIII.

THE BATTLE OF THE MACAR.

The next day Hamilcar drew from the Syssites two hundred and twenty-three thousand kikars of gold, and levied a tax of fourteen shekels on the Rich. Even the women were called upon to contribute, and a tax was exacted for the children; and—monstrous deviation from Carthaginian customs—he forced the colleges of priests to furnish money.

He likewise requisitioned all the horses, mules, and weapons. The possessions of those citizens who endeavoured to misrepresent their wealth, were confiscated and sold; and, in order to abash the avaricious, he personally contributed sixty armours, and twelve hundred gommers of meal,—as much as the Ivory Company.

He sent to Liguria to hire as soldiers, three thousand mountaineers, accustomed to fight bears, advancing to them six moons' pay, at four minæ per day.

Notwithstanding that it was necessary to form an army, he did not accept, like Hanno, all the citizens whosoever offered. In the first place he rejected people of sedentary occupations; next, those whose bellies were too gross, or whose appearance was cowardly; while he admitted dishonoured men, the dissolute of Malqua, the sons of Barbarians, and emancipated slaves. As recompense, he promised to the New Carthaginians the complete rights of the city.

His first task was to reform the Legion,—those fine young men, who considered themselves the military majesty of the Republic, and were self-governed. He reduced all the officers to the ranks; he treated the men roughly, making them run, leap, and ascend without halting the acclivity of Byrsa; hurl javelins, wrestle, and even sleep out of doors in the public squares. Their families seeing this, pitied them.

He directed that the glaives should be made shorter, and the brogues stouter; he restricted the number of attendants, and reduced the baggage.

In the temple of Moloch there was kept a treasure of three hundred Roman pilums, which he took despite the pontiff's protestation.

With the elephants which had returned from Utica, and those which were the personal property of citizens, he organised a phalanx of seventy-two, and by every device rendered them most formidable. Their conductors were provided with a mallet and chisel to split open the animals' skulls, if during a mêlée they became unmanageable.

He would not permit the Grand Council to name his generals. The Elders endeavoured to oppose the laws to him, but he overrode them, and not one dared murmur: all bent under the vehemence of his genius. He assumed the sole charge of the war, the government, and the finances; and, in order to prevent accusations against him, he demanded that the Suffete Hanno should be made examiner of his accounts.

To procure sufficient stones to repair the rampart he demolished the old interior walls, which were at present useless. But the differences of fortunes replacing the hierarchy of races, continued to maintain a demarcation between the sons of the vanquished and those of the victors; so that the patricians watched with an irritated eye the destruction of these ruins, while the plebeians, without well knowing why, rejoiced over it.

Armed troops from morning till night defiled through the streets; every moment the sound of trumpets could be heard; chariots passed loaded with bucklers, tents, and pikes; the courts were thronged with women making bandages; the ardour of one was communicated to another; the soul of Hamilcar pervaded the Republic.

He had distributed the soldiers in equal numbers of pairs, taking care to place along the lines alternately a strong and a weak man, so that the less vigorous or more cowardly was at the same time led and impelled by two others. But with his three thousand Ligurians and the best of the Carthaginians, he could only form a simple phalanx of four thousand and ninety-six hoplites, protected by bronze casques, and wielding ashwood sarissas fourteen cubits long. Two thousand young men were equipped with slings and a poniard, and shod in sandals. These he reinforced with eight hundred others, armed with round bucklers and Roman glaives.

The heavy cavalry was comprised of the nineteen hundred guards yet remaning of the Legion, mailed in vermilion bronze like the Assyrian Clinabarians. He had four hundred mounted archers, called Tarentines, wearing weasel-skin caps and leather tunics, and armed with a double-edged battle-axe. Finally, mixed with the Clinabarians were twelve hundred Negroes from the quarter of the caravans, whose duty it was to run alongside of the stallions, supporting themselves by clutching their manes with one hand.

All was ready; however, Hamilcar did not start.

Frequently at night he would leave Carthage unaccompanied, and go a distance beyond the Lagoon, towards the embouchures of the Macar. Did he wish to join the Mercenaries? The Ligurians camped in the Mappals surrounded his mansion.

These apprehensions entertained by the Rich appeared justifiable, when one day they beheld three hundred Barbarians approach the walls. The Suffete ordered the gates to be opened to admit them; they were deserters, and ran towards their master, impelled either by their fear or their fidelity.

Hamilcar's return had not astonished the Mercenaries, for in their mind this man could not die. He was returning to fulfil his promises—a hope which had in it nothing absurd, considering how deep the abyss was between the Republic and the army. Besides, they did not deem themselves culpable, for they had forgotten their depredations at the feast.

The spies whom they had surprised undeceived them. This was a triumph for the desperate; even the lukewarm became furious. The two sieges had overwhelmed them with weariness; nothing progressed; it were far better to engage in battle! Thus, many of the men disbanding, wandered over the country, but at the rumour of the armament they returned.

Mâtho leaped with joy, crying out:

"At last! At last!"

The resentment which he had centred upon Salammbô now vented itself upon Hamilcar. His hatred now perceived for its object a settled prey; and as vengeance became more easy to conceive, he almost fancied he had attained, and already rejoiced in it.. At the same time he was possessed by a deeper tenderness and devoured by a keener desire.

Now he saw himself in the midst of the soldiers, brandishing the Suffete's head upon a pike. Then in the chamber with the purple couch, holding the maiden in his arms, covering her face with kisses, stroking caressingly her splendid long black hair; and this vision, which he knew could not be realised, tortured him. He swore to himself, since his comrades had named him Schalischim, to carry on the war, and the certainty that he would never return from it made him determine to render it pitiless.

He sought out Spendius in his tent, and said to him:

"You take your men! I shall bring mine! Warn Autharitus! We are lost if Hamilcar attacks us! Do you hear me? Arise!"

Spendius remained stupified before this authoritative air. Mâtho had habitually permitted himself to be led, and the fits of passion he had previously evinced had always quickly subsided. But at present he seemed at once calmer and more terrible; a superb will flashed in his eyes like the flames of a sacrifice.

The Greek did not heed Mâtho's reasons. He occupied one of the pearl embroidered Carthaginian tents, spending his time drinking cool drinks from silver cups, playing at cottabus; let his hair grow long, and conducted the siege with slowness. In fact, he had established secret communications with the city, and did not wish to depart, knowing that before many days it would open its gates.

Narr' Havas, who constantly wandered between the three armies, at this juncture was found near Spendius. He supported the Greek's opinion, and even blamed Mâtho for being willing through an excess of courage to abandon their enterprise.

"Leave, then, if you are afraid!" cried Mâtho; "you have promised to supply us with pitch, sulphur, elephants, foot soldiers and horses, where are they?"

Narr' Havas reminded him that he had exterminated Hanno's last cohorts; as for the elephants, his men were now hunting for them in his forests; that he was equipping the infantry, and that the horses were on the march.

As he talked the Numidian kept caressing the ostrich plume that fell over his shoulder, rolling his eyes like a woman, all the time smiling in an aggravating manner. Mâtho stood before him unable to make any response.

Just then an unknown man entered, dripping with sweat, terrified, his feet bleeding, his girdle unfastened; and his laboured respiration shook his thin sides as if they would burst; he launched forth in an unintelligible dialect, with wide open eyes, as though he was recounting a battle.

The Numidian king sprang outside the tent and summoned his horsemen. They ranged themselves on the plain in the form of a circle before Narr' Havas, who was now mounted; he lowered his head and bit his lips. At last he divided his men in two sections, ordering the first section to await him; then, with an imperious gesture, leading the other section at a gallop, he disappeared on the horizon in the direction of the mountains.

"Master!" murmured Spendius,—"I do not like these extraordinary chances—the Suffete who returns, and Narr' Havas who goes off!"

"Well! what matter?" said Mâtho disdainfully.

This was another evident reason why they must forestall Hamilcar and rejoin Autharitus. But if they abandoned the siege of the cities the inhabitants would attack them in the rear, while they would have the Carthaginians in front of them. After many discussions they resolved upon the following plan, which was immediately executed.

Spendius with fifteen thousand men proceeded as far as the bridge over the Macar, three miles from Utica. The angles of it were fortified by four enormous towers upon which were planted catapults. With trunks of trees and masses of rock, barricades of thornbushes and stone walls, they blocked all the mountain paths and gorges. On the summits heaps of grass were piled up ready to be fired as signals; and shepherds trained to see at long distances were posted there at regular intervals.

Hamilcar doubtless would not take the road

by the Hot Springs Mountain as Hanno had done. He would certainly think that Autharitus, being master of the interior, could close the road against him. Then a check at the beginning of the campaign would ruin him, while a victory would only result in soon having to begin over again, as the Mercenaries would be further off. He could yet land at the Cape of Grapes and then march on to one of the cities; but he would find himself between the two armies: an imprudence of which he was incapable with such a small number of troops. Therefore he was bound to skirt the base of the Ariana and turn to the left to avoid the embouchures of the Macar, and march straight to the bridge. It was at this point Mâtho waited for him.

At night by torch-light he superintended the pioneers; anon he sallied forth to Hippo-Zarytus, to inspect the works in the mountains; returning, oppressed with his plans, he could not rest.

Spendius envied his tireless force, but for all details as to directing the spies, the choice of sentinels, the construction of machines, and all measures for defence, Mâtho listened docilely to his companion; henceforth they talked no more about Salammbô,—one not thinking of her, and the other restrained by a sense of shame.

Often Mâtho went in the direction of Carthage, endeavouring to see Hamilcar's army. He darted his eyes along the horizon, threw himself flat on the earth, and in the throbbing of his own arteries believed that he heard the tramp of troops.

He declared to Spendius, that if before three days

Hamilcar had not advanced, he should march with all his men to meet him and offer battle. Two days more passed, still Spendius detained him; but the morning of the sixth day he departed.

The Carthaginians were no less impatient for battle than the Barbarians. In the tents and in the houses all were moved by the same desire, by the same pangs; all asked themselves what kept Hamilcar back.

From time to time, the Suffete ascended the cupola of the temple of Eschmoûn and stood beside the Annunciator-of-the-Moon to observe the winds. One day, the third of the month of Tibby, he was seen descending the Acropolis with hurried steps. A great clamour was raised in the Mappals, quickly the streets were filled with commotion, and everywhere soldiers began to arm themselves, amid the cries of distracted women, who threw themselves upon the men's breasts. Once equipped, they ran to the square of Khamoûn and fell into their ranks. No one was permitted to follow or speak to the soldiers, or approach the ramparts: during some minutes the entire city was as silent as a vast tomb. The soldiers, leaning on their lances, dreamed, and those in the houses sighed.

At sunset the army marched through the western gate, but instead of taking the road to Tunis to gain the mountains in the direction of Utica, they continued along the sea-coast, and by this road they soon attained the Lagoon, where large round spots whitened with salt glistened like gigantic silver plates forgotten on the banks. Further on the puddles of water multiplied, the ground gradually became softer, the soldiers' feet sank beneath the surface; yet Hamilcar would not turn back. He always moved at the head of the troops, mounted on his horse, spotted yellow like a dragon, that kept tossing the froth about himself as he advanced by dint of stout efforts through the mire. Some of the soldiers cried out that they would perish; he snatched away the weapons from these whimperers and gave them to the servants.

At every step the mud became deeper and deeper; it was necessary for the men to mount the beasts of burden, others clung to the horses' tails; the robust pulled up the weak, and the Ligurians urged forward the infantry at the points of their spears. The obscurity increased: the road was lost: all halted.

Then the Suffete's slaves advanced to seek for the landmarks planted at certain distances by his orders; presently they shouted out through the darkness from a distance, and the army followed them.

Finally, the resistance of firm ground was felt under foot. Then a whitish curve became vaguely outlined, and they soon found themselves on the shores of the Macar. Notwithstanding the cold, the camp fires were not lighted.

In the middle of the night wind squalls arose. Hamilcar commanded the officers to arouse the soldiers, but not to sound the trumpets; therefore the captains quietly moved about, tapping the men on their shoulders.

A very tall man waded into the water, and as it did not reach to his girdle, the army could ford it.

The Suffete ordered that thirty-two of the elephants should be placed in the stream, one hundred paces apart, whilst others should be stationed below to stay the lines of men from being swept away by the current; and all the troops, holding their weapons above their heads, crossed over the Macar as between two walls. Hamilcar's observations had revealed the fact, that the westerly winds drove the sand so as to obstruct the stream by forming across it a natural causeway.

Now he was on the left bank facing Utica on a vast plain, an advantage for his elephants, which after all constituted the main strength of his army.

This stroke of genius aroused the enthusiasm of the soldiers, and an extraordinary confidence returned to them; they wanted to fall immediately upon the Barbarians; but the Suffete ordered them to rest for two hours.

As soon as the gun appeared the troops were again put in motion on the plains, in three lines, the elephants in front of the light infantry with the cavalry behind them, and at the rear marched the phalanx.

The Barbarians encamped at Utica, and the fifteen thousand around the bridge, were surprised to see in the distance the ground undulate. The wind, which blew very strongly, chased the dust in whirlwinds; they lifted themselves up, as if detached from the soil, in large golden pillars, then disintegrated into nothingness, always recommencing, thus hiding from the view of the Mercenaries the Punic army. In consequence of the effect produced by the horns placed on the side of the casques, some believed that they perceived a herd of cattle; others, deceived by the fluttering mantles, pretended to distinguish wings; and those who had travelled much shrugged their shoulders, explaining that it was the illusion of the mirage. Meanwhile something enormous continued to advance. Little vapours, tenuous as breaths, floated over the surface of the desert. The sun, now much higher, shone more powerfully; a fierce glare, which seemed to quiver, made the depth of the sky more profound, and affecting all objects, rendered the distance incalculable.

The immense plain developed on all sides until lost to view; and the almost invisible undulations of the ground were prolonged to the extreme horizon, closed in by the long blue line of the sea. The two armies went forth from their tents to behold; and the people of Utica, in order to see better, crowded upon the ramparts.

They distinguished many transverse bars bristling with even points; these became thicker and larger; black hillocks swayed; suddenly square bushes appeared: they were the elephants and the lances. A single yell burst forth:

"The Carthaginians!" and, without signal, without command, the soldiers at Utica and those stationed at the bridge made a dash pell-mell to fall together in one body upon Hamilcar.

At this name Spendius trembled and breathlessly repeated—"Hamilcar! Hamilcar!" And Mâtho was not there! What should he do? No means for flight!

The surprise of this event, the terror he experienced for the Suffete, and above all the urgency for an immediate resolution, upset him: he fancied that he saw himself slashed by a thousand swords, decapitated, dead.

Meanwhile they called for him. Thirty thousand men were about to follow his leadership; a fury against himself seized him as he fell back upon the hope of victory; it was full of delight, and he fancied himself braver than Epaminondas. To hide his pallor he daubed his cheeks with vermilion, then buckled on his greaves and cuirass, swallowed a cup of pure wine, and ran hotly after his troops, that had hastened towards those of Utica.

Both divisions united so rapidly that the Suffete had not time to range his men in line of battle. Gradually he slackened his pace.

The elephants stopped, swaying their heavy heads, covered with ostrich-plumes, as they struck themselves on their shoulders with their trunks.

At the back through the intervals could be distinguished the cohorts of velites, and further on, the large helmets of the Clinabarians with polished weapons that glittered under the sun's rays, cuirasses, plumes, and waving standards.

But the Punic army all told numbering only eleven thousand three hundred and ninety-six men, seemed scarcely to contain so many, for it formed a long square, narrowed at the flank and closed up on itself. In seeing them so weak the Barbarians were possessed by a disorderly joy, as they were three times the number of the enemy.

As yet no one could discern Hamilcar; he had perhaps remained behind? What difference any way? The disdain that they had for these merchant soldiers reinforced their courage, and before Spendius could command the manœuvre, it had all been anticipated and already executed.

They deployed in a long straight line that overlapped the wings of the Punic army, in order to completely envelope it. But when they were not more than three hundred paces apart, the elephants, instead of advancing, turned back; then behold, the Clinabarians wheeled round and followed them, and the surprise of the Mercenaries redoubled as they perceived all the archers running to rejoin them. The Carthaginians were then afraid and were flying! A formidable hooting burst out among the Barbarian troops, and from the back of his dromedary Spendius cried out:

"Ah, I knew it well! Advance! Advance!"

Then launched forth instantaneously through the air, streams of javelins and darts, and balls from whirring slings. The elephants, galled on their haunches by the flying arrows, were put in a rapid gallop and stirred up a great dust, that so completely enveloped them that they vanished like shadows in a cloud.

Now far beyond could be distinguished a loud noise of tramping, predominated over by the shrill blare of trumpets blown with fury. The spaces before the Barbarians, full of eddies and tumult, drew them in like a whirlpool, and some dashed headlong into it. The cohorts of infantry appeared; they closed their ranks, and simultaneously all the others saw the foot soldiers running with the galloping cavalry.

Hamilcar had commanded the phalanx to break its sections, for the elephants, light infantry, and cavalry to pass through these intervals, in order to quickly take up their station on the wings, and had so exactly calculated the distance from the Barbarians, that at the moment when they came within reach, the entire

Carthaginian army was re-formed in a great straight line. In the centre bristled the phalanx, formed in syntagmata or perfect squares, having sixteen men on each side. All the file leaders appeared between the long sharp points, which jutted unequally beyond them, as the first six ranks crossed their sarissas, holding them in the middle, and the ten inner ranks supported theirs on the shoulders of their comrades immediately before them.

Their faces half disappeared under the visors of their casques, bronze greaves covered their right legs, and broad cylindrical shields reached down to their knees; and this awful quadrangular mass, moving as a single piece, seemed to possess the life of an animal and the functions of a machine. Two cohorts of elephants regularly bordered it, and the huge creatures shuddered, to detach the splinters of the arrows sticking in their black hides. The Indians crouched on their necks amidst tufts of white plumes, guiding them with the spoon-shaped end of the harpoons they wielded; while in the towers men concealed as far as their shoulders, waved, behind the great bent bows, iron holders containing burning tow.

On the right and left of the elephants hovered the slingers, with a sling around their heads, another about their loins, and a third in their right hands. Then came the Clinabarians, each one flanked by a Negro, holding their lances between the ears of their horses, covered, like their riders, with gold. Following at certain spaces came the light-armed soldiers, with bucklers of lynx-skin, over which projected the points of the javelins they held in their left hands; and the Tarentines, managing two horses coupled together, finished off at both ends this wall of soldiers.

The Barbarian army, on the contrary, had not been able to maintain its allignment. Its enormous length wavered and opened out gaps. All panted breathless from running. The phalanx swayed heavily as it thrust forward all its sarissas; under this tremendous weight the Mercenaries' lines, too thin, gave way in the middle.

The Carthaginian wings spread out to seize them; the elephants followed: with lances held obliquely the phalanx cut the Barbarians in two; both the enormous fragments were shaken; the wings, with volleys of arrows and balls, drove them back against the phalangites. The cavalry failed to disengage itself, with the exception of two hundred Numidians, who charged the right squadron of the Clinabarians. All the others found themselves enclosed and could not escape from the lines. Destruction was imminent and a resolution urgent.

Spendius commanded an attack on the phalanx to be made simultaneously on the two flanks, to force a passage right through it. But the narrowest ranks glided within the longest ones, returned to their position, and the phalanx wheeled to meet the Barbarians, as terrible on its flanks as it had been just before on its front.

They struck against the shafts of the long sarissas; the cavalry in the rear foiled their attack, and the phalanx, supported by the elephants, kept closing up and extending, and presented successively a square, a cone, a rhombus, a trapezium, and a pyramid. A double interior movement was continually being made from its front to its rear, as those who were at the base of files ran towards the first ranks, while such of them as were fatigued or wounded fell back to the base. The Barbarians found themselves crowded on to the phalanx. It was impossible for it to advance; the field of action appeared like an ocean whereon were tossing red plumes and bronze scales, while the bright bucklers rolled like silver foam. Sometimes from end to end wide currents would descend and then ascend, while in the middle a dense mass remained immovable.

The lances inclined and rose alternately. Elsewhere, was a movement of naked blades so rapid that only the points could be distinguished, and the turms of cavalry swept in wide circles which closed up behind them in eddies.

Above the captains' voices the blare of the clarions and twanging of lyres, leaden bullets and almond-shaped pellets of clay whistled in their flight through the air, smiting swords from the hands that clasped them, and making brains leap from the skulls. The wounded, sheltering themselves with one arm under their shields, pointed their swords with the pommel rested on the ground, and others, writhing in pools of blood, turned to bite the passers' heels. The multitude was so compact, the dust so thick, the tumult so deafening, that it was impossible to clearly distinguish anything; the cowards who offered to surrender were not even heard. When men were disarmed they gripped body to body, and breasts cracked against the cuirasses, and the heads of the corpses hung backwards between two nerveless arms.

There was a company of sixty Umbrians who stood firmly on their legs, their pikes advanced before their eyes, unshaken and grinding their teeth as they cut down and forced back two syntagmata at once. The Epirote shepherds ran on to the left squadron of the Clinabarians, seized their horses by the manes, twisting their clubs in them, till the tortured animals, throwing their riders, fled across the plain. The Punic slingers, scattered here and there, stood agape. The phalanx began to waver, the captains ran about distracted, the rear ranks pushed on the soldiers, and the Barbarians had re-formed their lines. They returned to the charge; the victory was within their grasp.

But a cry, one frightful shriek, burst out, a roar of pain and rage; it was the seventy-two elephants charging down in a double line. Hamilcar had waited until the Mercenaries were massed in a single spot, before loosing the elephants upon them; the Indians had goaded them so vehemently that the blood ran over their large ears. Their trunks were bedaubed with minium, and they held them straight in the air like red serpents; their breasts were accoutred with a boar-spear, their backs with a cuirass, their tusks elongated with iron blades curved like sabres; and to render them more ferocious, they had been intoxicated with a mixture of pepper, pure wine, and incense. They shook their collars of bells, shrieking, and the elephantarchs lowered their heads to avoid the stream of flaming darts which began to fly from the tops of the towers.

In order to resist the charge more effectually the Barbarians closed up in a compact body; the elephants threw themselves impetuously into the middle. The boar-spears attached to their breasts like the prows of ships clove through the cohorts; they fell back in great waves; with their trunks the elephants kept strangling men, or, even snatching them from the ground, held them over their heads and delivered them to the soldiers in the tower; with their tusks they disembowelled their victims and tossed their bodies in the air, while long entrails hung from their ivory tusks like tangles of cordage from masts. The Barbarians endeavoured to gouge out their eyes, or hamstring them: even glided under their bellies and plunged their blades up to the hilts, but were crushed beneath the falling animals and perished; the more intrepid clutched on to their girths, under the down-pouring volley of flames, balls, and arrows, and continued to sever the leather till the wicker towers rolled off like a tower of stones. Fourteen elephants, placed on the extreme right, irritated by their wounds, turned on the second line; the Indians seized their mallets and chisels, and applying them to the neck-joint, with all their force struck one mighty blow.

The enormous animals sank down, falling one upon another, forming almost a mountain, and on the heap of carcasses and armour a monstrous elephant, called Fury of Baal, caught by the leg among the chains, trumpeted till evening with an arrow in his eye.

Meanwhile the others, like conquerors who delight in the extermination of foes, were overthrowing, crushing, stamping, venting their fury on the bodies and on the wrecks. In order to drive them back, the companies pressed around them in close circles, but they pivoted on their hind feet in a continual rotary movement, always advancing. The Carthaginians experienced a renewal of vigour, and the battle raged again.

The Barbarians weakened; some Greek hoplites threw away their weapons; a panic seized the others. Spendius could be seen leaning forward on his dromedary as he spurred it on the shoulders with two javelins. Then all dashed towards the wings and ran in the direction of Utica.

The Clinabarians, whose horses were exhausted, did not attempt to overtake them. The Ligurians, overcome by thirst, screamed for some one to carry them to the stream. But the Carthaginians placed in the middle of the syntagmata, and who had suffered least, stamped their feet with eagerness when they saw their vengeance escaping; already they were starting in pursuit of the Mercenaries; Hamilcar appeared.

He held in with silver reins his spotted horse, all covered with foam. The bandlets attached to the horns of his casque clattered in the wind behind him, and he had placed under his left thigh his oval buckler. With a movement of his three-pointed pike he checked the army.

The Tarentines sprang quickly from their first on to their second horses, and departed to the right and left towards the water and the city.

The phalanx easily exterminated all who remained of the Barbarians. When the swords came near, they closed their eyes and stretched out their throats. Others defended themselves to the death; they were struck down from a distance under a shower of stones, like mad dogs. Hamilcar had charged his men that they should take prisoners; but the Carthaginians obeyed him with rancour, as they experienced so much pleasure in plunging their swords into the Barbarians' bodies. As they felt the heat they set to work with naked arms like mowers, and when they stopped to take breath, they followed with their eyes across the country a horseman in pursuit of a runaway soldier. He succeeded in catching him by the hair and held him thus some moments, then clove him down with a blow of his battle-axe.

Night fell. The Carthaginians and Barbarians had disappeared. The elephants that had fled were wandering on the horizon, with their towers on fire, burning in the darkness here and there, like moving light-houses, half lost in the mist; and no other movement was noticeable over the plain than the rippling of the stream swollen by the corpses which it was carrying out to the sea.

Two hours after, Mâtho arrived. By the starlight he caught sight of long unequal heaps lying upon the ground. They were files of Barbarians. He stooped down; all were dead. He called afar; not one voice answered.

That same morning he had quitted Hippo-Zarytus with his soldiers to march on Carthage; he reached Utica, to find that Spendius's army had just gone, and the inhabitants had begun to fire the war-machines. All had been broken to pieces with fury. But the tumult that was raging in the direction of the bridge redoubled in an incomprehensible manner. Mâtho had hurried by the shortest route to cross the mountain, and as the Barbarians were flying by the plain, he had met no one.

In front of him small pyramidal masses stood out in shadow, and nearer, on this side of the stream, were motionless lights level with the ground. In fact, the Carthaginians had drawn back behind the bridge, and to deceive the Barbarians, the Suffete had established numerous posts on the other bank.

Mâtho continued to move forward, believing that he distinguished Punic ensigns, for some horses' heads which did not move appeared in the air fixed on the top of staves, thrust in invisible stacks of arms, and he heard in the distance a great uproar, the noise of songs and clinking of cups.

Then, ignorant where he was, or how to find Spendius, quite overcome by anguish, terrified and lost in the darkness, he most impetuously retraced his steps by the same route. The dawn was breaking, when from the mountain height he beheld the city, with the frames of the engines blackened by the flames leaning like giant skeletons against the walls.

All was hushed in an unusual silence and dejection. Amongst his soldiers outside the tents slept men almost naked, stretched out on their backs, or with their foreheads on their arms, supported by their cuirasses. Some of them were ungluing the bloody bandages from their legs. Those who were dying rolled their heads gently; others dragged themselves along to fetch their comrades a drink. Along the narrow paths sentinels patrolled to keep themselves warm, or kept their faces turned towards the horizon, with their pikes on their shoulders in a savage attitude.

Mâtho found Spendius sheltered under a piece of canvas that was hung from two poles driven into the ground, clasping his knees between his hands, his head lowered.

They remained some time without speaking. Finally Mâtho murmured:

"Vanquished!"

Spendius replied in a sombre voice:

"Yes; vanquished!"

And to all questions he answered only by gestures of despair.

Meanwhile, moans and death-rattles were heard on all sides. Mâtho partially drew aside the canvas. Then the spectacle of the soldiers recalled to him another disaster in the same place, and grinding his teeth, he exclaimed:

"Wretch! once already...."

Spendius interrupted him:

"But you were not there!"

"It is a curse!" cried Mâtho. "At last, however, I shall reach him. I shall vanquish him! I shall kill him! Ah, if I had only been there!...." The idea of having missed the battle stung him to greater desperation than the defeat. He pulled off his sword and threw it to the ground. "But how have the Carthaginians defeated you?"

The former slave recounted the manœuvres. Mâtho believed that he saw them, and was exasperated. The army of Utica, instead of running towards the bridge, should have fallen upon Hamilcar from behind.

"Alas! I know it," said Spendius.

"You ought to have doubled the depths of your

lines, and not to have engaged the phalanx with the light troops, and to have made way for the elephants. At the last moment you could have regained the field; nothing compelled you to retreat."

Spendius answered:

"I saw Hamilcar pass by in his large red mantle, his arms raised above the dust like an eagle flying on the flank of the cohorts, and at every gesture of his head they closed in or extended their ranks; the crowd drew us the one towards the other; he was looking at me; I felt in my heart a cold steel!"

"Perhaps he might have chosen the day?" Mâtho said in an undertone to himself.

They interrogated each other, trying to discover what had brought the Suffete at the most untoward juncture. They talked of the situation, and to extenuate his fault, or reimbue himself with courage, Spendius declared that there still remained some hope.

"Even though there remained none it would be of no consequence!" retorted Mâtho. "All alone I should continue the war!"

"And I, also!" cried the Greek. Bounding to his feet, he walked with long strides, his eyes flashing, and a strange smile wrinkled his jackal face.

"We will recommence; do not quit me again! I am not made for battles in the broad daylight; the flash of swords troubles my vision; it is a malady; I have lived too long in the *ergastulum*. But give me walls to scale at night, and I will penetrate to the citadels, and the corpses shall be cold before cock-crow! Show me some one,—something,—an enemy, a treasure, a woman," he repeated—"a woman, be she the daughter of a king, and I will quickly bring your desire at your feet. You reproach me for having lost the battle against Hanno; I nevertheless regained it—confess it! My drove of swine served us better than a phalanx of Spartans." And yielding to the wish to extol himself and take his revenge, he enumerated all that he had done for the cause of the Mercenaries.

"It was I, in the gardens of the Suffete, who incited the Gauls! Later on at Sicca I maddened them all with the fear of the Republic; Gisco was about to send the interpreters back, but I did not choose that they should be able to speak. Ah, how their tongues hung out of their mouths! Do you remember? I conducted you to Carthage; I stole the Zaïmph; I guided you to her presence; I will do still more; you shall see!" He burst into laughter like a madman.

Mâtho considered him with wide open eyes. He experienced a species of embarrassment before this man, who was at once so cowardly and so terrible.

The Greek resumed in a jovial tone, snapping his fingers:

"By Bacchus! After the rain the sun! I have worked in the quarries, and I have drunk Massic wine, in a ship which belonged to me, beneath a golden canopy like a Ptolemy. Misfortune ought to render us more capable. By force of toil one bends fortune. She loves the crafty; she will yield!"

He went up to Mâtho and took him by the arm.

"Master, at present the Carthaginians are sure of their victory. You have a whole army which has not been in combat, and your men obey you! Place them in the van. Be assured that my men, for vengeance' sake, will march. I have yet remaining three thousand Carians, twelve hundred slingers and archers, complete cohorts! We can even form a phalanx: let us return!"

Mâtho, stunned by the disaster, until now had thought of no way of escape. He listened with open mouth; the bronze plates encircling his sides rose and fell with the throbbing of his heart. He picked up his sword and cried out:

"Follow me! We march!"

But the scouts, when they returned, reported that the Carthaginian dead had been carried away, the bridge was in ruins, and Hamilcar had disappeared.

CHAPTER IX.

THE CAMPAIGN.

Hamilcar had thought that the Mercenaries would await him at Utica, or that they would return against him: finding that his forces were not sufficient to deliver or receive an attack, he had plunged to the south of the right bank of the river, which placed him at once beyond the danger of a surprise.

From the first, shutting his eyes to their revolt, he wished to detach all the tribes from the cause of the Barbarians; then, when they should be well isolated in the middle of the provinces, he would fall upon and exterminate them.

In fourteen days he pacified the region comprised between Thouccaber and Utica, with the cities of Tignicabah, Tessourah, Vacca, and others more to the west. Zounghar, built in the mountains, Assouras, celebrated for its temple, Djeraado, fertile in juniper-trees, Thapitis, and Hagour sent to him ambassadors.

The people from the country came laden with provisions, imploring his protection, kissing his feet and the feet of his soldiers, and uttering bitter complaints against the Barbarians. Some came offering in sacks the decapitated heads of Mercenaries whom they claimed to have killed, but which in fact they had cut from the corpses that they found, as numberless soldiers were lost in the retreat, and were afterwards picked up dead in different places, under the olive trees or in the vineyards.

To dazzle the people, Hamilcar, the first day after his victory, sent to Carthage the two thousand prisoners taken on the battle-field. They arrived in long companies each of a hundred men, their arms fastened behind their backs by a bronze bar which caught them at the nape of their necks; even the wounded, yet bleeding, were compelled to run, driven along by cuts from the whips of the horsemen riding behind them

There was a delirium of joy! It was reported that six thousand Barbarians had been killed, the others could not hold out, and the war ews terminated. People embraced one another in the streets, and rubbed butter and cinnamon on the faces of the *Dii-Patæci*, to express their thankfulness. These Gods, with their big eyes and their gross bellies, with their arms raised to their shoulders, seemed under the access of fresh paint to be alive, and to participate in the gladness of the people.

The Rich left their doors open; the city resounded with the beating of tambourines; the temples were illuminated nightly, and the handmaidens of the Goddess descended to Malqua, and established at the cross-roads tressels of sycamore where they prostituted themselves. Lands were voted to the conquerors; holocausts to Melkarth; three hundred golden crowns to the Suffete, and his partisans proposed to decree him new prerogatives and fresh honours.

Hamilcar had solicited the Elders to make overtures to Autharitus, offering to exchange all the Barbarian prisoners, if necessary, for old Gisco, and the other Carthaginians held by him. The Libyans and the Nomads who composed Autharitus's army scarcely knew the Mercenaries, who were men of Italiote or Greek race; and inasmuch as the Republic proffered so many Barbarians in exchange for so few Carthaginians, they resolved that it must be for the sole reason that the Barbarian captives possessed no value, whereas the others must have considerable. They feared a trap. Autharitus refused.

Forthwith the Elders issued a decree for the execution of their prisoners, although the Suffete had written not to put them to death, as he had planned to incorporate the best with his own troops, hoping by this step to encourage defection. But hatred swept away all prudence.

The two thousand Barbarians were fastened against the stelas of the tombs in the Mappals; then the pedlars, kitchen scrubs, embroiderers, and even women, the widows of the dead warriors, with their children, joined by all others who wished, came to kill them with arrows. In order to prolong their torture they slowly took deliberate aim. Each lowered their weapon, and raised it again by turns. The multitude crowded up, giving vent to yells.

The paralytics had themselves brought on stretchers; many prudently brought their provisions and stayed there till evening; others passed the night there. Drinking booths had been set up. Many gained large sums by hiring out their bows.

The crucified bodies were allowed to stand, resembling so many red statues on the tombs; and the pervading exultation reached as far as the people of Malqua, descendants of the Autochthonic tribes, who ordinarily were indifferent to events in the Republic. In recognition of the present pleasure afforded to them by the government, they were now concerned in her fortunes, feeling themselves to be Punic, and the Elders considered it crafty thus to have merged the entire people in the same vengeance.

The sanction of the Gods was not wanting, for from every quarter of the sky ravens descended, beating their wings as they circled in the air, with loud hoarse croaks, and making an enormous cloud which continually wheeled over itself. It could be seen from Clypea, from Rhades, and from the promontory of Hermiæum. Sometimes this mass would suddenly rift, widening afar its black spirals; it was an eagle which swooped into the middle, then soared away. On the terraces, on the domes, on the points of the obelisks, and on the pediments of the temples, here and there, big birds were perched holding in their reddened beaks shreds of human flesh.

In consequence of the odour the Carthaginians resigned themselves to release the bodies. Some were burned, others were thrown into the sea, and were driven by the north wind on the waves, to be washed upon the beach at the end of the gulf before the camp of Autharitus.

This chastisement had doubtless terrified the Barbarians; as from the roof of Eschmoûn they could be seen hastily pulling up their tents, rounding up their herds, and hoisting the baggage upon the asses, so that by the evening of the same day the entire army had decamped.

It was intended by marching and countermarching between the Hot Springs Mountain and Hippo-Zarytus, to close to the Suffete the approaches to the Tyrian cities, with a possibility of a return to Carthage.

During this period the two other armies endeavoured to reach him in the south, Spendius by the east, Mâtho by the west, so as to unite the three armies and then surprise and entrap him. A totally unlooked-for reinforcement astonished them, for Narr' Havas reappeared with three hundred camels laden with bitumen, twenty-five elephants, and six thousand horsemen.

In order to weaken the Mercenaries the Suffete had deemed it well to give Narr' Havas enough to do in his own distant kingdom. From the heart of Carthage he had come to an understanding with Masgaba, a Getulian brigand who sought to carve a realm for himself. Supported with Carthaginian silver, the adventurer had stirred the Numidian states to revolt, by the promise of their freedom. But Narr' Havas, warned by the son of his nurse, had surprised Cirta, poisoned the conquerors with the water in the cisterns, had struck off some heads, and reduced everything to order: and he now came more furious than the Barbarians against the Suffete.

The chiefs of the four armies agreed as to dispositions for the war. As it would be prolonged it was necessary to provide against every contingency.

It was agreed first to invoke the assistance of the Romans, and the mission was offered to Spendius; but as a fugitive, he did not dare to take charge of it, therefore twelve men from Greek colonies were selected to execute it, and embarked on a Numidian shallop at Annaba.

Then the chiefs exacted from all of the Barbarians an oath of complete obedience. Each day the captains inspected the clothing and shoes; even the use of bucklers was forbidden to the sentinels, for they often had been found to prop them against their lances and thus sleep whilst standing upright. Those who dragged about any baggage were constrained to get rid of it; everything, according to the Roman custom, must be carried on the back. By way of precaution against the elephants Mâtho instituted a corps of panoplied cavalry, in which both man and horse were concealed under a cuirass of hippopotamus hide bristling with nails; and to protect the horses' hoofs, they wore shoes of plaited espartograss.

It was forbidden to pillage the towns, or to tyrannise over the inhabitants of non-Punic race. As the country was being drained, Mâtho ordered the distribution of rations to the soldiers individually, without heeding the women; at first they shared with them, and from lack of sufficient food, many became weak. It was the occasion of incessant quarrels and invectives; many attracted the companions of others by bribes, or even by the promise of their rations. Seeing this, Mâtho commanded that all the women should be driven away without mercy. They took refuge in the camp of Autharitus; but the women of the Gauls and Libyans by force of outrages compelled them to leave.

At length they ventured under the walls of Carthage, imploring the protection of Ceres and of Proserpine; as there was in Byrsa a temple and priests, consecrated to these Goddesses, in expiation of the horrors committed formerly during the siege of Syracuse. The Syssites alleging their right to all strays, claimed the youngest to sell; and the New-Carthaginians took some of the blonde Lacædemonian women in marriage.

Some of the women obstinately followed the armies. They ran on the flank of the syntagmata beside the captains. They called to their men, and pulled them by their cloaks, struck themselves on their breasts as they uttered curses, and held out at arm's length their crying naked little babies. This sight softened the hearts of the Barbarians, yet they felt that the women were obviously a hindrance, a peril even. Frequently they were rudely pushed back, but they would persistently return. Mâtho ordered the cavalry of Narr' Havas to charge them with their lances, and when the Balearic warriors cried out to him that they wanted women,—"Myself! I have none!" he answered.

At present the genius of Moloch possessed him. Despite the rebellion of his conscience, he executed frightful deeds, and imagined that in so doing he obeyed the voice of a God. When he could not ravage them, he threw stones into the fields to render them barren.

By reiterated messages he pressed Autharitus and Spendius to hasten on. But the operations of the

Suffete were incomprehensible. He encamped successively at Eidous, at Monchar, at Tehent; the scouts believed that they espied him in the vicinity of Ischiil, near the frontier of Narr' Havas's dominion; and it was ascertained that he had crossed the stream above Tebourba, as if to return to Carthage. Scarcely was he in one place, when he removed to another. The routes that he took always remained unknown. Without giving battle, the Suffete kept his advantages; pursued by the Barbarians, he seemed to lead them on.

These marches and counter-marches fatigued the Carthaginians yet more; and Hamilcar's forces were not renewed, but day by day diminished. Now the people from the country brought provisions to him reluctantly. Everywhere he met a hesitation, a taciturn hatred; and in spite of his supplications to the Grand Council no succour came from Carthage.

Some said—and perhaps some believed—that he did not require aught. It was a ruse, or a useless complaint, and Hanno's partisans, in order to do an ill office to Hamilcar, exaggerated the importance of his victory. The troops that he had under his orders they were content to sacrifice, but they were not going to thus continually supply all of his demands. The war was quite heavy enough! it had cost too much; and, actuated by pride, the patricians of his faction supported him with slackness.

Then, despairing of the Republic, Hamilcar levied by force on the tribes for all that was requisite for the war: grain, oil, wood, animals, and men. At these demands the inhabitants were not tardy in taking flight. The towns that he traversed were

Q

deserted, cabins were ransacked without finding anything, and very soon a frightful solitude enveloped the Punic army.

The Carthaginians furiously pillaged the provinces, filled up the cisterns, burned the houses; the sparks carried by the wind scattered afar, and on the mountains entire forests burned, bordering the valleys with a crown of fire: to pass beyond, the troops were compelled to wait until they subsided. Then they resumed their march under the full sun, over the hot cinders.

Sometimes they saw by the roadside lurid gleams in the bushes like the eyeballs of a tiger-cat. It was a Barbarian crouching on his haunches, daubed with dust to blend his form with the colour of the foliage; or when they went along a ravine, those who were on the wings suddenly heard stones rolling, and in lifting their eyes perceived in the opening of the gorge a bare-footed man fleetly bounding by.

Inasmuch as the Mercenaries did not besiege them again, Utica and Hippo-Zarytus were free. Hamilcar commanded them to come to his aid. Not daring to compromise themselves, they replied by vague words, compliments, and excuses.

He abruptly marched back northwards, determined to obtain possession of one of the Tyrian cities, even if he had to besiege it. It was necessary for him to have a point on the coast in order to draw from the islands, or from Cyrene, supplies and soldiers, and he coveted the port of Utica as being the nearest to Carthage.

The Suffete accordingly left Zouitin, and cautiously skirted the lake of Hippo-Zarytus. But soon he was obliged to extend his regiments in a column, to climb up the mountain separating the two valleys. At sunset they descended into its summit, hollowed out like a funnel; when they perceived before them, level with the ground, bronze she-wolves, which seemed to run over the grass.

Suddenly large plumes of feathers rose into view; and to the rhythm of flutes a formidable chant burst forth. It was the army of Spendius: for the Campanians and Greeks, in their abhorrence of Carthage, had adopted Roman ensigns. At the same time on the left appeared long pikes, shields of leopard's skin, linen cuirasses, and naked shoulders. They were Mâtho's Iberians, Lusitanians, Balearics, and Getulians; the neighing of the horses of Narr' Havas was heard: they distributed themselves around the hill. Then came the irregular mob commanded by Autharitus, made up of Gauls, Libyans, and Nomads; and in their midst the Eaters-of-Unclean-Things could be recognised by the fishbones worn in their hair.

Thus the Barbarians had so exactly regulated their marches that they had simultaneously united. But, surprised themselves, they halted for some minutes motionless, and consulted.

The Suffete had collected his men in an orbicular mass, the form of which offered on every side equal resistance. Their high-pointed bucklers, stuck in the turf one against the other, surrounded the infantry. The Clinabarians remained outside; and further off, at intervals, the elephants were stationed. The Mercenaries were harassed with fatigue: it would be better to wait until the following day;

and, certain of their victory, the Barbarians occupied themselves during the entire night in eating.

They lighted huge bright fires, which while dazzling them, left the Punic army beneath them in the shade. Hamilcar caused a trench to be excavated around his encampment after the Roman method, fifteen feet wide and ten cubits deep; and a parapet to be thrown up with the earth thus dug out, on which were planted interlacing sharp stakes. At sunrise the Mercenaries were amazed to behold the Carthaginians thus entrenched as in a fortress.

They recognised in the midst of the tents Hamilcar, who walked about giving his orders. His body was encased in a brown cuirass fashioned of small scales. He was followed by his horse, and from time to time he paused, extending his right arm to point out something.

Then more than one recalled to himself similar mornings when to the din of clarions he had passed slowly before them, and how his looks had fortified them as cups of wine. A sort of tenderness seized them. Those, on the contrary, who did not know Hamilcar, were delirious in their delight at having caught him.

However, if all attacked at the same time they would inflict mutual damage in the contracted space. The Numidians could charge across, but the Clinabarians, protected by their cuirasses, would crush them; then how could they pass the palisades? As for the elephants, they were not sufficiently trained for them.

"You are all cowards!" cried Mâtho.

And with picked troops he dashed against the

entrenchments. A volley of stones repulsed them, for the Suffete had captured on the bridge their abandoned catapults.

This failure abruptly turned the unstable spirit of the Barbarians. Their excessive bravado disappeared; they wished to conquer, but with the slightest possible risk. According to Spendius, it was necessary to carefully guard the position they had secured, and famish the Punic army. But the Carthaginians began to dig wells, and as mountains surrounded the hill, they discovered water.

From the summit of their palisade they fired arrows, hurled earth, dung, and stones, which they tore up from the ground; whilst the six catapults were wheeled incessantly the length of the entrenchment.

But the springs might naturally dry up, the provisions would fail, the catapults might wear out; the Mercenaries were ten times their number, and would certainly triumph in the end. As a subterfuge to gain time, the Suffete thought that he would open negotiations, and one morning the Barbarians found within their lines a sheep-skin covered with writing. He justified himself for his victory: the Elders had forced him into the war; and, to show them that he kept his word, he now offered to them the plunder of Utica or Hippo-Zarytus, whichever they chose. Hamilcar, in conclusion, declared that he did not fear them, because he had won over some traitors, and that with their help he would easily make an end of them all.

The Barbarians were troubled; this proposition of an immediate booty made them ponder; they apprehended treason, not suspecting a snare in the boasting of the Suffete; and they began to regard each other with distrust. Every word was observed, every movement watched; and at night terrors awoke them. Many deserted their comrades, following their personal fancy in choosing the army to which they attached themselves: and the Gauls with Autharitus joined the men of the Cisalpine province, whose language they understood.

The four chiefs conferred every night in Mâtho's tent, and, squatting around a buckler, they moved forward and backward attentively the little wooden dummies, invented by Pyrrhus for reproducing military manœuvres. Spendius, explaining the resources of Hamilcar, entreated them not to throw away this opportunity, and swore by all the Gods. Mâtho in vexation walked about gesticulating. For him the war against Carthage was a personal affair, and he felt indignant that the others intermeddled without being willing to obey him. Autharitus divined his words from his face, and applauded. Narr' Havas raised his chin as a sign of disdain; not one measure was offered but he considered it fatal. Mâtho smiled no more: sighs escaped him as if he had forced back the anguish of an impossible dream, the despair of a lost enterprise.

While the Barbarians deliberated in their uncertainty, the Suffete increased his defences, dug a second trench on the inside of the palisades, erected a second wall, and constructed wooden towers at the corners; his slaves went to the middle of the advance-posts to bury caltrops in the ground. But the elephants, whose allowances were reduced, struggled in their shackles. To economise the fodder, he ordered the Clinabarians to kill the least robust of the stallions. Some of the men refusing to comply, were at once beheaded. The horses were eaten. The memory of this fresh meat during the following days was a great sorrow.

From the bottom of the amphitheatre, where the Punic army was confined, they saw all around them on the heights the four Barbarian camps full of movement. Women moved about balancing leather bottles on their heads; goats bleated, wandering under the stacks of pikes; the sentinels were going on or off duty, and men were eating their meals around the tripods. In fact, the various tribes furnished them with abundant supplies, and they had no idea how greatly their inaction terrified the Punic army.

From the second day, the Carthaginians had remarked in the camp of the Nomads a troop of three hundred men remote from the others. They were the Rich, retained as prisoners since the commencement of the war.

The Libyans ranged them all on the edge of the ditch, and, posted behind them, threw javelins, while making a rampart of their bodies. Scarcely could these wretched beings be recognised, to such a degree were their faces disfigured by vermin and filth. Their hair had been pulled out in spots, leaving bare ulcers on their scalps; and they were so thin and hideous that they resembled mummies in tattered shrouds. Some of their number trembled and sobbed in a stupid manner; others screamed out to their friends to fire upon the Barbarians.

There was one among these prisoners perfectly motionless, with head bent, who did not speak; his flowing white beard fell down to his hands, covered with chains. The Carthaginians felt from the depths of their hearts the downfall of the Republic as they recognised Gisco. Even though the place was dangerous they crowded there to see him. Some one had placed on his head a grotesque tiara, made of hippopotamus-skin studded over with stones. This had been a fancy of Autharitus, that thoroughly displeased Mâtho.

Hamilcar was infuriated, and ordered the palisades to be opened, determined to clear a way at any cost, and in a furious rush the Carthaginians charged half-way up, about three hundred paces. Such a torrent of Barbarians poured down, that they were driven back on their own lines.

One of the guards of the Legion was left outside, having stumbled against the stones. Zarxas ran up, knocked him down, and plunged his poniard into his throat; he drew out the weapon and threw himself upon the wound;—gluing his lips to it with grunts of delight and wild starts that shook him to his very heels, he sucked the blood in deep draughts, then tranquilly sat on the body with face uplifted, turning his head back to inhale the air, like a hind that has just drunk from a torrent. He struck up in a shrill voice a Balearic song, a vague melody, full of prolonged modulations, breaking off and replying to himself, like echoes answering echoes in the mountains; he called his dead brothers and invited them to a feast;—then, he let his hands fall listlessly between his knees, slowly bowed his head and wept. This atrocious deed filled the Barbarians, and especially the Greeks, with horror.

From this time the Carthaginians made no sortie; but they had no thought of surrender, being assured that they would perish under tortures.

Meanwhile, despite Hamilcar's care, the provisions diminished frightfully. For each man there remained not more than ten *k'hommer* of corn, three *hin* of millet, and twelve *betza* of dried fruits. No more meat, oil, or salt provisions, not one grain of barley for the horses; they could be seen bending down their emaciated necks to seek in the dust for trampled bits of straw.

Often the sentinels patrolling the terrace espied in the moonlight a dog belonging to the Barbarians prowling below the entrenchments in heaps of filth. They felled it with a stone, and by the aid of the straps of a buckler, lowered themselves down the length of the palisade, and without a word ate it. Occasionally a horrible baying was set up, and the venturesome never returned. In the fourth dilochia of the twelfth syntagma, three phalangites quarrelling about a rat, waxed so wroth that they killed each other with blows of their knives.

All longed for their families and their homes: the poor for their cabins shaped like bee-hives with shells placed at the thresholds, and a net suspended outside; and the patricians for their grand halls full of bluish shadows, wherein, during the warmest hour of the day, they had formerly sought repose, listening to the indistinct voices in the street, mingled with the rustling of leaves in their gardens, stirred by the breeze;—and, to better enter into these reveries, and thoroughly enjoy them, they half-closed their eyelids until the shock of a wound awakened them.

Every moment there was an engagement, a new alarm; the towers blazed, the Eaters-of-Unclean-Things leaped upon the palisades—their hands were cut off with axes; others ran up; a shower of iron fell upon the tents. Galleries of reed hurdles were erected to protect them from the projectiles. The Carthaginians shut themselves up and ventured out no more.

Each day the sun in its course above on the hill deserted from the early hours the depth of the gorge and enwrapped them in shadow. In front and behind rose the grey slopes of earth, covered with stones spotted over with scanty lichens, and over their head the sky, always cloudless, spread out more steely cold to the eye than a metal cupola. Hamilcar was filled with such a measure of indignation against Carthage, that he felt strongly disposed to join the Barbarians and lead them against her. Besides, now, even the porters, the sutlers, and slaves began to murmur; and neither the people, the Grand Council, nor anyone extended a solitary hope. The situation was intolerable, and especially so because of the idea that it would become worse.

At the news of this disaster Carthage heaved with anger and hatred; the citizens perhaps would have execrated the Suffete less if early in the war he had allowed himself to be vanquished.

But to hire other Mercenaries there was neither time nor money. As for recruiting soldiers in the city, how could they equip them? Hamilcar had taken all the weapons! And who would command new troops? The best captains were now in the campaign with him. Meanwhile, messengers despatched by the Suffete arrived in the streets and cried out for help. The Grand Council was perturbed, and made arrangements for their disappearance.

This was a useless precaution: all accused Barca for having acted with too much leniency. He should have annihilated the Mercenaries after his victory. Why had he ravaged the tribes? However, they already had imposed on themselves sacrifices quite heavy enough! And the patricians deplored their contribution of fourteen shekels, the Syssites theirs of two hundred and twenty-three thousand kikar of gold, and those who had given nothing lamented as bitterly as the others.

The populace was jealous of the new Carthaginians, to whom Hamilcar had promised the complete rights of the city; and even the Ligurians, who had fought so dauntlessly, were confounded with the Barbarians, and like them were cursed; their race became a crime, a complicity. The shopkeepers on the door-sills of their shops, journeymen who walked about with their leaden rules in their hands, pedlars of pickle rinsing their baskets, bathmen in the sweating baths, and the vendors of hot drinks, all discussed the operations of the campaign. They traced in the dust with their fingers the plans of battle; and there was not a vagabond so low that he did not dare vouchsafe to correct Hamilcar's military errors.

The priests averred that all his misfortunes were

a chastisement for his long impiety. He had not offered holocausts, he had not purified his troops, he had even refused to take with him augurs;—and the scandal of the sacrilege strengthened the violence of restrained hatreds, the rage of hopes betrayed. They recalled the disaster of Sicily, and all the burden of his pride that they had borne so long. The colleges of pontiffs did not pardon him for seizing their treasure, and they exacted from the Grand Council a pledge to crucify him if he ever returned.

This year the heat of the month of Eloul, which was most excessive, was a fresh calamity. From the lake shore nauseous odours arose and were diffused through the atmosphere with the smoke of the spices circling up at the street corners. Hymns constantly resounded. Streams of people crowded the stairways to the temples; the walls were draped with black veils; tapers burned constantly in front of the *Dii-Patæci;* and the blood of the camels slaughtered as sacrifices ran along the flights of steps, forming red cascades.

A funereal delirium agitated Carthage. From the extremity of the narrowest alleys, and from the blackest dens, pale faces issued forth—men with profiles like vipers, who ground their teeth. The shrill shrieks of women filled the dwellings, and escaping through the lattices, made those who stood chatting about the squares turn around. Sometimes it was believed that the Barbarians were coming: some one had seen them behind the Hot-Springs Mountain. Then it was rumoured that they were encamped at Tunis. And the voices multiplied, swelling till merged in one confusing clamour. Then a universal silence reigned. Some of the people remained clinging to the pediments of the edifices with one hand shielding their eyes, while others, lying flat at the foot of the ramparts, strained their ears. The fear having passed, their wrath broke out afresh. But the conviction of their powerlessness soon threw them back into the same sadness.

It redoubled every evening, when all mounting the terraces, uttered, while bowing nine times, a vast cry of salutation to the sun, as it sank slowly behind the Lagoon, then suddenly disappeared in the mountains in the direction of the Barbarians.

They were looking forward to the coming of the thrice holy feast, when from the top of a pyre an eagle soared towards the sky—a symbol of the resurrection of the year, a message from the people to its supreme Baal which they considered as a kind of union, a means of attaching themselves to the power of the Sun.

Besides, filled now with hatred, the people naturally turned towards Moloch, the Man Slayer, and all deserted Tanit. In effect, the Rabbetna, no longer possessing her veil, was despoiled of a part of her power. She refused the blessing of her waters. She had forsaken Carthage; she was a deserter, an enemy. Some, to outrage her, threw stones at her. But even while cursing many pitied her. She was still cherished, and perhaps more profoundly than ever.

All their misfortunes came from the rape of the Zaïmph. Salammbô had indirectly participated in this crime; therefore she was included in the same rancour; she must be punished. The vague idea of an immolation, quickly circulated amongst the people. To appease the Baalim, undoubtedly they must offer something of incalculable value—a beautiful being, young, a virgin of an ancient family, descended from the Gods,—a human Star.

Daily unknown men invaded the gardens of Megara, and the slaves, trembling for themselves, did not dare resist them. However, they did not pass on to the stairway of the Galleys, but always stopped below with eyes uplifted to the last terrace; they waited for Salammbô, and for hours cried out against her, like dogs barking at the moon.

CHAPTER X.

THE SERPENT.

These clamours of the populace did not frighten the daughter of Hamilcar; she was disturbed by loftier inquietudes—for her great serpent, the black Python, languished: and for the Carthaginians a serpent was not only a national, but a personal fetich. They believed every serpent to be an offspring of the slime of the earth, inasmuch as it emerged from the depths, and it needed no feet to walk upon; its movements recalled the undulations of the streams; its temperature ancient darkness, clammy, full of fruitfulness; and the orb that it described in biting its tail, the complete planetary system, the intelligence of Eschmoûn.

Salammbô's serpent had frequently of late refused the four living sparrows offered to it at the new and full of each moon. Its beautiful skin, covered like the firmament with spots of gold on a dead black surface, was now yellow, flabby, wrinkled, and too large for its body; about its head was spreading a downy mould; and in the corners of its eyes appeared little red points that seemed to move.

From time to time Salammbô drew near to its silver filigree basket, and withdrew the purple curtain, cast aside the lotus leaves and down—but it was continually coiled upon itself, more motionless than a withered vine. Under the influence of her intense observation she ended by feeling in her heart a spiral like another serpent, which was gradually rising up to her throat and strangling her.

She was in despair at having seen the Zaïmph; and yet she experienced a sort of joy, a peculiar pride. A mystery eluded her in the splendour of its folds; it was the mist enveloping the Gods, the secret of universal existence; and Salammbô, while horrified at herself, regretted that she had not lifted it.

Almost always she was crouching on the floor of her room, her hands clasped around her left knee, her mouth half opened, chin lowered, and eyes fixed. She recalled with terror her father's face. She yearned to make a pilgrimage in the mountains of Phœnicia, to the temple of Aphaka, where Tanit had descended under the form of a star. All manner of imaginations allured and alarmed her; besides, each day a greater loneliness environed her. She did not even know what had become of Hamilcar.

Wearied of her thoughts she arose; and in moving about, the soles of her tiny sandals clattered against her heels at every step as she walked at random in the large, silent room. The amethysts and topazes bedighting the ceiling quivered here and there in luminous points, and Salammbô, as she walked, turned her head slightly to view them. She took the suspended amphoras by their necks; she refreshed herself under the broad fans, or even amused herself by burning cinnamon in hollowed pearls.

At sundown Taanach drew back the lozenges of black felt which closed the openings in the wall; then Salammbô's doves, rubbed with musk like the doves of Tanit, at once flew into her presence, and their pink feet slipped over the glossy pavement in the midst of the grains of barley which Salammbô scattered to them in handfuls, as a sower in a field. But suddenly she burst out in sobs, and remained extended full length on the great couch of cowhide straps, without moving, repeating one word, always the same, with her eyes open, pale as death, insensible, cold; and yet she heard the cries of the apes in the clumps of palm trees, and the continuous grinding of the great wheel raising through the stories a stream of pure water up into her porphyry basin.

Sometimes during many days she refused to eat. She dreamed that she saw dim stars passing beneath her feet. She summoned Schahabarim; and when he came she had nothing to say to him.

She could not live without the solace of his presence; but her spirit revolted against this domination; she felt for the priest, at the same time, terror, jealousy, and hatred, and an emotion akin to love, in recognition of the singular delight she experienced whenever she found herself near to him.

He had recognised the influence of Rabbet, skilled as he was to distinguish which were the Gods who sent illnesses; and to cure Salammbô he ordered that her room should be sprinkled with lotions of vervain and adiantum, and that she should eat mandrake every morning, and sleep with her head on a sachet of aromatics mixed by the pontiffs. He had even employed hazelwort, a fire-coloured root, by which fatal spirits are driven back in the north. Finally, he turned towards the polar star, and murmured in triads the mysterious name of Tanit. But as Salammbô continued to suffer, his anguish deepened.

No one in Carthage was as learned as this priest. In his youth he had studied in the college of the Mogbeds at Borsippa, near Babylon; then had visited Samothrace, Pessinus, Ephesus, Thessaly, Judea, and the temples of the Nabathæans, which are lost in the sands; and he had journeyed on foot along the banks of the Nile, from the cataracts to the sea. With his face covered with a veil, and waving torches, he had cast a black cock on a fire of sandarack before the breast of the Sphinx—Father-of-the-Terror. He had descended into the caverns of Proserpine; he had witnessed the five hundred columns of Lemnos turn, and had seen the brightness of the candelabrum of Tarentum, which carried on its standard as many sconces as there are days in the year.

Occasionally at night he would receive Greeks to question them. The constitution of the world did not cause him less solicitude than the nature of the Gods; with the armillary placed in the portico of Alexandria he had observed the equinoxes, and accompanied as far as Cyrene the bematists of Euergates, who measured the heaven by calculating the number of their paces. So that now there was growing up in his thoughts a subjective religion, without a defined formula, and for this very reason full of ecstasies and fervour.

He no longer believed that the earth was shaped like a pine-cone, but he believed it to be round, and eternally falling in space with such prodigious velocity that no one could perceive its fall.

From the position of the sun above the moon, he concluded that Baal was supreme; the orb was only his reflection and visage. Moreover, all terrestrial things which he then saw forced him to recognise as supreme the male destroying principle. Then, he secretly accused Rabbet for the misfortune of his life. Was it not for her that in former days the grand pontiff had advanced amid a tumult of cymbals and taken his future virility? And he followed with a melancholy gaze the men who abandoned themselves to pleasures with priestesses in the depths of the turpentine groves.

His days were spent in inspecting the censers and gold vases, tongs and rakes used for the cinders of the altar, and all the robes of the statues, even to the bronze pins used to frizz the hair of an old Tanit in the third chapel, close to the emerald vine. Regularly, at the same hours, he raised before the same entrances the grand tapestries, which fell back again. He remained with his arms open in the same attitude, prayed prostrated upon the same stones; and about him, through the lobbies filled with eternal twilight, moved only a population of barefooted priests.

But over the barrenness of his life Salammbô came as a flower in the chink of a sepulchre. Yet he was harsh to her, and never spared her either penances or bitter speeches. His condition established between them the equality of a common sex; and yet, his wishes towards the maiden would have been rather to have the power of possessing her, than to find her so fair and, above all, so pure. Often he clearly saw that she tried in vain to follow his thoughts. Then he turned away more sadly, and felt himself more forsaken, more lonely, and more useless.

Strange words frequently escaped his lips, and passed before Salammbô as broad flames illuminating abysses.

It was night, on her terrace, when alone these two observed the stars, and Carthage spread itself below their feet, whilst the gulf and open sea were vaguely obscured in the colour of the darkness.

He revealed to her the theory of souls which descended on the earth, following the same track as the sun by the signs of the zodiac. With extended arm he pointed out in Aries the entrance of the human generation; in Capricorn the entrance for the return towards the Gods; and Salammbô strove to perceive them, for she took these conceptions for realities, accepting as actualities pure symbols, and even figures of speech, a distinction which was no longer clearly defined for the priest.

"The souls of the dead," he said, "resolve themselves in the moon as do the corpses in the earth. Their tears compose her humidity; it is a dark abode full of mire, wrecks, and tempests."

She asked what would become of her.

"At first you will languish, light as a vapour that

floats on the waves; and after trials and most prolonged agonies, you will enter the centre of the sun to the very source of the Intelligence!"

However, as he did not mention Tanit, Salammbô imagined he was restrained through shame for his vanquished Goddess, and called her by a commonplace name, that designated the moon. But she continued to pour forth benediction upon the planet so fertile and benign. At last he exclaimed:

"No! no! she draws from the sun all her fruitfulness! Have you not seen her vagrantly wandering around him like an amorous woman who runs after a man in a field?"—and without cessation he exalted the virtues of the grand luminary.

Far from weakening her mystic desires, on the contrary, he stimulated them, and he even seemed to take pleasure in harassing her by his revelations of a pitiless doctrine. Salammbô, despite the throes of her love, threw herself upon them with rapture.

But the more Schahabarim felt a doubt concerning Tanit the more he desired to believe in her. In the depths of his soul remorse checked him. It was necessary that he should have some proof, a manifestation of the Gods; and in the hope to obtain such, he imagined an undertaking that should at the same time save his country and his belief.

From this moment he set himself to deplore before Salammbô the sacrilege and consequent misfortunes even in the regions of the sky. Then abruptly he announced the peril threatening the Suffete, who was assailed by three armies commanded by Mâtho, —for, because of Mâtho's possession of the veil, he was, in the eyes of the Carthaginians, king of the Barbarians; adding that the preservation of the Republic, as well as her father's safety, depended upon her alone.

"Upon me!" she exclaimed. "What can I do?"

But the priest, with a smile of disdain, said:

"Never will you consent!"

She supplicated him to explain. Finally Schahabarim said to her:

"It is necessary that you go to the Barbarians' camp and retake the Zaïmph."

She sank down upon the ebony stool, and remained with her arms stretched out between her knees, shuddering throughout her entire frame like a victim at the foot of an altar awaiting the blow of the axe. Her temples throbbed violently; she saw circles of fire burning before her eyes, and in her stupor comprehended nothing more than that she certainly must be on the eve of her death.

But if Rabbetna triumphed,—if the Zaïmph was brought back and Carthage delivered—of what importance the life of one woman! thought Schahabarim. Then she might perhaps obtain the veil and not perish.

For three days he did not return to her; the evening of the fourth day she sent for him.

To more surely inflame her heart, he reported all the invectives that were openly hurled in the Council upon Hamilcar; he told her she had sinned, and that she should make reparation for her crime, and that Rabbetna ordered this sacrifice.

Often a great clamour crossed over the Mappals, and reached Megara. Schahabarim and Salammbô went quickly out, and looked from the top of the stairway of the galleys.

It was occasioned by the people congregated in the square of Khamoûn, who yelled out for weapons. The Elders did not wish to furnish them, as they esteemed this effort unavailing, for others who had gone without a general had been massacred. At last the crowd was permitted to sally forth; and from a kind of homage for Moloch, or a vague wish for destruction, they pulled up in the groves of the temple large cypress trees, and having lighted them in the torches of the Cabiri, carried them through the streets while they sang. These monstrous flames advanced swaying gently, casting reflections on the glass globes at the crest of the temples, on the ornaments of the colossi, on the beakheads of the ships, passed beyond the terraces, and appeared like suns revolving in the city. They descended the Acropolis. The gate of Malqua opened.

"Are you ready?" exclaimed Schahabarim, "or have you recommended them to say to your father that you abandon him?" She hid her face in her veil, and the great lights receded, till gradually they sank to the edge of the waves.

An indefinable terror held her; she was afraid of Moloch, afraid of Mâtho. That man of giant stature, and who was master of the Zaimph, dominated Rabbetna, even as the Baal did, and he appeared to her surrounded with the same splendours. Then she remembered that the spirit of the Gods sometimes visited the bodies of men. Had not Schahabarim, in speaking of him, declared that she ought to conquer Moloch? They were mingled the one with the other: she confounded them: both pursued her.

She wished to know the future, and approached her serpent,—for auguries were often drawn from the attitude of the serpents. The basket was empty. Salammbô was troubled.

She found it coiled up by its tail to one of the silver balustrades near the suspended couch, rubbing itself, to disengage itself from its old yellowish skin; meanwhile its body, shining and bright, was gradually extending, like a blade partially drawn from the scabbard.

The following days, according as she allowed herself to be convinced she was more disposed to succour Tanit, the Python grew better and larger, and seemed to revive.

The certitude that Schahabarim expressed the will of the Gods established itself in her conscience. One morning she arose determined, and asked the priest what it was necessary for her to do to compel Mâtho to give back the veil.

"Reclaim it," said Schahabarim.

"But if he refuses?" she resumed.

The priest contemplated her attentively, and with such a smile as she had never before seen.

"Yes; what shall I do?" repeated Salammbô.

He rolled between his fingers the ends of his bandelets that fell down from his tiara over his shoulders, his eyes downcast, immobile; finally perceiving that she did not comprehend, he said:

"You will be alone with him."

"And then?"

"Alone in his tent."

"And what then?"

Schahabarim bit his lips; he sought for some roundabout phrase.

"If you must die it will be later," said he; "much later! fear nothing! and whatever he attempts, do not call out! do not be frightened! You should be humble, you understand, and submissive to his desire, for it is the order of Heaven!"

"But the veil?"

"The Gods will care for it," responded Schahabarim.

She added:

"Oh, father, if you would only accompany me?"

"No!"

He made her kneel, and keeping her left hand raised and her right one extended, he swore on her behalf to bring back to Carthage the veil of Tanit. With fearful imprecations, she consecrated herself to the Gods, and each time that Schahabarim pronounced a word she faintingly repeated it.

He indicated to her all the purifications and fasts she ought to perform, and what paths to pursue, in order to reach Mâtho's tent; besides, he told her that a servitor familiar with the roads should accompany her.

She felt herself freed. She dreamed of naught but the happiness of reseeing the Zaïmph; and now she blessed Schahabarim for his exhortations.

It was the season when the doves of Carthage migrated to the mountain of Eryx in Sicily, there nesting about the temple of Venus. Previous to their departure, during many days, they sought each other, and cooed to reunite themselves; finally one evening they flew, driven by the wind, and this large, white could glided in the heaven very high above the sea.

The horizon was crimson. They seemed gradually to descend to the waves, then disappear as though swallowed up and falling, of their own accord, into the jaws of the sun. Salammbô, who watched them disappear, lowered her head. Taanach, believing that she surmised her mistress's grief, tenderly said:

"But, mistress, they will return."

"Yes! I know it."

"And you will see them again."

"Perhaps!" Salammbô said, as she sighed.

She had not confided to anyone her resolution, and for its discreet accomplishment she sent Taanach to purchase, in the suburbs of Kinisdo (instead of requiring them of the stewards), all the articles it was necessary she should have: vermilion, aromatics, a linen girdle, and new garments. The old slave was amazed by these preparations, without daring to ask any questions; and so the day arrived fixed by Schahabarim when Salammbô must depart.

Towards the twelfth hour, she perceived at the end of the sycamores an old blind man, whose hand rested on the shoulder of a child who walked before him, and in the other hand he held, against his hip, a species of cithara made of black wood.

The eunuchs, the slaves, the women had been scrupulously sent away; no one could possibly know the mystery that was being prepared.

Taanach lighted in the corners of the room four tripods full of *strobus* and cardamom, then she spread out great Babylonian tapestries, and hung them on cords all round the room,—for Salammbô did not wish to be seen even by the walls. The player of the kinnor waited crouching behind the door, and the young boy, standing up, applied his lips to a reed flute. In the distance the street clamour faded, the violet shadows lengthened before the peristyles of the temples, and on the other side of the gulf the base of the mountain, the olive fields, and the waste yellow ground indefinitely undulated till finally lost in a bluish vapour; not a single sound could be heard, and an indescribable oppression pervaded the air.

Salammbô crouched on the onyx step on the edge of the porphyry basin; she lifted her wide sleeves and fastened them behind her shoulders, and began her ablutions in a methodical manner, according to the sacred rites.

Next Taanach brought to her an alabaster phial, containing something liquid, yet coagulated; it was the blood of a black dog, strangled by barren women on a winter's night in the ruins of a sepulchre. She rubbed it on her ears, her heels, and the thumb of her right hand, and even the nail remained tinged a trifle red, as if she had crushed a berry. The moon rose, then both at once the cithara and the flute commenced to play. Salammbô took off her ear-rings, laid aside her necklace, bracelets, and her long white simarra; unknotted the fillet from her hair, and for some minutes shook her tresses gently over her shoulders to refresh and disentangle them. The music outside continued; there were always the same three notes, precipitous and furious; the strings grated, the flute was high-sounding and sonorous. Taanach marked the cadence by striking her hands; Salammbô, swaying her entire body, chanted her prayers, and one by one her garments fell around her on the floor.

The heavy tapestry trembled, and above the cord that sustained it the head of the Python appeared. He descended slowly, like a drop of water trickling along a wall, and glided between the stuffs spread out, then poised himself on his tail; he lifted himself perfectly straight up, and darted his eyes, more brilliant than carbuncles, upon Salammbô.

A shudder of cold, or her modesty perhaps, at first made her hesitate. But she recalled the order of Schahabarim, so she went forward; the Python lowered himself, alighting upon the nape of her neck in the middle of his body, allowing his head and tail to hang down like a broken necklace, and the two ends trailed on the floor. Salammbô rolled them around her sides, under her arms, between her knees; then taking him by the jaw, she drew his little triangular mouth close to her teeth; and with half-closed eyes she bent back under the moon's rays. The white light seemed to enshroud her in a silvery fog; the tracks of her wet feet shone on the stones; stars twinkled in the depths of the water; the Python tightened against her his black coils, speckled with spots of gold. Salammbô panted under this too heavy weight; her loins gave way, she felt that she was dying: the Python patted her thighs softly with his tail; then the music ceased, and he fell down.

Taanach drew near to Salammbô, and after arranging two candelabras, of which the lights burned in two crystal globes filled with water, she tinted with henna the inside of the hands of her mistress, put vermilion on her cheeks, antimony on her eyelids, and lengthened her eyebrows with a mixture of gum, musk, ebony, and crushed flies' feet.

Salammbô, sitting in a chair mounted with ivory, abandoned herself to the care of her slave. But the soothing touches, the odour of the aromatics, and the fasts she had kept, enervated her: she became so pale that Taanach paused.

"Continue!" said Salammbô; and as she drew herself up in spite of herself, she felt all at once reanimated. Then an impatience seized her; she urged Taanach to hasten, and the old slave growled:

"Well! well! mistress! . . . You have no one waiting for you elsewhere!"

"Yes!" responded Salammbô, "some one waits for me."

Taanach started with surprise, and in order to know more, she said:

"What do you order me to do, mistress, if you should remain away?" . . . .

But Salammbô sobbed, and the slave exclaimed:

"You suffer! What is the matter with you? Do not go! Take me! When you were a little one and wept, I held you to my heart and suckled you, and made you laugh by tickling you with my nipples. Mistress!" she struck her withered breasts, exclaiming: "You sucked them dry. Now I am old! I can do nothing for you! You do not love me any more! You hide your troubles from me, you disdain your nurse!" With fondness and vexation the tears coursed down her face, in the scars of her tattooing.

"No!" said Salammbô, "no; I love you; be comforted!"

Taanach, with a smile like the grimace of an old monkey, recommenced her task. Following the directions of the priest, Salammbô ordered her slave to make her magnificent. Taanach complied, with a barbaric taste full of elaboration and ingenuity.

Over a first fine wine-coloured tunic she placed a second one, embroidered with birds' plumes. Golden scales were fastened to her hips, from her wide girdle flowed the folds of her blue, silver-starred petticoat-trousers. Then Taanach adjusted an ample robe of rare stuff from the land of the Seres, white variegated with green stripes. She attached over Salammbô's shoulders a square of purple, made heavy at the hem with beads of *sandastrum;* and on the top of all these vestments she arranged a black mantle with a long train. Then she contemplated her, and proud of her work, she could not keep from saying:

"You will not be more beautiful the day of your nuptials!"

"My nuptials!" repeated Salammbô in a reverie, as she leaned her elbow on the ivory chair.

Taanach held up before her mistress a copper mirror, wide and long enough for her to view herself completely. She stood up, and with a light touch of one finger put back a curl that drooped too low on her forehead. Her hair was powdered with gold, crimped in front, hanging down her back in long twists, terminating in pearls. The light from the candelabra heightened the colour on her cheeks, the gold throughout her garments, and the whiteness of her skin. She wore around her waist, on her arms, hands, and feet such a profusion of jewels that the mirror, reflecting like a sun, flashed back prismatic rays upon her :—and Salammbô stood beside Taanach, leaning and turning around on all sides to view herself, smiling at the dazzling effect.

She walked to and fro, embarrassed by the time that she needs must tarry.

Suddenly the crow of a cock was heard. She quickly pinned over her hair a long yellow veil, passed a scarf around her neck, and buried her feet in blue leather buskins, saying to Taanach :

"Go, see under the myrtles, if there is not a man with two horses."

Taanach had scarcely re-entered before Salammbô descended the stairway of the galleys.

"Mistress!" called out the slave. Salammbô turned around and placed one finger on her lips, in sign of discretion and silence.

Taanach crept quietly the length of the prows as far as the base of the terrace, and in the distance by the moonlight she distinguished in the cypress avenue a gigantic shadow moving obliquely to the left of Salammbô : this was a foreboding of death.

Taanach went back to her room, threw herself on the floor, tore her face with her finger-nails, pulled out her hair, and uttered shrill yells at the top of her voice.

Finally the thought came to her that some one might hear; then she was quiet, and sobbed very low, with her head between her hands and her face laid flat on the stones.

CHAPTER XI.

IN THE TENT.

The man sent by Schahabarim to guide Salammbô conducted her up the road leading beyond the lighthouse towards the Catacombs, then descended the long suburb of Molouya, full of steep by-ways.

The sky began to whiten. Sometimes palm-beams jutting beyond the walls obliged them to lower their heads. The two horses, pacing carefully, kept slipping; and they thus arrived at the gate of Teveste.

Its heavy valves were half open; they passed; it slowly swung to behind them.

For some time they followed along the foot of the ramparts, and at the top of the cisterns they took a road by the Tænia, a narrow ribbon of yellow land, which separating the gulf from the lake, was prolonged as far as Rhades.

No one appeared in or about Carthage, either on the sea or in the surrounding country. The clay-coloured waves rippled softly, as the gentle wind tossed the foam over the sweep of the breakers and flecked them o'er with broken splashes of white.

Notwithstanding the profusion of her wraps, Salammbô shivered in the freshness of the morning, and was made dizzy by the unaccustomed motion of the horse and the open air. Then the sun rose; it bit the back of her head, and involuntarily she became a trifle drowsy. The two horses ambled along side by side, burying their hoofs in the mute sand.

When they passed the Hot-Springs Mountain, they proceeded at a more rapid gait as the ground became firmer.

Although it was the season for ploughing and sowing, the fields as far as the eye could span were as forsaken as a desert; heaps of grain were spread out from place to place; elsewhere the reddened barley shed itself from the ear; and on the clear horizon, villages appeared in black, with incoherent and mutilated outlines.

Now and again a half-calcined piece of wall stood up on the roadside. The cabin roofs were falling in, exposing the interiors, where could be seen fragments of pottery, tatters of clothing, all sorts of utensils, and unrecognisable shattered objects. Frequently a being covered with rags, evidently startled by the equestrians, emerged from the ruins, its face incrusted with dirt, and eyes flaming, but always quickly took to its heels, or disappeared in a hole. Salammbô and her guide did not halt.

Abandoned plains succeeded each other. Over wide stretches of yellow earth spread out in uneven streaks, a black charcoal dust, lifted by their horses' feet, rose behind them in clouds. Sometimes they came to peaceful nooks, a brook that ran amid long

s

grasses, and on climbing up the opposite bank, Salammbô, to refresh her hands, would pluck the wet leaves.

At the corner of a wood of laurel-roses she was nearly unseated by her horse shying at a corpse stretched upon the ground in the roadway. The slave readjusted her on the cushions. He was one of the servitors of the temple of Tanit, a man whom Schahabarim employed in perilous missions. With an excess of precaution he now went on foot beside her, between the two horses, now and then touching them up with the end of a leather lash, wound around his arm; or pulled from a pannier hung on his breast balls of wheat, dates, and yolks of eggs, wrapped up in lotus leaves, which he would proffer to Salammbô, without speaking or pausing.

In the middle of the day, three Barbarians dressed in animals' skins crossed their path; gradually others appeared, wandering in bands of ten, twelve, or twenty-five, many driving she-goats or cows, which limped. Their heavy clubs were studded with brass points; cutlasses glittered on their filthy savage clothing. Seeing the riders, they opened their eyes wide with a menacing and amazed air.

As they passed along, some shouted after them a commonplace benediction, others obscene pleasantries; and the guide replied to each group in their own idiom, telling them that he was conducting an ill youth to be healed at a distant temple.

Meantime the day fell. The baying of a dog was heard, and they directed their steps towards the sound. Through the twilight they perceived an enclosure of uncemented stones surrounding a shapeless building. A dog ran along on the wall; the slave stoned it, and they entered a high, vaulted hall. In the centre a crouching woman was warming herself at a brushwood fire, the smoke from which curled up, making its escape through a hole in the roof. Her white hair, which fell to her knees, half concealed her, and without caring to answer the guide, she mumbled in an idiotic manner words of vengeance against the Barbarians and the same against the Carthaginians.

After the guide had ferreted about from right to left, he came back to the old woman, and demanded something to eat. She shook her head, keeping her eyes fixed on the fire, and murmured:

"I was the hand; the ten fingers are cut off. The mouth can eat no more."

The guide showed her a handful of gold pieces; she threw herself upon them, but quickly resumed her motionless attitude.

Finally he drew a poniard from his girdle, and placed it across her throat; then she tremblingly went and lifted up a large slab, and brought out from concealment an amphora of wine and some fish preserved in honey from Hippo-Zarytus.

Salammbô turned away from this unclean food, and, being sorely fatigued, slept on the caparisons taken from her horse, and heaped in a corner of the hall.

Before daybreak the guide awoke her.

The dog growled, and the guide stole softly up behind it, and with a single well-directed blow with his poniard, cut off its head. He rubbed the blood on the horses' nostrils to reanimate them

The old hag threw after them a curse. Salammbô perceived it, and pressed the amulet she wore to her heart.

They retook their journey. Urged by impatience, now and again she asked the guide if they should not soon reach their destination. The road rolled over little hills. The chirping of the cicadas was alone audible. The sun heated the yellowed grasses. The ground was riven by crevices, which divided it into immense slabs.

Sometimes a viper crawled by, or an eagle flew overhead. The guide always ran alongside of Salammbô, who mused beneath the veils, and, despite the heat, refrained from casting them aside, fearful of soiling her beautiful vestments.

At regular distances towers loomed up, built by the Carthaginians for the purpose of watching the movements of the tribes. From time to time the two travellers entered one of these, to avail themselves of the shade, but, when once refreshed, started on again.

The previous day, by way of precaution, they had made a wide detour, but at present they met no one; as the region was barren, the Barbarians had not passed this way.

Gradually the devastation commenced anew; and sometimes in the midst of a field there appeared a mosaic floor, the sole relic of a vanished château. The olive-trees, stripped of foliage, seemed in the distance like broad thorn-bushes. They passed through a town where all the houses had been burnt flat to the ground. Along on the wall-sides could be seen human skeletons, as well as those of dromedaries and mules; and half-devoured carrion blocked the streets.

Night fell; the sky hung low, covered with clouds. During the space of two more hours they ascended in a westerly direction; when all at once appeared before them quantities of small flames.

At the bottom of an amphitheatre, here and there golden plates gleamed as they moved about. These were the polished cuirasses of the Clinabarians in the Punic camp. Then they distinguished in the same vicinity other and more numerous lights, for the armies of the Mercenaries were now combined and massed together, extending over a vast area.

Salammbô made a movement to advance, but the guide led her further on, and they skirted the terrace that enclosed the Barbarians' camp. A breach was discovered: the slave disappeared.

At the top of the entrenchments patrolled a sentinel, carrying a bow in one hand and a pike over his shoulder.

Salammbô continued to advance. The sentinel knelt down, and a long arrow pierced the end of her mantle. Then she halted, motionless; he called out, asking what she wanted.

"To speak to Mâtho," she replied. "I am a fugitive from Carthage."

He whistled; the signal was repeated again and again in the distance.

Salammbô waited; her frightened horse snorted and wheeled.

When Mâtho arrived, the moon was rising behind her, but her face was concealed under a yellow veil covered with black flowers, and so many ample draperies enveloped her entire body, it was impossible to divine aught of it. From the top of the terrace he contemplated this vague form rising like a phantom through the evening shadows.

At length she said to him:

"Take me to your tent. I wish it."

A recollection which he could not clearly define passed through his memory. He felt his heart beat. This air of command intimidated him.

"Follow me!" said he.

The barrier was lowered; soon she was within the Barbarians' encampment

It was replete with a great tumult and a surging crowd. Fires burned brightly under suspended camp kettles, and their crimson reflections weirdly illuminated certain places, while permitting others to remain in complete darkness.

People were shouting and calling on all sides; the horses were tethered in long, straight rows between the tents, that were round or square, constructed of leather or canvas; there were also reed huts, and holes dug in the ground, like burrows of animals.

The soldiers were carting faggots for the fires, or were squatting on the ground, or, wrapped up in their mats, were disposing themselves for sleep; and Salammbô's horse, in order to step over their forms, sometimes was forced to stretch out his legs and leap.

Salammbô recalled having previously seen these very same men; but now their beards were much longer, their faces more tanned, and their voices harsher. Mâtho walked in front of her, and at a gesture of his arm that lifted his red mantle, the men scattered. Some kissed his hands, others bowed down and accosted him, to request his commands, as he ranked now as the veritable, the only Chief of the Barbarians: Spendius, Autharitus, and Narr' Havas had been discouraged, but he had shown such audacity and determination, that all obeyed him.

Salammbô in following him traversed the entire camp, as his tent was pitched at the end, and only three hundred paces distant from Hamilcar's entrenchments.

She noticed on the right a broad ditch, and it seemed to her that faces leaned on the edge at the level of the ground, resembling decapitated heads; yet their eyes moved, and from their half-opened mouths moans in the Punic language escaped.

Two Negroes, holding cressets filled with burning resin, stood on either side of Mâtho's tent. He advanced, and brusquely casting aside the fall of canvas, entered. She followed him. It was a deep tent, supported by a pole in the middle, and lighted by a large sconce in the form of a lotus, filled with yellow oil, on which floated handfuls of burning tow; in the shadows could be distinguished shining military accoutrements. A naked blade leaned against a stool, beside a buckler; whips of hippopotamus hide, cymbals, little bells and collars, were thrown pell-mell into baskets of esparto-grass; crumbs of black bread soiled a felt coverlet; in one corner, on a round stone, copper money was carelessly heaped; and through the rents of the tent-canvas the wind brought from without the dust, and the scent of the elephants, which could be heard rattling their chains as they were feeding.

"Who are you?" asked Mâtho.

Without reply she slowly looked round the tent, and her glance was arrested at the far end, where, on a bed of palm-branches, la_ something bluish and scintillating.

She advanced quickly: a cry escaped her. Mâtho, behind her, stamped his foot.

"What brings you? Why do you come?"

She replied, pointing to the Zaïmph:

"To take it!" and with the other hand pulled off her veils. Mâtho recoiled, his elbows thrown back, with mouth open, and almost terrified.

She felt herself sustained as if by the power of the Gods, and gazing at him face to face, she demanded the Zaïmph, claiming it with profuse and haughty words.

Mâtho did not hear: he was contemplating her, and her garments, that were to him blended with her body: the sheen of the fabrics was like the splendour of her skin, something special, appertaining to her alone: her eyes and her diamonds equally sparkled; the polish of her finger-nails continued the lustre of the jewels that bedecked her fingers; the two agraffes fastening her tunic raised her breasts a trifle up and pressed them closer; he lost himself in a reverie as his eye followed a slender thread that fell between them, to which was suspended an emerald medallion that he perceived revealing itself lower down under the violet gauze. She wore for ear-rings two tiny balances of sapphires, supporting a hollow pearl filled with liquid perfume, which percolated through minute perforations and from moment to moment fell in a drop, which moistened her bare shoulders. Mâtho with fascination watched it slowly trickle down.

An indomitable curiosity attracted him, and like a child who puts its hand on an unknown fruit, tremblingly he touched her lightly with the tip of his finger on the upper part of her bosom; at the touch her flesh, slightly cold, yielded with an elastic resistance.

This contact, although scarcely perceptible, shook Mâtho to the depths of his soul. An insurrection of his whole being impelled him towards her. He desired to envelope her, absorb her, drink her. His breast heaved, his teeth chattered.

He took her by the wrists and gently drew her to him, and then sat down on a cuirass beside the couch of palm-branches, covered with a lion's skin, while she remained standing. Thus holding her between his knees, he scanned her from head to foot, repeating:

"How beautiful you are! How beautiful you are!"

His eyes continually fixed on hers, made her suffer, and this embarrassment, this repugnance, increased in a manner so keen that Salammbô had to restrain herself from screaming out. The thought of Schahabarim came to her; she resigned herself.

Mâtho kept holding her little hands in his, and from time to time, in spite of the priest's edict, she averted her face, and tried to throw him off by shaking her arms. He dilated his nostrils to inhale more freely the perfume exhaled from her person—an indefinable emanation, fresh, yet it made him dizzy, like the fumes from a censer—a diffusion of honey, pepper, incense, roses, and yet another odour.

But, how came he to find her thus beside him in his tent, at his discretion? Some one doubtless had brought her. She had not come for the Zaïmph? His arms fell, and he lowered his head, overwhelmed by a sudden reverie.

In order to move him, Salammbô said, in a plaintive voice:

"What, then, have I done, that you wish my death?"

"Your death!" he exclaimed.

She resumed:

"I saw you one night, by the flames of my burning gardens, between the steaming cups and my slain slaves; and at that time your wrath was so fierce that you bounded towards me, and made me fly! Then a terror entered Carthage—devastation of the cities—burning of the countries—massacre of the soldiers. It is you who have destroyed them! It is you who have assassinated them! I hate you! Your name alone gnaws me like remorse! You are more execrable than the pest! Aye, than the Roman war! The provinces quake before your fury; the ditches are full of dead! I have followed the trace of your fires as though I walked behind Moloch!"

Mâtho rose at a bound; a tremendous pride swelled his heart; he felt himself lifted to the height of a God.

With palpitating nostrils, and teeth set, she continued:

"As if there had not already been enough of your sacrilege, you came to my palace during my sleep, enveloped in the Zaimph! Your words I did not comprehend; but I saw very well that you desired to drag me towards something frightful—to plunge me to the bottom of an abyss!"

Mâtho, wringing his hands, cried out:

"No! no! It was to give the Zaimph to you! To render it back to you! For it seemed to me that the Goddess had left her vestment for you, and that it belonged to you! In her temple or in your mansion, what matter? Are you not all-powerful, immaculate, radiant and beautiful as Tanit?" And with a look full of infinite admiration:

"At least—perhaps—if you may not be Tanit herself?"

"I, Tanit!" Salammbô exclaimed to herself.

They talked no more. The distant thunder rumbled. The sheep bleated, frightened by the storm.

"Oh! come near!" he resumed. "Come near; fear nothing!

"Formerly I had been but a soldier, confounded among the common Mercenaries, and even so mild that I freely carried upon my back the wood for my comrades. Do I trouble myself about Carthage? The crowd of her men tosses to and fro as though lost in the dust of your sandals, and all the Carthaginian treasures, with her provinces, her waters, and her islands, do not entice me like the freshness of your lips and the turn of your shoulders. But I wanted to pull down her walls, in order that I might come near to you and possess you! Besides, while I wait I revenge myself! At present, I crush men like shells. I throw myself on the phalanxes; I scatter the sarissas with my hands, and arrest the stallions by their nostrils; a catapult even is powerless to kill me! Oh! if you only knew how in the midst of this war I have thought of you! Sometimes the memory of a gesture—of a fold in your robes, has suddenly seized me and entangled me like a net! I perceived your eyes in the flames of the fire-lances and above the gilding of the shields. I hear your voice in the resounding of the cymbals; I turn round—you are not there! And then I plunge again into the thick of battle!"

He lifted his arms in his emotion, and the swollen veins intercrossed like ivy creeping over the branches of trees; the perspiration rolled down on his chest between his squared muscles, while his rapid breathing made his sides heave beneath his belt of bronze, fitted with straps that hung to his knees, which were firmer than marble. Salammbô, accustomed to the eunuchs, allowed herself to be overcome by the force of this man.

It was the chastisement of the Goddess, or the influence of Moloch, circulating around her in the five armies. Overwhelmed by a certain lassitude, she indistinctly heard through her stupor the intermittent call of the sentinels answering one another.

The flames of the lamp wavering fitfully under gusts of warm air, became at moments bright flashes of light, then almost extinguished, intensifying the obscurity; and she saw only Mâtho's eyeballs like two glowing coals in the night. Now she felt, indeed, that a fatality encompassed her, that she had attained a supreme moment which was irrevocable, and with one effort went towards the Zaïmph, and raised her hands to seize it.

"What are you doing?" cried Mâtho.

She answered with placidity:

"I return to Carthage with the Zaïmph."

He advanced, and folded his arms with an air so terrible that she was immediately as nailed to the ground.

"You return with it to Carthage!" he stammered; and repeated, grinding his teeth: "You return with it to Carthage! Ah! you came to take the Zaïmph, to conquer me, then to disappear! No! no! you belong to me! and at present, no one can tear you from here! Ah! I have not forgotten the insolence of your large, tranquil eyes, and how you crushed me with your haughty beauty! Ah! it is my turn now! You are my captive, my slave, my servant! Call, if you will, your father, and his army, the Elders, the Rich, and your entire execrable people! I am the master of three hundred thousand soldiers! I will go and seek them in Lusitania, among the Gauls, and in the depths of the desert. I will overthrow your city, and burn all its temples! The triremes shall float on streams of blood! I do not choose that a single house, a stone, or a palm-tree remain! And if men fail me, I will draw the bears from the mountains, and turn the lions upon your people! Do not attempt to fly, or I shall kill you!"

Ghastly, and with fists clenched, he quivered like a harp when the over-tense strings are about to snap. Suddenly sobs suffocated him, and he sank down on his haunches before her.

"Ah! forgive me, I am a wretch, viler than the

scorpions, than the mud or the dust! Just now, as you were speaking, your breath passed over my face, and I delighted in it as a dying man who, prone on his face, drinks at the edge of a stream. Crush me, that I may feel your feet! Curse me, that I may hear your voice! Do not go! Pity me! I love you! I love you!"

He fell upon his knees on the ground before her, and encircled her waist with his arms, his head thrown back and his hands wandering listlessly about her; the gold discs suspended from his ears shone on his bronzed throat; large tears rolled in his eyes, like silver balls; he sighed in a caressing manner, and murmured vague speeches lighter than a breeze, as savoury as a kiss.

Salammbô was invaded by a softness in which she lost all consciousness of herself. Something at once from within, and from on high, an order of the Gods, forced her to self-abandonment; clouds lifted her up, and fainting she fell back on the couch in the midst of the lion's skin. Mâtho seized her in a frantic embrace; her golden chainlet snapped, and the two ends flew apart, striking against the tent like two leaping vipers. The Zaïmph fell and enveloped her. Seeing Mâtho's face bending over her, she exclaimed:

"Moloch, thou burnest me!" and the kisses of the soldier, more devouring than fire, coursed over her. She was as if lifted up in a storm, or as consumed by the force of the sun.

He kissed all the fingers of her hands; her arms, her feet, and the long tresses of her hair from end to end.

"Take the Zaïmph," he said; "how can I resist?

Take me with it! I will renounce everything! Beyond Gades, twenty days by sea, there has been found an island covered with gold-dust, with verdure, and birds. On the mountains large flowers full of perfume swing mid-air, fuming like eternal censers; in citron trees taller than the cedars, milk-white serpents with the diamonds of their jaws make the fruit fall to the ground. The air is so soft that it wards off death. Aye, I will find it; you shall see this haven. We shall live in crystal grottos hewn out at the foot of the hills. No one has ever inhabited this country, where I shall become king."

He brushed off the dust from his cothurnes; then besought her to allow him to put a quarter of a pomegranate between her lips; he piled up clothing behind her head to make a pillow; in fact he sought in every imaginable way to serve her, to humiliate himself, and even went so far as to spread over her knees the Zaïmph as a simple rug.

"Do you still keep," said he, "those little gazelle horns on which your necklaces are suspended? Give them to me! I love them!" Joyous laughter escaped him, and he talked as though the war was at an end; and the Mercenaries, Hamilcar, and all obstacles, had now disappeared.

Through an opening in the tent they saw the moon as she glided between two clouds.

"Ah! but I have passed nights in contemplating her! She seemed to me a veil which hid your face; you looked at me through it; memories of you were mingled with her rays. Then I could distinguish you there no more!" And with his head upon her bosom, carried away again by his emotion, he wept freely.

"Then this is he," she thought, "the formidable man who makes Carthage tremble!"

Finally he slept; then, disengaging herself from his arms, she placed one foot on the ground, when she saw that her chainlet was broken.

In grand families the virgins were accustomed to respect these little shackles with almost the same reverence as though they were religious symbols. Salammbô blushingly rolled around her ankles the two ends of her dishonoured gold chainlet. Carthage, Megara, her mansion, her room and the tract of country through which she had recently traversed, rushed in whirlwinds through her memory, in images tumultuous, and yet withal distinct. But a supervening abyss removed them far from her, to an infinite distance.

The storm was passing away: rare heavy drops of rain, spattering one by one, made the tent-top sway.

Mâtho slept as a man intoxicated, extended on his side, one arm flung out beyond the edge of the couch; his pearl bandeau, thrust a trifle up, exposed his forehead. A smile parted his lips, disclosing his glittering teeth in the midst of his black beard, and in his half-closed eyes lurked a silent, almost outrageous gaiety. Salammbô regarded him, her head down, her hands clasped, motionless.

At the head of the couch a poniard lay on a cypress table; the sight of this shining blade inflamed her with murderous desire. Lamenting voices came from afar through the darkness, and like a choir of spirits solicited her. She drew near and seized the haft of the weapon, but at the rustle of her robe Mâtho partially opened his eyes, moved his lips over her hands, and the poniard dropped.

Screams burst out; a frightful light flashed behind the tent. Mâtho lifted the tent cloth; they perceived that a vast conflagration enveloped the Libyan camp. Their reed cabins were burning, the stems twisting, splintered through the smoke, flying like arrows; over the red horizon black shadows ran frantically beyond. Yells issuing from those within the cabins were heard; the elephants, the cattle, and the horses leaped and plunged among the distracted crowd, crushing the soldiers with the munitions and baggage that they dragged out of the fire. Trumpets sounded the alarm. Voices called out:

"Mâtho! Mâtho!" Men tried to enter, shouting:

"Come! come! Hamilcar is burning the camp of Autharitus."

At this he made one bound. Salammbô now found herself alone.

Then she closely examined the Zaïmph; after she had contemplated it well, she was surprised not to experience that measure of happiness she had formerly thought should be hers. She remained melancholy before her dream accomplished.

Just then the end of the tent was lifted and a hideous form appeared. At first Salammbô could only discern two eyes, and a long white beard, which hung down to the ground, for the rest of the body, entangled in the rags of a tawny garment, dragged along the earth: and at every forward movement the

T

two hands were buried in his beard, and then fell back. In crawling thus he gradually arrived at Salammbô's feet, and she recognised old Gisco.

In fact, the Mercenaries, to prevent the captive Elders from escaping, had broken their legs with a metal bar, then had thrown them all promiscuously to rot in a ditch of filth. The most robust, when they heard the rattle of the bowls, used to raise themselves up and yell: it was thus that Gisco had perceived Salammbô.

When Mâtho led Salammbô across the camp to his tent Gisco had seen her, and had conjectured her to be a Carthaginian woman by the little beads of *sandastrum* that clattered on her buskins, and actuated by the presentiment of some great mystery, with the aid of his companions he had succeeded in getting out of the ditch, and he had dragged himself on his hands and elbows twenty yards or more to Mâtho's tent.

"It is you!" finally she said, almost appalled.

Lifting himself up on his hands, he replied:

"It is I! All believed me to be dead, is it not so?"

She bowed her head, and he continued:

"Ah! why have not the Baals granted me this grace!"—and he drew so close that he touched her robe—"they would have thus spared me the pain of cursing you!"

Salammbô threw herself quickly backward; she had such fear of this unclean being, who seemed as hideous as a larva and as terrible as a phantom.

"I shall soon be one hundred years old," he said. "I have seen Agathocles, I have also seen Regulus and the Roman eagles pass over the Punic harvest fields! I have seen all the horrors of battles, the sea encumbered with the wrecks of our fleets! The Barbarians whom I formerly commanded have captured and chained me by my four limbs like a homicide slave; my companions one by one are dying about me; the odours of their corpses awaken me at night; I drive away the birds that swoop down to peck out their eyes; and yet not for one single day have I despaired of Carthage! Although I should have seen all the armies pitted against her and the flames of the siege overtop the temples, even then I should have believed in her eternity! But now all is ended! All is lost! The Gods curse her! Malediction on you who have hastened her ruin by your ignominy!"

She opened her lips.

"Ah! I was there!" cried he. "I heard you pant with lust as a prostitute, when he told you of his passion, and you permitted him to kiss your hands! But if the madness of your unchastity impelled you, at least you should have behaved as well as the wild beasts, which hide themselves to couple, and you would not thus have displayed your shame almost before the eyes of your father!"

"What?" she exclaimed.

"Ah, then you do not know that the two entrenchments are within sixty cubits one to the other,—that your Mâtho, from excess of audacious pride, has established himself in front of Hamilcar? Your father is just there behind you, and if I could only have crawled up the pathway leading to the platform I could have cried, 'Come now, see your daughter in the embrace of a Barbarian! She has put on the vestments of the Goddess to please him, and abandons her body to his lust; thus she betrays the glory of your name and the majesty of the Gods, the vengeance of her country, even the salvation of Carthage!'"

The movements of his toothless mouth agitated his long white beard to its very end; his eyes were fastened upon her and seemed to devour her, as he said:

"Oh! Sacrilege! Be accursed! Accursed! Accursed!"

Salammbô cast aside at arm's length the tent cloth, held it thus uplifted without answering Gisco. She looked in the direction of Hamilcar's encampment.

"It is this way, is it not?" she asked.

"What matter is it to you? Turn aside! Away with you! Rather crush your face against the earth! It is a holy place, which your look would profane!"

She hastily threw the Zaïmph around her waist, gathered up her veils, mantle, and scarf—"I go there!" she ejaculated, and disappeared.

At first she ran along in the darkness without meeting anyone, as all had rushed towards the fire, and the uproar increased as the far-reaching flames of the conflagration impurpled the sky behind. Presently a long terrace hindered her progress. She turned from right to left at hazard, searching for a rope, a ladder, a stone, anything, in fact, to help her to mount over the wall. She was afraid of Gisco, and it seemed that cries and steps pursued her. The day began to dawn. She discerned by the feeble light a pathway in the entrenchments; taking her robe between her teeth, as it greatly encumbered her, with three bounds she attained the platform.

A sonorous signal sounded below her in the shade, the same signal that she had heard at the foot of the stairway of the galleys. Leaning over the terrace, she recognised the man sent by the priest Schahabarim, holding two saddled horses.

All night he had wandered between the two entrenchments, but becoming greatly disquieted by the conflagration, he had gone back, trying to discover what happened in Mâtho's camp; and as he knew that this place was nearest to his tent, in obedience to the priest's orders he had not left the vicinity, but there awaited Salammbô.

He mounted and stood upright on the back of one of the horses, and Salammbô slipped down from the terrace to him; at once they spurred their horses into a sharp gallop, making the circuit of the Punic camp, searching for an entrance.

Mâtho re-entered his tent. The smoking lamp scarcely burned, and as he believed Salammbô slept, he patted delicately all over the lion's skin spread out on the couch of palm-branches. Not finding her, he called, and she answered not; he quickly jerked down a strip of canvas to admit the daylight. The Zaïmph had disappeared.

The earth trembled under the tread of the multitude. Yells, neighs, the clash of armours sounded through the air, and the fanfare of the clarions rung out the signal for a charge. All was like a fierce hurricane eddying around him. An inordinate fury overtook him; he seized his weapons and madly dashed outside.

Long files of Barbarians were descending the mountain sides double quick, and the Punic squares advanced against them with a heavy, regular oscillation. The fog, torn by the sun's rays, formed little detached clouds that hung in the air, and gradually rising, disclosed standards, helmets, and the points of pikes. Under the rapid evolutions, portions of the field still in shadow seemed to change place as a single piece. Elsewhere it appeared as if torrents were crossing each other, and between them thorny masses remained motionless. Mâtho distinguished the captains, the soldiers, and the heralds, as far as to the range of varlets in the rear who were mounted on asses. But Narr' Havas, instead of holding his position and covering the foot-soldiers, abruptly wheeled to the right, as though he deliberately aimed to be crushed by Hamilcar's troops.

His cavalry passed beyond the elephants, which had slackened their speed, and all the horses stretched out their heads, uncurbed by reins, galloping at a pace so furious that their bellies fairly seemed to graze the earth. Then suddenly Narr' Havas rode resolutely towards a sentinel, threw down his sword, his lance, his javelins, and vanished thus unarmed in the midst of the Carthaginians.

The king of the Numidians entered Hamilcar's tent and said to him, pointing out his men, who had halted at a distance:

"Barca! I bring them to you—they are for you!"

Then he prostrated himself on the ground in sign of subjugation; afterwards recalled, as proof of his fidelity to Hamilcar, his line of conduct since the beginning of the war.

At first, he recounted how he had prevented the siege of Carthage and the massacre of the Punic captives; then, how he had not profited by the victory over Hanno after the defeat at Utica. As to the Tyrian cities, they were on the frontier of his own realm. In short, he had not participated at the battle of Macar, had even absented himself expressly, to avoid the obligation of combatting the Suffete.

In truth, Narr' Havas had ever desired to aggrandise himself by encroachments on the Punic provinces, and, according to the chances of victory, he had succoured or forsaken the Mercenaries. But seeing that Hamilcar would ultimately be the strongest, he had determined to ally himself to him; and perhaps there might also be in his present defection a grudge against Mâtho, either because he was in command, or by reason of his former love.

Without interruption the Suffete listened, for this man who presented himself thus with all his forces in an army to which he owed a debt of vengeance, was an auxiliary not to be disdained. Hamilcar divined at once the utility of such an alliance for the advancement of his great projects. For with the Numidians he would at once extricate himself from the Libyans, then he could draw with him the West to the conquest of Iberia: hence, without asking why he had not come sooner, or remarking any of his falsehoods, Hamilcar kissed Narr' Havas, clasping him three times to his breast.

As a last resort and in despair Hamilcar had fired the Libyans' camp. This army came to him like succour from the Gods; but dissimulating his joy, the Suffete craftily rejoined:

"May the Baals favour you! I know not what the Republic will do for you, but know this, that Hamilcar is not ungrateful."

The tumult redoubled; the captains entered; he armed himself while speaking:

"Let us go! Return, you with your cavalry will destroy their infantry, between your elephants and mine! Courage! Exterminate them!"

Narr' Havas was dashing forth just as Salammbô appeared. She quickly dismounted and threw open her wide mantle, and spreading her arms she displayed the Zaïmph.

The leathern curtain of the tent, looped up at the four corners, allowed the entire circuit of the mountains covered with soldiers to be seen, and as it stood in the centre, from all sides Salammbô was beheld. An immense clamour burst forth, a long cry of triumph and of hope. Those who were moving stopped; the dying leaned on their elbows, and turned round to bless her.

All the Barbarians now knew that she had retaken the Zaïmph; from the distance they saw her, or believed that they saw her, and their yells of rage and vengeance also resounded, despite the applause of the Carthaginians. Thus these five armies swarming on the mountains stamped and howled with joy or rage on all sides of Salammbô.

Hamilcar, powerless to speak, thanked him by nodding his head. His eyes alternately scanned her and the Zaïmph; and he remarked that her chainlet was broken. Then he quivered, seized by a terrible suspicion. But quickly resuming his impassibility, he considered Narr' Havas askance without turning his face.

The king of the Numidians held himself apart in a discreet attitude; on his forehead was a little dust where he had touched the ground when he had prostrated himself. Finally the Suffete advanced towards him, and, with an air full of gravity:

"In recompense for the services that you have rendered me, Narr' Havas, I give you my daughter!" adding, "Be my son, and protect your father!"

Narr' Havas made a gesture of great surprise, afterwards, throwing himself before Salammbô, covered her hands with kisses.

Salammbô, calm like a statue, seemed not to comprehend: she blushed slightly and dropped her eyes, and her long lashes made shadows upon her cheeks. Hamilcar desired to unite them immediately by an indissoluble betrothal. In Salammbô's hands a lance was placed, which she offered to Narr' Havas; their thumbs were tied together by a leather lace, then corn was poured over their heads, and the grains which fell around them rang, like hail, rebounding.

CHAPTER XII.

THE AQUEDUCT.

Twelve hours after, there only remained of the Mercenaries heaps of wounded, dying, and dead.

Hamilcar had suddenly issued from the bottom of the gorge, and descended again upon the western slope looking towards Hippo-Zarytus, whither, as the field broadened out, he had taken care to attract the Barbarians Narr' Havas with his cavalry had surrounded them; the Suffete meanwhile drove them back, and crushed them. Furthermore, they were conquered in advance by the loss of the Zaïmph; even those who did not actually care for it, felt a distress akin to weakness. Hamilcar not making it a point of honour to remain in possession of the battle-field, had drawn off a little to the left upon the heights, whence he commanded the enemy.

The outline of the camps could be recognised by their bent-down palisades. A long mass of black cinders smoked on the site of the Libyans' camp; the upturned ground undulated like the waves of the sea, and the tents, with their flapping rags of canvas, resembled rudderless ships, half lost among the breakers. Cuirasses, pitchforks, clarions, fragments of wood, iron, and brass, grain, straw, and clothing, were strewn amid the corpses. Here and there some stray fire-lance on the point of extinction was burning against a pile of baggage. The earth in certain places was hidden under the bucklers; the carcases of horses succeeded each other in heaps, like a chain of hillocks. One could perceive legs, sandals, arms, coats-of-mail, and heads in their helmets, kept together by the chin-pieces, which rolled about like balls. Human hair hung on the thorn-bushes. In pools of blood disembowelled elephants lay struggling in death-agonies, with their towers yet upon their backs. One trod upon glutinous things; and even though the rain had not fallen, there were pools of mud.

This confusion of corpses occupied the entire surface of the mountain from top to bottom.

Those who survived did not stir any more than the dead, but crouched in irregular groups, looking at one another, too much terrified to speak.

At the end of a long prairie, the lake of Hippo-Zarytus shone under the rays of the declining sun; to the right, close-packed groups of white houses stood out above a girdle of walls; the sea beyond spread out indefinitely; and with their chins in their hands, the Barbarians sighed as they thought of their home land. A cloud of grey dust settled down. The evening wind blew, refreshing and inflating their lungs. As the coolness gradually increased, the vermin could be seen leaving the dead bodies, which were growing cold, and crawling along on the warm sand; and ravens perched motionless on the top of large stones, turned towards the dying.

When night fell, dogs with yellow hair, the unclean beasts which follow armies, came stealing softly amid the Barbarians. At first they licked the clotted blood from the yet warm stumps of limbs, but soon they set to devouring the bodies, always attacking the bowels first.

One by one, like shadows, the fugitives appeared; the women also ventured to return, for there were still some of them left, especially with the Libyans, despite the frightful massacre which the Numidians had perpetrated.

Some lighted the ends of ropes to serve as torches; others held their pikes crossed, upon which their dead were placed and carried apart.

The dead were extended on their backs in long rows, open-mouthed, with their lances hard by, or else were piled up in confusion; and often, in the endeavour to discover the missing, it became necessary to dig through quite a heap. Then the torches were moved slowly over the faces: the hideous weapons had inflicted complicated wounds; greenish shreds of flesh hung from their foreheads: they were cut in pieces, or cloven to the marrow, bluish from strangulation, or deeply gashed by the elephants' tusks.

Even though they had expired almost at the same time, there existed marked differences in the progress of decomposition. Men from the north were bloated with livid swellings; and the Africans, who were more wiry, seemed to have been smoked, and were already drying up.

The Mercenaries were known by the tattooings on

their hands; the veterans of Antiochus displayed a sparrow-hawk; those who had served in Egypt, the head of a cynocephalus; those who had done duty under the princes of Asia, a battle-axe, a pomegranate, or a hammer; and those who had served in the Greek Republics, the profile of a citadel or the name of an Archon; and there were some whose arms were entirely covered by numerous symbols, blending with the cicatrices of old and new wounds.

For the bodies of men of Latin race—namely, the Samnites, Etruscans, Campanians, and the Bruttians—four large funeral pyres were established.

The Greeks dug pits for their dead with the points of their swords; the Spartans took off their own cloaks to wrap about their fallen comrades; the Athenians turned the bodies of their dead so as to face the rising sun; the Cantabrians buried their slain under heaps of stones; the Nasamones doubled the corpses in two, lashing them together with leathern straps; and the Garamantians went away to bury their dead upon the shore, that the waves might perpetually lave them. But the Latins were in despair, because they could not collect the ashes in urns; the Nomads regretted the absence of the hot sands in which bodies were mummified; and the Celts missed the three rough stones under a rainy sky at the end of a gulf full of islets.

Loud cries were raised, followed by a long silence. This was to force the departed souls to come back. Then the clamour was perseveringly resumed at regular intervals.

They excused themselves before the dead for being unable to accord them honours, as the rites prescribed; for owing to this privation they were doomed to wander during infinite periods, and to go through all manner of perils and metamorphoses. They questioned them, they asked what they desired, while others overwhelmed them with abuse for allowing themselves to be conquered.

The light from the great funeral pyres cast a weird pallor over the bloodless faces, upturned here and there upon the fragments of armour; and tears excited tears, till sobs became more poignant, recognitions and embraces more frantic. The women threw themselves upon the bodies, mouth to mouth and forehead against forehead; they were only forced away with blows when the earth was thrown into the pits over the bodies. They blackened their cheeks; they cut their hair; they drew their blood and shed it in the graves. They even gashed upon themselves counterparts of the wounds disfiguring their dead.

Groans penetrated through the clashing uproar of the cymbals. Some pulled off their amulets and spat upon them. The dying rolled in the bloody mire, furiously biting their mutilated fists; and forty-three Samnites, a devoted band, all in the sacred springtime of their youth, cut each other's throats like gladiators. Presently the wood for the funeral pyres failed; all the fires died down; all the ditches were filled; and, wearied with crying, enfeebled, tottering, they slept beside their dead brothers, some clinging tenaciously to a life full of troubles, and others desirous that they might never awaken.

In the whiteness of dawn there appeared, outside

the lines of the Barbarians, soldiers defiling with their helmets uplifted on the points of spears : saluting the Mercenaries, they asked if they had no message to send back to their countries.

Others drew near, and the Barbarians recognised many of their old comrades.

The Suffete had proposed to all of the captives to serve in his troops. Many had intrepidly refused ; and as he was quite resolved not to feed them, or hand them over to the Grand Council, he had dismissed them, binding them not to again fight against Carthage. He had distributed the enemies' weapons to those whom fear of torture had rendered tractable, and now they presented themselves to the vanquished, less to win them over, than from an impulse of pride and curiosity.

They began with a recountal of the good treatment bestowed upon them by the Suffete. Much as the Barbarians despised these traitors, they listened to them with envy. Then, at the first words of reproach, the cowards lost temper, displaying from afar their own captured swords and cuirasses ; and defied them with insults to come and take them. At which the Barbarians picked up stones: all fled ; and nothing more could be seen at the top of the mountain than their spear-points projecting above the palisades.

Then a pang heavier than that caused by the humiliation of a defeat overtook the Barbarians ; they reflected upon the manity of their courage, and remained with eyes fixed, grinding their teeth.

The same idea spontaneously took possession of all : they rushed in a tumultuous crowd upon the

Carthaginian prisoners whom by chance the soldiers of the Suffete had failed to discover; and as he had withdrawn from the battle-field, they were still secure in the deep pit. These victims were now ranged on a flat stretch of ground, while sentinels made a circle around them, and the women were permitted to enter the enclosure by thirties and forties successively. Eager to profit by the short time allotted to each group, they ran from one victim to another, uncertain, palpitating; then leaning over the poor wretches, pounded them with all their might, like washerwomen beating linen; crying aloud their husbands' names, they tore them with their nails, and dug out their eyes with their hairpins.

Afterwards the men tortured them: from their feet, which they cut off at the ankles, to their foreheads, from which they tore crowns of skin to place upon their own heads. The Eaters-of-Unclean-Things were atrocious in their imaginations: they inflamed the wounds by pouring into them dust, vinegar, and potsherds; others were waiting behind them; the blood flowed, and they made merry as do the vintagers around the fuming vats.

In the meantime Mâtho sat on the ground in the same place where he was when the battle had ended. His elbows on his knees, and his temples pressed between his hands, he saw nothing, heard nothing, and thought no more.

At the shouts of joy uttered by the crowd, he raised his head. Before him, upon a pole, hung a rag of canvas trailing on the ground, partially screening disordered baskets, rugs, and a lion's skin. He recognised his tent; and he rivetted his eyes upon the ground, as if on that spot the daughter of Hamilcar, in vanishing from him, had been engulfed in the earth.

The tattered canvas beat in the wind ; sometimes the long strips fluttered before his face, whereon he could see a red mark like the print of a hand— aye, the imprint of the hand of Narr' Havas, the sign of their alliance. Then Mâtho arose ; he seized a yet smoking brand, and threw it disdainfully upon the wreck of his tent. Then with the toe of his cothurne he kicked into the flames the articles which were scattered about, so that all should be consumed.

Suddenly, without anyone having the power to divine from what point he sprang, Spendius appeared. The former slave had two splints of a broken lance-butt bound upon his thighs, and he limped about in a piteous way, giving vent to dolorous moans.

"Take those off," said Mâtho to him. "I know that you are a brave!" He was so crushed by the injustice of the Gods, that he had not sufficient force to be indignant with mortals.

Spendius made a sign to him, and led him to the hollow of a peak, where Zarxas and Autharitus were in concealment.

They had taken flight like the slave—the one, cruel as he was, and the other despite his valour. But who could have expected the treason of Narr' Havas, or the burning of the Libyans' camp, or the taking of the Zaïmph, or the sudden attack of Hamilcar, and above all, his manœuvres, forcing them to return to the heart of the mountain, under the direct attack of the Carthaginians? Spendius would not

U

confess his terror, and persisted in the assertion that his leg was broken.

Finally the three chiefs and the *Schalischim* consulted as to what course they should determine upon in their present strait.

Hamilcar closed their road to Carthage; they were caught between his soldiers and the provinces of Narr' Havas; the Tyrian cities would join the conquerors, and this would at once drive them to the sea-coast; and all the united forces would crush them. This was what would infallibly befall them.

No means offered to avoid the war, hence they must pursue it to the uttermost. But, how could they make the necessity for an interminable struggle comprehensible to those discouraged people with their wounds yet bleeding?

"I charge myself with that," said Spendius.

Two hours after a man came from the direction of Hippo-Zarytus, and climbed the mountain at a run. He waved tablets at arm's-length, and as he shouted loudly, the Barbarians surrounded him.

He bore despatches from the Greek soldiers of Sardinia, recommending their comrades in Africa to keep a surveillance over Gisco, also over the other captives. A merchant of Samos, a certain Hipponax, coming from Carthage, had apprised them that a conspiracy was organised for their escape, and the Barbarians were notified to provide against the emergency, as the Republic was powerful.

Spendius' strategy did not at first succeed as he had anticipated. This assurance of a new peril, far from exciting fury, aroused fears. They recalled

Hamilcar's warning, thrown but lately in their midst; they now expected something unforeseen, that would be most terrible. The night was passed in great anxiety; many even took off their arms, to mollify the Suffete whenever he might present himself.

But on the morrow, at the third watch of the day, a second courier appeared, yet more breathless and begrimed with dust than the first. Spendius jerked from his hands a papyrus scroll covered with Phœnician characters, wherein the Mercenaries were supplicated not to be discouraged, for the braves of Tunis were coming at once to support them with large reinforcements.

Spendius first read this letter three times successively; and sustained by two Cappadocians, who held him sitting upon their shoulders, he was transported from place to place, reading it. For seven consecutive hours he harangued.

He recalled to the Mercenaries the promises made by the Grand Council; to the Africans the cruelties of the intendants; to all the Barbarians the general injustice of Carthage. The Suffete's gentleness was an allurement to capture them. Those who should surrender would be sold as slaves; the vanquished would perish in tortures. As for flight, what road was open? No people would receive them. Whereas, if they persisted in their efforts, they would obtain at once their liberty, revenge, and money! And they would not be compelled to wait long, since the people of Tunis and the entire of Libya were hurrying to their help.

He displayed the unrolled papyrus, saying, "Look

upon this! Read! Here are their promises! I do not lie!"

Dogs prowled, their black muzzles plastered with red. The high sun heated the bare heads. A nauseous odour exhaled from the imperfectly buried dead; some of the corpses protruded from the ground to their waists. Spendius called them to bear witness to the truth of what he said; then menacingly raised his fists in the direction of Hamilcar.

Mâtho was watching him, and, in order to mask his true cowardice, he made a display of anger, by which he was himself gradually overtaken: he dedicated himself to the Gods, while he heaped curses upon Carthage. "The torture of captives was mere child's-play. Why, therefore, spare them, only to drag after the army these useless cattle? No! we must make an end of them! their projects are known. Only one escaping could betray us! No quarter! The good men will be recognised by the fleetness of their legs, and the strength of their blows."

Then they returned to the captives, many of whom were still in death-throes; they finished them by thrusting their heels into the victims' mouths, or else stabbed them with javelins. Finally they thought of Gisco; no one had seen him anywhere; this caused them uneasiness. All desired to be convinced of his death, and to participate in its consummation. At last three Samnite herdsmen discovered him at twelve paces from the site where recently Mâtho's tent had stood; they recognised him by his long beard, and called the others.

Lying down on his back, his arms against his hips, and his knees pressed together, he had the appearance of one dead, laid out for the sepulchre. However, his thin sides rose and fell, and his eyes opened widely, contrasting with the pallor of his face, as he glared with a fixed, intolerable stare.

At first the Barbarians contemplated him with great astonishment. During the period that he had lived in the pit almost everyone had forgotten him; disturbed by old memories, they kept at a distance, not daring to lift a hand against him.

But those who were behind, murmured and thrust themselves forward; when a Garamantian passed through the crowd, brandishing a sickle, all understood his intent; their faces grew crimson, and seized with shame, they yelled, "Yes! yes!"

The man with the sickle went up to Gisco, took him by the head, and leaning it on his knee, he reaped it with a few rapid strokes; it fell, and two great gushing jets of blood made a hole in the dust. Zarxas had sprung upon it, and, more agile than a leopard, he ran towards the Carthaginians.

Then, when he was two-thirds up the mountain, he pulled Gisco's head from his breast, and holding it by the beard, twirled his arm rapidly many times, and the head finally launched forth, describing a long parabola, and disappeared behind the Punic entrenchment.

Very soon on the edge of the palisades were erected two standards intercrossed, an acknowledged sign for reclaiming the dead. Then four heralds, chosen because of their deep voices, came forward with large clarions, and through the brass trumpets they declared that henceforth there could be nothing more between the Carthaginians and the Barbarians, neither faith, nor pity, nor Gods ; that they refused in advance all overtures, and that all messengers of truce should be returned with their hands cut off.

Immediately afterwards, Spendius was deputed to Hippo-Zarytus, in order to arrange for provisions. The Tyrian city sent them supplies the same evening. They ate greedily ; and when thus comforted, they quickly packed up the remnants of their baggage and their broken weapons, placing the women in the centre, and, without heeding the wounded wailing behind them, they started by the river-bank at a quick march, like a pack of departing wolves.

They marched upon Hippo-Zarytus, deciding to take it, as they very much needed a city.

Hamilcar saw the Barbarians from the distance, and was overtaken with despair, in spite of the pride he felt to see them fly before him. He should have been able to attack them at once with fresh troops. Another such a day, and the war was at an end ! If events dragged, the enemy would return stronger, as the Tyrian cities would doubtless join them. His clemency to the vanquished had served for nothing, therefore he was resolved henceforth to be merciless

The same evening he sent to the Grand Council a dromedary laden with bracelets gathered from the dead enemy; and, with horrible threats, he ordered that they should despatch another army to him.

For a long time all believed him to be lost, so that when they learned of his victory, they experienced a stupefaction that amounted almost to a terror. The vaguely announced return of the Zaimph completed the marvel. Thus the Gods and the strength of Carthage seemed now to belong to Hamilcar.

Not one amongst his enemies dared venture a complaint or a recrimination. By the enthusiasm of his friends, and the pusillanimity of his enemies, before the prescribed time had elapsed an army of five thousand men was ready.

This reinforcement promptly gained Utica to support the Suffete in the rear, while three thousand of the most important citizens embarked on vessels which were to land at Hippo-Zarytus, whence they proposed to drive the Barbarians back.

Hanno had accepted the command, but he confided the army to his lieutenant, Magdassan, in order to conduct the naval forces himself, as, in consequence of his malady, he could no longer endure the jolting of his litter. His disease had eaten away his lips and nostrils, and had thus made a large hole in his face, so that at ten paces the back part of his throat was visible. Knowing himself that he was hideous, he wore a veil, like a woman, to conceal his head.

Hippo-Zarytus heeded not his summons, neither did it that of the Barbarians; but each morning the inhabitants let down to them baskets filled with provisions, and calling from the height of the towers, excused themselves on account of the exigencies of the Republic, and implored them to be gone. They addressed by signs the same protestations to the Carthaginians stationed on the sea.

Hanno contented himself with blockading the port, without risking an attack. Meantime, he persuaded the judges of Hippo-Zarytus to receive in the city three hundred soldiers. Afterwards, he sailed towards the cape of Grapes, making a long detour in order to surround the Barbarians,—an inopportune and even dangerous proceeding. His jealousy hindered him from aiding Hamilcar: he arrested the Suffete's spies, disturbed all his plans, and compromised his enterprise. At length Hamilcar wrote to the Grand Council to relieve Hanno of his command, and he was therefore recalled to Carthage, furious against the baseness of the Elders and the folly of his colleague. Then, after so much hope, they found themselves in a situation even more deplorable; but they all endeavoured not to reflect, and even avoided speaking on the topic.

As if they had not for the time being enough misfortunes, they learned that the Mercenaries of Sardinia had crucified their general, had seized the fortified towns, and everywhere had slain the men of Canaanite race. The Romans threatened the Republic with immediate hostilities if she did not give them twelve hundred talents, with the entire island of Sardinia. Rome had accepted an alliance with the Barbarians, and had sent to them flat boats freighted with flour and dried meats. The Carthaginians pursued them, and captured five hundred men; but, three days later, a fleet coming from the country of Bysancium, carrying provisions to Carthage, foundered in a tempest. The Gods evidently were against Carthage.

Then the citizens of Hippo-Zarytus, feigning an alarm, made Hanno's three hundred men mount on the walls, when they surprised them from behind, seized them by the legs, and suddenly hurled them over the ramparts. Those who were not instantly killed, being pursued, drowned themselves in the sea.

Utica was suffering from the presence of the soldiers, for Magdassan had acted like Hanno, and according to his orders he surrounded the city, deaf to Hamilcar's prayers. His soldiers were given wine mixed with mandrake, and during their sleep, their throats were cut. At the same time the Barbarians arrived, and Magdassan took flight. The gates were opened, and from this moment the two Tyrian cities showed a persistent devotion for their new friends, and an inconceivable hatred for their former allies.

This abandonment of the Punic cause was a warning and an example. Hopes of future deliverance were rekindled. Populations heretofore uncertain, hesitated no more. All gave way. The Suffete learned it, and expected no succour. He was now irrevocably lost.

At once he dismissed Narr' Havas, who had to defend, henceforth, the boundaries of his own kingdom. For his own part he resolved to return to Carthage and obtain soldiers to recommence the war.

The Barbarians established at Hippo-Zarytus perceived his army as it descended the mountain.

Whither were the Carthaginians going? Doubtless hunger drove them; and maddened by their sufferings, despite their weakness, they were coming to offer battle. But they turned to the right: then it must be that they were retreating. They could be reached and utterly crushed. The Barbarians dashed in pursuit.

The Carthaginians were retarded by the stream;

it was swollen wide, and the west wind had not been blowing. Some swam across, others floated on their bucklers, and they resumed their march. Night fell. They could no longer be seen.

However, the Barbarians did not pause, but ascended the stream, searching for a shallow place to ford. The people of Tunis hurried up to help them, bringing those of Utica with them At every clump of bushes their number increased, and the Carthaginians, lying on the ground, could hear the tramp of feet in the darkness. From time to time, in order to make their pursuers slacken their pace, Barca fired back upon them a volley of arrows, thereby killing many. When day broke they were in the Mountains of Ariana, at the point where the road made an elbow.

Then Mâtho, marching at the head of his troops, believed that he distinguished in the horizon something green on the summit of an eminence. The earth sloped; obelisks, domes, and houses appeared! It was Carthage! His heart beat so furiously, that he supported himself against a tree to keep from falling.

He thought of all that had happened in his existence since the last time that he had passed there ' It was an infinite surprise, an amazement. Then a joy carried him away at the idea that he should again see Salammbô. His past reasons for execrating her now flooded his memory, but he peremptorily rejected them. Quivering in every fibre, and with straining eyes, he contemplated beyond Eschmoûn the high terrace of a palace above the palms. An ecstatic smile illumined his face, as though some great radiant light had fallen over him; he opened his arms, and sent kisses on the breeze, murmuring, "Come! Come!" A sigh swelled his bosom, and two tears, long, like pearls, fell upon his beard.

"What restrains you?" cried Spendius. "Hasten! March on! The Suffete will escape us! But your knees shake, and you look to me like a drunken man!"

Stamping his feet with impatience, he urged Mâtho to advance, and blinking his eyes, as at the approach to an end seen far away, he cried: "Ah! we are there! We are there! I hold them!"

He had such a convincing, triumphant manner, that Mâtho, surprised out of his torpor, felt himself drawn on. These words coming unexpectedly in the crisis of his distress, drove his despair to vengeance, and opened a field for his wrath. He sprang on one of the camels in the baggage train, tore off the halter, and with the long cord he struck with his full force the laggards, running alternately from right to left in the rear of the troops, like a dog driving a flock.

At his voice of thunder the men closed up the lines, and those on crutches hastened their steps: half-way across the isthmus the interval diminished. Then the vanguard of the Barbarians marched in the dust of the Carthaginians. The two armies drew nearer and nearer, until they almost touched. But the gates of Malqua and Tagaste, and the great gate of Khamoûn, spread open their ponderous valves. The Punic squares divided; three columns were therein swallowed up and eddied under the porches. Soon the masses closed in too much upon themselves, and were choked in the entrances, so that they could not advance. Spears struck against spears in the air, and the Barbarians' arrows splintered against the walls.

Hamilcar was seen on the threshold of Khamoûn; he turned, and cried to his men to scatter; then he dismounted, and with his sword pricked his horse on the crupper, letting him loose upon the Barbarians. It was an Orynx stallion, nourished on balls of flour, and so well trained that he would bend his knees to permit his master to mount him. Why, then, did he thus send away this fine animal? Was this a sacrifice?

The noble horse galloped amidst the lances, knocking over the men, and entangling his feet in their entrails; he fell down, then struggled up on his feet with furious bounds; and while they scattered, endeavoured to arrest him, or looked at him full of surprise, the Carthaginians rejoined their lines and entered the enormous gate, that resoundingly reclosed behind them.

It did not yield; the Barbarians plunged and battered against it; and during the lapse of some minutes the entire length of the army presented an oscillation that became gentler and gentler, and at last entirely subsided.

The Carthaginians having stationed soldiers on the aqueduct, commenced hurling stones, balls, and beams. Spendius averred that it was useless to persist; therefore they pitched their encampment at a greater distance from the walls, fully resolved to besiege Carthage.

Meanwhile the rumour of the war had travelled

beyond the confines of the Punic dominion; and from the Pillars of Hercules, as far as the other side of Cyrene, the herdsmen guarding their herds dreamed of it, and the caravans talked about it at night in the starlight. This grand Carthage, Mistress of the Sea, splendid as the sun, awful as a God, had found men who dared to attack her! Even her downfall had frequently been reported, and all had believed it probable, as all were longing for it, —the subject peoples, tributary villages, allied provinces, and independent tribes: those who cursed her for her tyranny, or who were jealous of her power, or who coveted her wealth.

The bravest had very quickly joined themselves to the Mercenaries. The defeat at the Macar, however, prevented all the others. Finally they regained confidence, and gradually making advances, had come nearer; and now the inhabitants of the eastern regions had posted themselves in the sand-hills of Clypea, on the other side of the gulf.

As soon as the Barbarians appeared, they showed themselves.

These were not the Libyans from the environs of Carthage, who had for a long time constituted the third army, but the Nomads from the plateau of Barca, bandits of the cape of Phiscus and the promontory of Derne, and those from Phazania and from Marmarica. They had crossed the desert, sustaining themselves by drinking from the brackish wells built of camels' bones: the Zuæces, covered with ostrich plumes, had come in their quadrigæ; the Garamantes, masked with black veils, riding far back on their painted mares; others mounted on asses on onagers, on zebras, or on buffaloes; and some dragged the roofs of their cabins, shaped like a shallop, with their families and idols.

There were also Ammonians, whose limbs were wrinkled by the hot water of the fountains; the Atarantes, who cursed the sun; the Troglodytes, who laughingly interred their dead under branches of trees; and the hideous Auseans, who ate locusts; the Achrymachidas, who ate lice; and the Gysantes, painted over with vermilion, and who ate monkeys.

All were ranged on the sea-coast in a great, straight line. They advanced in succession, like whirlwinds of sand raised by the wind. In the middle of the isthmus their crowd stopped; the Mercenaries established before them near the walls did not wish to move.

Then from the direction of Ariana appeared men from the west, the people of Numidia,—for, in fact, Narr' Havas only governed the Massylians; and furthermore, a custom permitting them after a reverse to abandon their king, they had reassembled on the Zainus, then at the first movement Hamilcar had made, they had crossed it. First were seen running all the hunters of the Malethut-Baal and of the Garaphos, clothed in lions' skins, and driving with the shafts of their pikes little, thin horses with long manes; following these came the Gaetulians, encased in breast-plates made of serpents' skins; then the Pharusians, wearing tall crowns made of wax and resin; these were followed by the Caunians, Macares, and Tillabares, each holding two javelins and a round buckler of hippopotamus hide. They halted at the base of the Catacombs, near the first pools of the Lagoon.

But when the Libyans had moved off, on the ground that they had occupied there appeared, like a cloud, lying flat on the earth, a multitude of Negroes: they had come from White-Haroush and Black-Haroush, from the desert of Augila, and even from the vast country of Agazymba, which was four months' journey to the south of the Garamantes, and even more distant! In spite of their redwood ornaments, the filth on their black skins made them resemble mulberries that had been rolled a long time in the dust.

They wore breeches made from the fibres of bark, tunics of dried grass, and on their heads the muzzles of wild animals: they howled like wolves, shaking triangles ornamented with dangling rings, and brandished cow-tails on the end of a pole by way of banners.

Behind the Numidians, the Maurusians, and the Gaetulians, thronged the yellow men who were scattered over the country beyond Taggir in the cedar forests. Cat-skin quivers beat over their shoulders, and they led in leashes enormous dogs as tall as asses, which never barked.

In short, as if Africa had not sufficiently emptied itself, and in order to gather up more furies, they had even recruited the lowest races: in the rear of all the others could be seen men with profiles of animals, who laughed in an idiotic manner, wretches ravaged by hideous diseases, deformed pigmies, mulattoes of doubtful sex, Albinos blinking their pink eyes in the sunlight,—all stammering unintelligible sounds, and putting a finger in their mouths to signify their hunger. The medley of weapons was not less confused than the people, or their apparel. Not a deadly invention that could not be found here, from wooden poniards, stone battle-axes, ivory tridents, to long sabres toothed like saws, slender, and made of a pliable sheet of copper. They wielded cutlasses divided in many branches, like antelopes' horns; they carried bill-hooks attached to cords, iron triangles, clubs and stilettoes.

The Ethiopians of Bambotus hid in their hair tiny poisoned darts. Many had brought stones in sacks; others, who were empty-handed, gnashed their teeth.

A continual surging swayed this multitude. Dromedaries, daubed with tar like the hulls of ships, upset the women who carried their children on their hips. Provisions were spilled out of their baskets; and in walking one stepped on morsels of rock salt, packages of gum, rotten dates, and gourou-nuts. Sometimes on a bosom alive with vermin could be seen, suspended from a fine cord, a diamond, a fabulous gem worth an entire empire, which satraps had coveted. The majority of these people did not know what they desired: a fascination, a curiosity impelled them: the Nomads, who had never seen a city, were frightened by the vast shadows cast by the massive walls.

Now the isthmus was obscured by this multitude of men, and the long span of tents, resembling cabins during an inundation, spread out to the first lines of the other Barbarians, who were streaming with metal, and symmetrically established on the two flanks of the aqueduct.

The Carthaginians were still in terror of those who had already arrived, when they perceived coming straight towards the city, like monsters, and like edifices, with their shafts, weapons, cordage, articulations, capitals, and carapaces—the engines sent for the siege by the Tyrian cities: sixty *carrobalistas*, eighty onagers, thirty *scorpions*, fifty *tollenones*, twelve rams, and three gigantic catapults, with the capacity of throwing rocks weighing fifteen talents.

Masses of men clutched at their base, pushed, pulled, and toiled to propel the engines, that quivered and shook at each step: thus they came in front of the walls.

But it would still require many days to complete the preparations for the siege. The Mercenaries, forewarned by their previous defeats, did not wish to risk themselves in fruitless engagements; and on neither one side nor the other was there any hurry, as all knew that a terrible action was about to ensue, which would result either in victory or complete extermination.

Carthage could hold out for a long time; her broad walls offered a series of salient and re-entering angles—an arrangement full of advantages for repelling an assault.

However, on the side of the Catacombs a portion of the wall had crumbled; and during obscure nights, between the disjointed blocks could be seen the lights in the dens of Malqua. In certain places they overlooked the top of the ramparts, and here lived those who had taken for new wives the women of the Mercenaries chased by Mâtho out of the camp. When the women saw again their own people, their hearts melted, and they waved from afar long scarves; then they came in the darkness to chat with the soldiers through the rift in the walls, and the Grand Council were apprised one morning that they had all taken flight. Some had crawled between the stones; others, more intrepid, had descended by ropes.

Spendius finally resolved to accomplish his cherished project.

The war, by keeping him at a distance, had, up to the present, debarred him from it; and since they had returned before Carthage, it seemed to him that the townsmen suspected his enterprise; but soon they diminished the sentinels on the aqueduct, as they did not possess too many guards for the defence of the enceinte. During many days the former slave practised aiming arrows at the flamingoes standing on the lake shore. Then one evening, when the moon shone bright, he entreated Mâtho to have lighted during the middle of the night a huge bonfire of straw, and cause all his men simultaneously to utter shrieks; then taking Zarxas, he went off by the shore of the gulf in the direction of Tunis.

When abreast of the last arches, they turned back, going straight towards the aqueduct. As the road was exposed, they advanced, creeping along up to the base of the pillars. The sentinels on the platform patrolled tranquilly.

High flames darted up; clarions were sounded. The soldiers in the watch-towers, believing that it was an assault, rushed towards Carthage.

One man remained. He appeared as a black figure against the dome of the sky; the moonlight was behind him, and his disproportionate shadow fell afar on the plain, like a moving obelisk. They waited until he was exactly in front of them. Zarxas seized his sling, but Spendius stayed him, actuated by prudence or ferocity, and whispered: "No! the whirring of the ball will make a noise! I will do it!" Then he strung his bow with all his might supporting the end against his left instep, took aim and the fatal arrow flew.

The man did not fall. He disappeared.

"If he were wounded we should hear him," said Spendius, and he sprang fleetly up, story after story, as he had done the first time, by the aid of the harpoon and cord, and when he reached the top, beside the corpse, he let the cord fall. The Balearian fastened to it a pick and mallet, and returned. The trumpets no longer sounded: all had subsided into perfect quiet. Spendius had lifted one of the stones, entered the water, and replaced the stone over himself.

Estimating the distance by paces, he came exactly to the spot where he had previously noticed a slanting fissure, and for three hours—in fact, till morning—he worked in a continuous, furious way, breathing with great difficulty through the interstices of the superior stones; assailed with violent pains, twenty times he believed he was dying.

At last a cracking was heard, an enormous stone bounded on the inferior arches and rolled down to the bottom—and all at once a cataract, an entire river of great volume, fell as from the sky into the plain! The aqueduct, cut in the middle, was emptying itself. This was the death of Carthage and the victory of the Barbarians.

In an instant, the Carthaginians, aroused in terror, appeared on the walls, the house-tops, and on the temples. The Barbarians gave vent to joyous shouts, danced around the vast waterfall in delirium, and in the extravagance of their delight wetted their heads in the rushing water.

At the summit of the aqueduct a man was perceived wearing a torn, brown tunic, leaning over the edge, his hands upon his hips, gazing beneath him to the very bottom, as though astonished at his own work.

Then he stood erect, traversing the horizon with a proud, impressive air, which seemed to say—"Behold! this is all my work!" Applause burst from the Barbarians. At last the Carthaginians comprehended the cause of their disaster, and howled in despair. Spendius ran from end to end of the platform, distracted by pride, raising his arms, like the driver of a victorious chariot in the Olympian games.

CHAPTER XIII.

MOLOCH.

The Barbarians had no need to circumvallate on the side toward Africa, as it belonged to them. But to render the approach to the walls easier, they pulled down the entrenchments bordering the moat. Afterwards Mâtho divided the army into large semi-circles, as a method to more effectually beleaguer Carthage. The hoplites of the Mercenaries were stationed in the front rank; behind them, the slingers and cavalry; at the rear, the baggage, the chariots, and the horses; and in front of this multitude, at three hundred paces from the towers, bristled the war-engines, designated by an infinity of names that changed frequently in the course of ages; however, they could always be reduced to two systems—those which acted like slings, and the others which operated like bows.

The first, the catapults, were composed of a square frame with two vertical standards and a horizontal bar at the top. At its anterior portion a cylinder wound with cables held down a large beam carrying a ladle to receive the projectiles; the base of the beam was caught in a hank of twisted horse-hair; and when the cords were loosened, the beam flew up, struck against the bar, which, checking it by a sudden shock, multiplied its force.

The second system offered a more complicated mechanism. On a small column a cross-piece was fixed by its centre, where ended a channel at right angles to it: at the ends of the cross-piece rose two frames, which contained a twisted hank of hair: two small beams were fastened therein to hold the ends of the cord, which was drawn to the bottom of the channel over a bronze tablet; by a spring, this plate of metal was detached, and sliding over grooves, drove out the arrows in all directions.

Catapults were as frequently called onagers, because they were like wild asses which threw stones by kicking; and the ballistas were called scorpions because of a hook fastened on the tablet, which, on being lowered with a blow, disengaged the spring.

Their construction required the calculations of experts. The timber must be selected of the hardest grain; the gearing was all of brass. They were tautened with levers, pulleys, capstans, or drums; strong pivots changed the direction of their aim. They were moved forward on cylinders; and those of the largest size, which were transported in sections, were remounted in front of the enemy.

Spendius placed the three large catapults to face the three principal angles; before each gate he placed a ram, before each tower a ballista; and farther back were wheeled the *carrobalistæ*. But it was necessary to preserve them from being fired by the besieged, and also to fill up the moat which separated them from the walls.

They pushed forward galleries made of green wattles and oaken ribs, like enormous bucklers sliding on three wheels; little cabins, covered with fresh hides and padded with wrack, sheltered the workmen. The catapults and ballistas were protected by curtains of cordage that had been soaked in vinegar to render them incombustible.

The women and the children went to the beach to gather stones, which they collected with their hands and brought to the soldiers.

The Carthaginians also made preparations for the siege.

Hamilcar had very quickly reassured them, by declaring that there yet remained enough water for one hundred and twenty-three days. This affirmation, his presence in their midst, and that of the Zaimph, above all, imparted great hope. Carthage recovered from her dejection, and those who were not of Canaanite origin were carried away by the passion of the others.

The slaves were armed, the arsenals were emptied, each citizen had his allotted post and employment. Twelve hundred men survived of the refugees: the Suffete made them all captains; and the carpenters, armourers, blacksmiths, and the silversmiths were appointed to superintend the engines. The Carthaginians had retained some of these implements, notwithstanding the conditions of the Roman peace. Understanding their construction, they repaired them readily.

The northern and eastern sides, being protected by

the sea and the gulf, were inaccessible. On the wall facing the Barbarians were placed trunks of trees, mill-stones, vases full of sulphur, and vats full of oil, and furnaces were built. Stones were heaped up on the platforms of the towers, and the houses immediately adjoining the rampart were crammed with sand to increase its strength and thickness.

The sight of all these preparations irritated the Barbarians. They desired to engage in combat at once. The weights they put into the catapults were of such an exorbitant size that the beams broke, thereby retarding the attack.

Finally, on the thirteenth day of the month of Schabar, at sunrise, a tremendous bang was heard at the gate of Khamoûn.

Seventy-five soldiers were hauling ropes arranged at the base of a gigantic beam horizontally suspended by chains, descending from a gallows, and terminating in a brazen ram's head It was swaddled in hides; bands of iron encircled it from place to place, and it was three times larger than a man's body, one hundred and twenty cubits long, and advanced or receded under the crowd of naked arms, pushing it forward or hauling it backwards, with a regular swing.

The rams before the other gates also began to move, and in the hollow wheels of the drums men could be seen going up step by step. Pulleys and capitals creaked; the cordage screens were lowered, and volleys of stones and arrows simultaneously shot forth. All the scattered slingers ran up; some of them approached the ramparts, carrying hidden under their shields pots of ignited resin; then they hurled them with all their might upon the enemy. This terrific hail of balls, darts, and fire passed beyond the front ranks, and made a curve which fell within the walls. But on their summits were erected huge cranes used for masting vessels; from them descended enormous pinchers, which ended in two semicircles, toothed on the inside edge. These bit fast to the rams. The soldiers, clinging to the beam, dragged it back. The Carthaginians panted in their efforts to draw it up, and the struggle continued till evening.

When the Mercenaries resumed their task the next day they found the top of the walls entirely hung with bales of cotton, cloth, and cushions; the battlements were closed with mattings, and between the cranes could be distinguished lines of pitchforks and sharp blades set in sticks. Immediately a furious resistance began.

Tree-trunks fastened to cables fell and rose alternately, battering the rams; grappling-irons shot past the ballistas, and tore off the roofs of the cabins; and from the platforms of the towers torrents of flint and pebbles poured down.

At length the rams burst the gate of Khamoûn and that of Tagaste; but the Carthaginians had heaped the inner side with such an abundance of materials that the valves could not open: they remained upright.

Tenebras were then forced against the walls, and applied to the joints of the massive blocks until they were loosened. The engines were governed the better because their crews worked in relays; from morning till evening they plied uninterruptedly, with the monotonous precision of a weaver's loom.

Spendius never wearied managing these engines. He personally tautened the cordage of the ballistas. In order that there should be an exact equality in their twin tensions, their cords were wound up and tapped in turn on the right and left side till both sounded in unison. He mounted on their frames, and delicately tapped them with the end of his foot, bending his ear, like a musician tuning a lyre. Then when the beam of the catapult rose, when the columns of the ballista trembled at the shock of the spring, as the stones poured out in streams, and the arrows darted forth like rays, he leaned his entire body over the platform, throwing his arms up in the air, as if he would follow the flight of the missiles.

Admiring his skill, the soldiers willingly executed his orders. In the gaiety of their labour they made jokes on the names of the engines. Thus the pinchers for seizing the rams were called wolves, and the covered galleries, vines; they were lambs, they were going to the vintage; and in loading their pieces they said to the onagers, "Go now, kick well!"—and to the scorpions, "Go through the enemies' hearts!" This facetiousness, always the same, sustained their courage.

However, the engines did not demolish the rampart. It was formed of a double wall and filled with earth; they battered down its upper works, but the besieged each time built them up again. Mâtho ordered the construction of wooden towers of an equal height with the enemies' stone towers. Into the moat were thrown turf, stakes, and chariots with the wheels on, to fill it up more rapidly; before it was full the immense crowd of Barbarians undulated over the plain in a single movement, and advanced to batter the base of the walls like an inundating sea.

They brought forward rope-ladders, straight ladders, and *sambucæ*, which were composed of two masts from which were lowered by tackles a series of bamboos ending in a movable bridge. They were all ranged in numerous straight lines, supported against the walls, and the Mercenaries in file, one after another, mounted, holding their weapons in their hands. Not one Carthaginian was espied until they had attained two-thirds of the height of the ramparts. Then the battlements opened, vomiting forth like dragons' jaws fire and smoke; sand scattered, filtering through the joints of their armour; the petroleum adhered to their clothing, the molten lead skipped over their helmets, burning cruel holes in their flesh; a shower of sparks flashed into their faces,—and orbits without eyes seemed to weep tears as large as almonds. The hair of some men, yellow with oil, was blazing. They started to run, and set the others on fire. From a distance cloaks soaked in blood were thrown over their faces and extinguished the flames. Some who were not wounded remained motionless, stiffer than stakes, with open mouth and both arms thrown out.

For many successive days the assault continued, and the Mercenaries hoped to triumph by excess of force and audacity.

Sometimes a man, standing on the shoulders of

another, drove an iron pin between the seams of the stones to serve as a step to reach higher, where he drove a second, and a third, and so on, protected by the overhanging eaves of the battlements; by this means they gradually climbed up: but ever at a certain height they were smitten and fell.

Presently the broad ditch became so full of human beings that it overflowed; under the feet of the living the wounded were heaped pell-mell with the dead and dying. Amid entrails, oozing brains, and pools of blood, calcined trunks made black spots; arms and legs, half protruding from a heap, stood straight upright like vine-stakes in a burnt vineyard.

As the ladders proved insufficient, they employed the *tollenones*—instruments constructed with a long beam placed transversely on an upright post, and carrying at the extremity a square basket, in which thirty foot-soldiers fully equipped could be held.

Mâtho wanted to go up in the first that was ready, but Spendius prevented him.

Men turned a small wheel, and responsively the large beam became horizontal, then appeared almost vertical; but being too heavily laden at the end, it bent like a reed. The soldiers, concealed up to their chins, crowded together; nothing but the plumes waving over their helmets could be seen. Finally, when the basket was fifty cubits in the air, it swayed from right to left several times, then fell; and like the arm of a giant holding on his hand a cohort of pigmies, it deposited on the edge of the wall the basketful of men, who leaped out in the midst of the enemies, but never returned.

All the other *tollenones* were speedily stationed; but it would require a hundred times as many to take the city. They were utilised in a murderous manner: Ethiopian archers were stationed in the baskets; then the cables were so adjusted that they should remain suspended mid-air, while the occupants fired upon the foe poisoned arrows. The fifty *tollenones* thus dominated the battlements surrounding Carthage like monstrous vultures, and the Negroes laughed to see the guards on the ramparts die in horrible convulsions.

Hamilcar immediately despatched hoplites thither, and made them each morning drink the juices of certain herbs which were well-known antidotes for poisons.

One evening, during a dark period, Hamilcar embarked the best of his soldiers on lighters and rafts, and turned to the right of the port, landing on the Tænia. From thence they advanced as far as the first lines of the Barbarians, and, taking them in the flank, made a terrible carnage. Men suspended by ropes descended the walls during the night, and set fire to the Mercenaries' works, and remounted in safety.

Mâtho was enraged; each obstacle, in fact, plunged him deeper in wrath; terrible and extravagant things befell him. Mentally he entreated Salammbô for a rendezvous; then waited for her. She did not come: this was a new treason, and henceforth he cursed her. And perhaps if he had seen her dead body he might have gone away.

He doubled his outposts, planted pitchforks at the base of the rampart, buried caltrops in the ground, and commanded the Libyans to bring to him an entire forest, in order to set fire to Carthage and burn it like a den of foxes.

Spendius persisted in the siege, seeking to invent frightful machines such as had never been constructed before. The other Barbarians who were encamped at a distance on the isthmus were amazed at these delays. They murmured; they were let loose.

Then they rushed forward, battering against the gates with their cutlasses and javelins. But the nakedness of their bodies made it easy to wound them, and the Carthaginians freely massacred them, while the Mercenaries exulted over it, doubtless from greed of the plunder. There resulted quarrels and fights between themselves. The country being now laid waste, stung by hunger they soon wrested the provisions from each other. They became discouraged. Numerous hordes went away; but the crowd was so dense that their absence was not noticed.

The best of the men endeavoured to dig mines; the ground, badly propped, caved in; then they would begin again elsewhere. Hamilcar always discovered the direction of their operations by applying his ear to a bronze buckler. He dug counter-mines under the road over which the wooden towers had to be wheeled, so that when they were moved they would be buried in the holes.

At length all acknowledged that the city was impregnable unless they erected a long terrace to the height of the city walls, which should permit them to combat on the same level; the top should be paved, in order to facilitate the shifting of the engines. Then it would be impossible for Carthage to resist.

Carthage began to suffer from thirst. Water valued at the outbreak of the siege at two *kesitah* a barrel sold now for a shekel of silver. The supplies of meat and grain were also being exhausted ; they feared a famine ; some even talked of useless mouths, which terrified everyone.

From the square of Khamoûn as far as the temple of Melkarth, corpses encumbered the streets ; and as it was the end of summer, large black flies tormented the combatants. Old men transported the wounded off the field, and the devout people continually performed fictitious funeral rites for their relatives and friends deceased far away during the wars. Statues of wax with hair and clothes were laid out before the house entrances. These images were melted by the heat of the tapers burning close to them, and the paint trickled down over their shoulders ; and tears coursed the cheeks of the living as they intoned lugubrious hymns beside these effigies. During these times the crowd ever ran hither and thither ; troops were constantly in motion ; captains shouted orders, and the shocks of the rams battering the rampart were incessantly heard.

The temperature became so heavy that the dead were too swollen to be placed in the coffins, and were burned in the middle of the courts. But these fires in the too confined spaces ignited the neighbouring walls, and long flames suddenly escaped from the houses, like blood spurting from an open artery. Thus Moloch possessed Carthage, he embraced the ramparts, he rolled through the streets, he even devoured the dead.

Men who wore in sign of despair mantles of rags, picked up anywhere, stationed themselves at the convergence of the streets, declaiming against the Elders and against Hamilcar, predicting total ruin for the entire people, and inviting them to general destruction and licence. The most dangerous were the drinkers of henbane, who in their crises fancied themselves to be wild beasts, and sprang upon the passers-by, whom they mangled cruelly. Mobs collected around them, forgetting the defence of Carthage. The Suffete conceived the idea of paying others of their class to support his policy.

In order to retain the Genii of the Gods in the city, their images were covered with chains, black veils were thrown over the *Dii Patæci*, and sackcloth around the altars. Some endeavoured to excite the pride and jealousy of the Baals by dinning in their ears, "You will be conquered! The other Gods are more powerful than you, perhaps! Show your power! Aid us! in order that the peoples may not say, 'Where are now their Gods?'"

A constant anxiety disturbed the pontiffs; those of Rabbetna were especially frightened, for the re-establishment of the Zaïmph had not sufficed; they remained sequestered in the third enclosure, as inexpugnable as a forest; only one of their number, the high priest, Schahabarim, risked going outside.

He went to Salammbô's palace, but remained silent, ever contemplating her with fixed gaze; or else lavished upon her words of reproach, harder than ever.

By an inconceivable contradiction, he did not pardon this young girl for having followed his orders. Schahabarim had divined all—and this besetting idea heightened the jealousy of his impotency. He accused her of being the cause of the war. Mâtho, according to his account, was besieging Carthage to recapture the Zaimph; and he poured forth imprecations and sarcasms upon this Barbarian for essaying to possess sacred objects. That, however, was not what the priest wanted to say.

At this period Salammbô did not experience any terror of the priest. The agonies she formerly suffered had all vanished, being now replaced by an ineffable tranquillity; even her gaze was less wandering, and burned with a limpid light.

Meanwhile the Python had again fallen ill, and as, on the contrary, Salammbô appeared to improve, the aged Taanach rejoiced over it, feeling sure that by its decline it had taken the weakness from her mistress.

One morning the slave found it behind the cowhide couch, coiled up on itself, colder than marble, its head hidden under a mass of worms. At her screams Salammbô came, and turned it over for some time with the toe of her sandal; her indifference amazed the slave.

Hamilcar's daughter no longer prolonged her fasts with her former fervour or rigour. She spent her days on the top of her terrace, leaning on her elbows over the balustrade, amusing herself watching the objects before her. The top of the walls at the end of the city cut against the sky irregular zig-zags, and the sentinels' lances all along looked like a border of

Y

spikes. She could see beyond, between the towers, the manœuvres of the Barbarians. On the days when the siege was suspended she could even distinguish their occupations, as they mended their weapons, or oiled their hair, or washed their bloody arms in the sea. Their tents were closed, and the beasts of burden were eating; and far away the scythes of the chariot wheels, ranged in a semicircle, seemed like a silver scimitar extended at the base of the hills.

Schahabarim's discourses revolved through her brain. She waited for her betrothed, Narr' Havas. Despite her hatred, she had a lurking wish to see Mâtho again. Of all the Carthaginians, she was, perhaps, the only person who had spoken to him without fear.

Frequently her father came into her room and sat on the cushions, considering her with an air almost tender, as though he found in the spectacle an immunity from his fatigues. Sometimes he interrogated her as to the incidents of her journey to the camp of the Mercenaries, asking her if no one had by chance compelled her to go thither; and with a shake of the head, she answered, "No," so proud was Salammbô of having rescued the Zaïmph.

But the Suffete always reverted to Mâtho, under the pretext of acquiring military information. He could not comprehend how she had employed the hours passed in his tent. In fact, Salammbô did not speak of Gisco; for as words contain in themselves an effective power, curses that are repeated to anyone else might return to their detriment. She likewise kept silent concerning her desire to assassinate

Mâtho, fearful lest she should be censured for not having yielded to it. She said that the *Schalischim* appeared furious, that he had shouted a good deal, and afterwards went to sleep. Salammbô told nothing more about it, perhaps from shame, or possibly from an excess of innocence, which did not allow her to attach any importance to the kisses of the soldier. Besides, it all floated through her melancholy and misty brain like the remembrance of an overwhelming dream, and she would not have known in what manner or by what words to express it.

One evening, when father and daughter were thus facing each other in conversation, Taanach, all amazement, entered, announcing that an old man, accompanied by a child, was in the courts, and wanted to see the Suffete.

Hamilcar turned pale, but promptly replied:

"Let him come up."

Iddibal entered, without prostrating himself, holding by the hand a young boy covered with a cloak of goat's skin, and at once raising the hood which concealed the boy's face, said:

"Here he is, master! Take him!"

The Suffete and the slave retired to a corner. The boy remained standing in the middle of the room with a gaze more attentive than astonished: he looked at the ceiling, the furniture, the pearl collars hung over purple draperies, and at the majestic young woman who leaned forward towards him.

He was, perhaps, ten years old, and no taller than a Roman sword; his curly hair overshadowed his convex forehead; his eyes seemed to penetrate space;

his thin nostrils dilated widely, and over all his person spread that indefinable splendour belonging to those beings destined for grand careers. When he had thrown aside his heavy cloak, he remained clad in a lynx-skin fastened around his body, and stood resolutely pressing his small, bare feet, white with dust, upon the pavement. Doubtless he surmised that important topics were being discussed by those present, as he maintained a motionless posture, holding one hand behind his back, his chin lowered on his breast, with one finger in his mouth.

At last Hamilcar attracted Salammbô's attention by a sign, and said in a low voice to her:

"Keep him with you. Do you understand? No one, not even of the household, must know of his existence."

Then retiring behind the door, he again asked Iddibal if he was certain that no one had noticed them.

"No one," said the slave; "the streets were deserted."

As the war filled all the provinces with danger, he had feared for the safety of his master's son. Then, not knowing where to securely hide him, Iddibal had brought him along the coast in a shallop, and for three days they had cruised about in the gulf, watching the ramparts; finally, upon this evening, when the neighbourhood of Khamoûn seemed deserted, he had ventured to slowly cross the channel and land in the vicinity of the arsenal, —the entrance to the port being free to all.

But soon the Barbarians established, opposite the port, an immense raft, to prevent the Carthaginians leaving it. They threw up the proposed terrace, and erected the wooden towers.

Communication between the city and the outside was intercepted, and an intolerable famine began.

All the dogs, mules, and asses were killed; afterwards the fifteen elephants that the Suffete had brought back. The lions of the temple of Moloch became furious, and the keepers no longer dared approach them; at first they were fed with wounded Barbarians; then corpses yet warm were thrown to them; but these they refused; and finally they all perished. At twilight people wandered along the old enclosures, plucking from between the stones grasses and flowers, which they boiled in wine, as wine was less costly than water. Others slipped up to the advanced posts of the enemy, and, crawling under the tents, stole food. Sometimes the Barbarians were so stupefied by this audacity that they permitted them to get away unmolested.

At length a day came when the Elders resolved between themselves to slaughter the horses of Eschmoûn, the sacred animals in whose manes the Pontiffs braided gold ribbons, and whose existence signified the movements of the sun—the idea of fire under its most exalted form. Their flesh was divided into equal portions, and secreted behind the altar; then every evening the Elders, alleging some religious service, ascended to the temple, regaled themselves in secret, and brought back, concealed under their tunics, some morsels for their children.

In the deserted quarters far from the walls, the less miserable inhabitants, from fear of the rest, had barricaded themselves.

The stones from the catapults, and the demolitions ordered for their defences, had accumulated heaps of ruins in the streets.

During the most tranquil hours, masses of people suddenly rushed out, yelling at the top of their voices; and from the summit of the Acropolis fires appeared, like purple rags contorted by the wind, dispersed over the terraces.

The three great catapults did not stop: their ravages were extraordinary; for instance, a man's head rebounded on the pediment of the Syssites; in the street of Kinisdo a woman in accouchement was crushed by a block of marble, and her infant, with her couch, were carried as far as the forum of Cynasyn, where the coverlet was found.

The slingers' balls proved to be the most vexatious missiles; these fell upon the roofs, into gardens, and the middle of courtyards, while the people were at table before their meagre repasts, with their hearts swollen with anguish. These atrocious projectiles were engraved with letters that left an imprint on the victim's flesh; on the dead could be read such appellations as "*swine*," "*jackal*," "*vermin*," and sometimes such pleasantries as "*catch!*" or "*I have quite merited it!*"

That portion of the rampart extending from the angle of the ports abreast of the cisterns was battered in. Then the people of Malqua found themselves caught between the old enceinte of Byrsa in the rear, and the Barbarians in front. Hamilcar had enough to do to strengthen the wall and raise it as high as possible, without troubling himself about the emergencies of these people. They were abandoned, and all perished; and although they were generally hated, in consequence of this calamity the Carthaginians conceived a great horror for Hamilcar.

The following day he opened the pits wherein he had stored his corn: his intendants gave it freely to the people, and for three days they gorged themselves. However, their thirst only became more intolerable, and they always saw before them the long cascade of pure water falling from the aqueduct: while under the sunshine, the fine mist floated up from its base with a rainbow beside it, and a little serpentine stream flowed over the plain and into the gulf.

Hamilcar did not give way, for he was counting upon an event—something decisive and extraordinary. His own slaves tore off the silver plates from the temple of Melkarth. Four long boats were taken from the port and dragged by means of capstans to the foot of Mappals, the wall abutting on the shore was pierced, and they departed to Gallia, to hire Mercenary soldiers, no matter at what price.

In the meantime Hamilcar was disturbed, because he could not communicate with the Numidian king, as he knew full well that he was stationed behind the Barbarians, and ready to fall upon them. But Narr' Havas's forces were too weak to risk making an attack alone.

The Suffete caused the rampart to be heightened twelve palms, all the munitions of war in the arsenals to be collected in the Acropolis, and the engines to be repaired once more.

They were wont to use for the cordage of the catapults tendons taken from the necks of bulls, or else from the legs of stags; but in Carthage there no longer existed either bulls or stags, therefore Hamilcar demanded from the Elders their wives' tresses; and though all made the sacrifice, the quantity was insufficient. There were, in the buildings of the Syssites, twelve hundred marriageable slaves, destined for the brothels of Greece and Italy, whose hair had become peculiarly elastic from the constant use of unguents, and was admirably suited for the war machines. But later on the loss would be too considerable. Then it was determined to select the finest heads of hair among the wives of the plebeians. Regardless of their country's needs, all the women cried out in despair when the servitors of the Hundred came with scissors to lay hands upon them.

A redoubled fury animated the Barbarians, for from a distance they could be seen taking out the fat from the dead bodies, to oil their machines, and pulling out the finger and toe nails of the corpses, which they sewed one over-lapping another, to make breastplates for themselves.

They conceived the idea of charging their catapults with vases full of vipers brought by the Negroes; these clay vessels shattered, in falling upon the paving-stones, and the serpents crawling about were so numerous that they seemed to swarm, and to come naturally out of the walls. Discontented with this invention, they perfected it, and threw all kinds of filth—such as human excrement, morsels of carrion, and corpses—upon their enemy. The plague broke out. The teeth of the Carthaginians dropped out, and their gums became colourless, like those of the camels after a too protracted journey.

The Barbarians' war machines were mounted upon the new terrace, even though it failed as yet to attain at every point the height of the rampart. In front of the twenty-three towers on the fortifications were erected twenty-three wooden towers; all the *tollenones* were remounted, and in the centre, a little further back, loomed up the formidable *helepolis* of Demetrius Poliorcetes, which Spendius had at last reconstructed. Pyramidal, like the lighthouse at Alexandria, it was one hundred and thirty cubits high and twenty-three wide, with nine stages that diminished towards the top, and were protected by brass scales pierced by numerous sally-ports, and filled with soldiers; on the topmost stage a catapult flanked by two ballistas was erected.

Hamilcar planted crosses upon which to crucify all those who talked of surrender. Even the women were formed in brigades. People slept in the streets, and wailed, full of anguish.

Then one morning, a little before sunrise, on the seventh day of the month of Nyssan, they heard a loud cry uttered simultaneously by all the Barbarians; the lead trumpets blared, and the great Paphlagonian horns bellowed like bulls. There was a universal rush for the rampart.

A forest of lances, pikes, and spears bristled at its base; it leaped against the walls, ladders were grappled on, and in the openings of the battlements Barbarians' heads appeared.

Beams, carried by long files of men, battered the

gates; and in spots where the terrace was wanting, the Mercenaries, in order to breach the wall, arrived in close cohorts, the first line crouching down, the second bending their hips, while the others rose in succession, in gradual inclinations of their bodies, until the last stood bolt upright; while elsewhere, to climb up, the tallest advanced at the head, the shortest in the rear; and they all supported with their left arms above their helmets their shields, locked together so closely by the rims that they appeared like an assemblage of large tortoises. The projectiles slid over these slanting masses.

The Carthaginians hurled mill-stones, pestles, vats, casks, couches, everything, in fact, that could make a weight and crush. Some watched in the embrasures with fishing nets, and when a Barbarian came up he found himself entangled in the meshes, and struggled like a floundering fish. They themselves demolished their own battlements; portions of the walls crumbled down, and in their passage stirred up a blinding dust. The catapults on the platform and those on the rampart fired one against the other, the stones clashed together and shattered into a thousand fragments, falling in a wide shower upon the combatants.

Presently the two crowds formed but one thick chain of human bodies, overflowing in the intervals of the terrace, and a little relaxed at the two ends, revolved perpetually without advancing.

They grappled each other, lying flat on the ground like wrestlers, and were crushed. Women leaned over the battlements and screamed. They were dragged forward by their veils, and the whiteness of their sides, suddenly uncovered, shone between the arms of the Negroes, as they plunged their poniards into them.

Some corpses were too closely packed in the crowd to fall, but, borne up by the shoulders of their comrades, they moved for some minutes quite upright, their eyes staring wide open.

Some, pierced through and through both temples with javelins, swayed their heads like bears; their mouths opened to scream, but remained silently agape ; hands that were cut off flew through the air. There were mighty blows, of which the survivors spoke many a long day afterwards.

Meanwhile arrows were flying from the tops of the wooden and stone towers. The long yards of the *tollenones* moved rapidly ; and as the Barbarians had pillaged the ancient cemetery of the Autochthones beneath the Catacombs, they hurled the tombstones upon the Carthaginians. Under the weight of the baskets, too heavily laden, the cables sometimes broke, and numbers of men, wildly throwing up their arms, fell from a great height.

Until the middle of the day the veterans of the hoplites had fiercely attacked the Tænia, in order to penetrate the Port and destroy the fleet. Hamilcar had lighted on the roof of Khamoûn a fire of humid straw, the smoke from which blinded them ; they fell back to the left, increasing the horrible crowd which struggled in Malqua. Some syntagmas, composed of robust men expressly chosen, had forced three of the gates. Then high barriers, constructed with boards studded with nails, barred their way; a fourth entrance readily yielded ; they darted beyond, and ran forward, only to roll into a moat in which snares had been hidden.

At the south-east corner Autharitus and his men beat down the rampart, where the fissure had been stopped up with bricks. The ground behind rose; they slowly climbed up, but found on the top a second wall, composed of stones and long beams lying flat, alternating like the squares on a chessboard. This was a Gallic mode adapted by the Suffete to the requirements of the situation. The Gauls thought that they were in front of a city of their own country. Their attack was languidly made, and consequently they were repulsed.

From the street of Khamoûn to the Vegetable Market, all the circuit of the walls now belonged to the Barbarians, and the Samnites finished the dying with blows of their spears, or even with one foot on the wall wonderingly contemplated beneath them the smoking ruins, and in the distance the battle which recommenced.

The slingers distributed in the rear fired incessantly, but from long use the springs of the Acarnanian slings were broken, so, like herdsmen, many slung the stones with their hands, others shot the lead balls with the handles of whips. Zarxas, with his long black hair covering his shoulders, bounded about everywhere and led on the Baleares; two pouches were suspended from his hips, into one of which he kept plunging his left hand, while his right arm whirled like the revolving wheel of a chariot.

Mâtho at first withheld from the combat, to command more effectually all his forces at once. He had been seen along the gulf shore with the Mercenaries; near the Lagoon with the Numidians; then on the border of the lake amongst the Negroes; at the end of the plain he pushed forward masses of soldiers, who kept incessantly coming up against the line of the fortifications. Gradually he approached them; the odour of blood, the spectacle made by the carnage, and the fanfare of clarions, had ended in making his heart bound. Then he entered his tent, threw aside his cumbersome breastplate, taking instead his lion-skin, which he found more convenient for battle. The muzzle adapted itself to his head, and surrounded his face with a circle of fangs; the two fore-paws crossed over his breast, and the claws of the hind-paws reached down to his knees.

He kept on his strong sword-belt, in which flashed a double-edged battle-axe; then, holding his large sword in both hands, he plunged impetuously through the breach. Like a pruner lopping off willow branches, who endeavours to cut as many as possible in order to gain the more money, he moved about, mowing down Carthaginians on all sides of him. Those who tried to seize him by the sides he knocked down with blows of the pommel of his sword; when they attacked him face to face he pierced them through; and if they took flight he slashed them down.

Two men simultaneously jumped upon his back: he recoiled at one bound against a door, crushing them. His active sword rose and fell; at last it shattered against an angle of the wall. Then he took his heavy axe, and from behind and in front he disembowelled the Carthaginians like a flock of sheep. They scattered more and more before him, and, slaying right and left, he arrived alone, before the second enclosure, at the foot of the Acropolis.

Materials that had been hurled from the summit encumbered the steps, and overflowed beyond the walls. Mâtho, in the midst of these ruins, turned around to call his comrades; he saw their plumes scattered through the multitude—they were being surrounded: they would perish. He dashed towards them; then the vast crown of red plumes congregating, quickly rejoined, and surrounded him. But the lateral streets disgorged an enormous throng, and he was taken up by his hips and carried away to the outside of the rampart, in a spot where the terrace was high.

Mâtho shouted a command: all the bucklers were levelled above the helmets; he leaped on the top to catch hold of something that might enable him to scale the walls and re-enter Carthage, and brandished his terrible battle-axe as he ran over the bucklers, that resembled bronze waves, like a marine God on the billows shaking his trident.

Meanwhile a man in a white robe strode on the edge of the rampart, impassive and indifferent to the death surrounding him. At times he extended his right hand to shade his eyes, as if he sought for some one. Mâtho passed beneath him. All at once his eyes flamed, his livid face contracted, and he lifted his meagre arms, shouting out words of abuse.

Mâtho heard them not; but he felt a look so cruel and furious enter his heart, that he gave vent to a moan. He hurled his long axe towards this man; people threw themselves about Schahabarim, and

Mâtho, seeing him no more, fell backwards exhausted.

A fearful creaking drew near, mingled with the rhythm of hoarse voices singing in cadence.

A vast throng of soldiers encompassed the *helepolis;* they dragged it with both hands, hauled it with ropes, and pushed it with their shoulders—for the slope rising from the plain to the platform, though it was extremely gentle, proved impracticable for machines of such prodigious weight. Notwithstanding that it had eight iron-bound wheels, since morning it had advanced thus slowly; it was like a mountain being elevated to the top of a mountain.

From the base of this machine an enormous ram projected; along the three sides facing the city the ports were lowered, and in the interior appeared mailed soldiers, like iron columns, who could be seen climbing and descending the two stairways that traversed the stories. Some of these men held themselves in readiness to spring the moment the grapples of the ports should touch the wall. In the middle of the upper platform the skeins of the ballistas were twisting, and the great beam of the catapult kept descending.

Hamilcar was at this moment standing on the roof of Melkarth; he judged that the beam would come directly towards him, against the most invulnerable portion of the wall, and on that account denuded of sentinels. Already for a long time his slaves had been carrying leather water-bottles to the circular road, where two transverse partitions of clay had been constructed to form a sort of basin. The water insensibly ran over the terrace, and it was most extraordinary that Hamilcar did not seem disturbed by this waste.

But when the *helepolis* had attained to about thirty paces of the wall, he commanded that boards should be placed between the houses over the streets, from the cisterns down to the rampart, and that the people should form in a file and pass from hand to hand helmets and amphoras filled with water, that were continually emptied. The Carthaginians waxed indignant at this exorbitant waste of water. The ram demolished the wall, suddenly a fountain escaped from the disjointed stones, when the brazen structure of nine stages, containing more than three thousand soldiers, began to sway gently, like a ship rocking on the billows.

In fact, the water had penetrated the terrace and had undermined the road before the machine; the wheels were imbedded in mire. Between the leather curtains on the first stage, Spendius's head appeared, blowing lustily through an ivory horn. The mammoth machine convulsively moved perhaps ten more paces; but the ground became softer and softer, the mire reached up to the axle-trees, then the huge *helepolis* stopped, leaning frightfully over on one side. The catapult rolled to the edge of the platform, and, carried away by the weight of its beam, toppled off, crushing the inferior stages in pieces beneath it. The soldiers standing in the ports slid into the abyss, or by chance some held on at the extremities of the long beam, and by their weight increased the inclination of the *helepolis*, which was now going to pieces and cracking in all its joints.

The other Barbarians rushed to rescue them, crowding in a compact mass; seeing which, the Carthaginians descended over the rampart and assailed them from behind, killing them at their ease. But the chariots armed with scythes came speedily up, galloping around the outside of this multitude; they remounted the walls. Night fell, and the Barbarians gradually retired.

Nothing could be seen over the plain but a sort of black, swarming mass, from the bluish gulf to the glittering white Lagoon; and the lake, into which blood had flowed, spread out beyond like a great purple pool.

The terrace was now so encumbered with the dead that it might have been constructed out of human bodies. In the centre stood the *helepolis* covered with armour, and from time to time enormous fragments became detached from it, like stones from a crumbling pyramid. Broad tracks made by the streams of molten lead could be distinguished on the walls; a wooden tower here and there had tumbled over, and was burning, and the houses appeared indistinctly like the tiers in a ruined amphitheatre. Heavy clouds of smoke curled up, through which whirled trails of sparks that were ever lost in the black sky.

Meantime, the Carthaginians, who were devoured by thirst, had rushed to the cisterns. They broke open the doors: a muddy puddle spread over the bottom.

What would now become of them? The Barbarians were innumerable, and when they had recovered from their fatigue, would begin again.

z

All night the people deliberated in groups at the corners of the streets. Some declared that they must send away the women, the sick, and the aged. Others proposed to abandon the city, and found a new colony far away. But ships were wanting; and the sun rose before any decision had been arrived at.

That day there was no fighting, everyone being too wearied. While the people slept they appeared to be dead.

When the Carthaginians reflected upon the cause of their disasters, they recalled the fact that they had neglected to send to Phœnicia the annual offering due to the Tyrian Melkarth, at which an immense terror overtook them. The Gods were indignant with the Republic, and would doubtless pursue her with vengeance.

The divinities were considered in the light of cruel masters, only to be appeased with supplications, and who allowed themselves to be corrupted by gifts. All were weak before Moloch—the devourer. Human existence, even the flesh of mankind, belonged to him; therefore, to preserve it, the Carthaginians were wont to offer him a portion, which calmed his wrath. Children were burned on their foreheads, or on the nape of their necks, with woollen wicks; and this custom of seeking to satisfy the Baal brought considerable money to the priests, who rarely failed to recommend the easiest and least painful method of sacrifice.

However, it was now a question of the very existence of the Republic. And as every profit must be purchased by some loss, and every transaction is regulated by the wants of the weaker and the demands of the stronger, there was no suffering too considerable for the God, since he took delight in the most horrible, and they all now lay at his mercy. He must therefore be completely glutted. The precedents showed that carnal sacrifices to him had compelled the scourge to disappear. Besides, they believed an immolation by fire would purify Carthage. The ferocity of the people was enlisted beforehand, inasmuch as the choice of victims must fall exclusively on the grand families.

The Elders assembled. Their session was long. Hanno had come, but as he was now unable to sit up, he remained lying near the entrance, half lost in the fringes of the lofty tapestry; and when the pontiff of Moloch asked if those convened consented to deliver up their children, his voice suddenly broke forth from the shadows as the roaring of a spirit out of the depths of a cavern, saying, that he regretted that he had none of his own blood to give, and he significantly looked at Hamilcar, who faced him at the other end of the hall.

The Suffete was so disturbed by this gaze that he dropped his eyes. All, however, approved by nodding their heads successively; and, according to the rites, he had to reply to the high priest, "Yes, so mote it be!" Then the Elders decreed the sacrifice by a traditional periphrasis—for there are things more troublesome to speak than to execute.

Almost immediately this decision was known throughout Carthage, and lamentation resounded. Everywhere the women were heard crying, and their husbands either consoling them or heaping invectives upon them for offering remonstrance.

Three hours afterwards an extraordinary news spread about among the people: the Suffete had discovered springs at the base of the cliff. All ran thither: holes had been dug in the sand, showing the water; and already some were lying flat on their bellies, drinking.

Hamilcar did not himself know whether it was a counsel from the Gods or the indistinct recollection of a revelation his father had formerly made to him, but, on quitting the conference of Elders, he had gone down to the beach with his slaves, and begun digging in the gravel.

He distributed clothing, shoes, and wine, and the balance of the grain stored in his vaults; he even made the populace enter his palace, opening the kitchens, magazines, and all the rooms except Salammbô's. He took occasion to announce that six thousand Gallic Mercenaries were coming, and that the king of Macedonia was also sending soldiers to them.

As early as the second day after the discovery of the springs, the volume of water had considerably diminished, and the evening of the third day they were completely dry. Then the Elders' former decree circulated anew on all lips, and the priests of Moloch commenced preparations for the sacrifice.

Men in black robes presented themselves at the houses; many of the inhabitants had previously deserted them on pretence of business, or of some dainty that they must go and buy. The servitors of Moloch surprised and took the children. Other parents, stupidly scared, delivered them up. The victims were all conveyed to the temple of Tanit, to the priestesses, who were ordered to amuse and feed them until the solemn day.

They arrived suddenly at Hamilcar's palace, and finding him in his gardens, said:

"Barca! we come for that you wot of—your son!" They added, that some people had met the boy one night during the last moon, crossing the middle of Mappals, led by an old man.

At first he felt as if suffocating; but very quickly understanding that denial would be in vain, he inclined his head, and introduced them into his house of commerce. His slaves, at a gesture from him, ran to keep watch over its neighbourhood.

He entered Salammbô's room, bewildered, seized Hannibal by one hand, and with the other tore from a trailing robe some strings, with which he fastened the boy's hands and feet together, placing the ends of the strings in his mouth as a gag, and concealed him under the cowhide couch, adjusting some wide drapery so that it fell all about the couch to the floor.

Then he paced the room from right to left, lifted his arms, turned around, bit his lips; then he halted, with his eyes fixed, and gasping as though he was dying.

At length, he clapped his hands three times. Giddenem appeared.

"Listen!" said he. "Go and take from amongst the slaves a male child of eight or nine years, with black hair and projecting forehead! Bring him! Hasten!"

Giddenem soon returned, and presented a boy.

He was a poor child, at the same time thin and bloated; his skin greyish, like the noisome rags that clung to his loins. He hung his head, and rubbed with the back of his hands his eyes, which were full of flies.

"How could anyone possibly mistake him for Hannibal! and time fails to choose another!" Hamilcar looked at Giddenem with the desire to strangle him.

"Go!" cried he; and the Master of Slaves fled.

The sorrow which the Suffete had for so long a time apprehended had come, and he sought with immeasurable efforts to discern if there was no manner, no way of averting it.

Abdalonim all at once spoke from the other side of the door: the servitors of Moloch were becoming impatient, and demanded the Suffete.

Hamilcar suppressed a cry; he experienced a pang akin to the seething burn from a red-hot iron; he began anew to pace the floor like a madman; then he sank down near the balustrade, and with his elbows on his knees, pressed his temples between his clenched hands.

The porphyry basin in the centre yet contained a small quantity of clean water for Salammbô's ablutions. Despite his repugnance and all his pride, the Suffete plunged the child into the basin, and like a slave merchant washed and scrubbed the boy with strigils and red earth. Afterwards he took from the cases surrounding the walls two squares of purple; of these he put one on his breast, the other on his back, pinning them over the collar-bone with two diamond agrafes; he poured perfumes over his head, clasped an electrum necklace around his throat, and thrust his plebeian feet into sandals with pearl heels—his daughter's own sandals; but he stamped with shame and rage. Salammbô, who was eagerly assisting him, was quite as pale as he. The child smiled, pleased with these splendours, and even growing bolder, commenced to clap his hands and leap with glee, when Hamilcar led him forth.

He held him firmly by the arm, as though he feared he should lose the boy; and the child, hurt by his fierce grasp, whimpered slightly as he ran beside the Suffete.

Abreast of the *ergastulum*, under a palm tree, a voice rose, a lamenting, supplicating voice, murmuring, "Master! oh, master!"

Hamilcar turned, and saw at his side a man most abject in appearance—one of the wretches who lived at hazard in his gardens.

"What do you want?" asked the Suffete. The slave, trembling horribly, stammered:

"I am his father!"

Hamilcar kept on walking; the slave followed, with bent back, and head thrust forward; as his loins seemed to give way, his face was convulsed by an indescribable agony, and his suppressed sobs stifled him, so strong was his desire at once to question him and to cry out "Mercy!"

At length he dared to touch the Suffete's elbow lightly with one finger.

"Do you take him to the . . . . . ?" He had not the strength to finish, and Hamilcar stopped, amazed by this outburst of grief.

He had never thought—so immense was the gulf separating the one from the other—that there could be anything in common between them. It even appeared to him to be a sort of outrage, an encroachment on his own privileges. He replied by a look, colder and more crushing than the axe of an executioner; the slave fainted, falling in the dust at his feet. Hamilcar stepped over him.

The three black-robed men waited for the Suffete in the great hall, standing against the stone disc. All at once he tore his garments, and rolled upon the stones, uttering sharp cries.

"Ah! poor little Hannibal! Oh! my son! my consolation! my hope! my life! kill me also! Take me! Misery! misery!" he ploughed his face with his finger-nails, and tore out his hair, howling like the mourners at the funerals. "Take him away! I suffer too much! Go! go! kill me with him!" The servitors of Moloch were astonished that the great Hamilcar possessed such a faint heart. They were almost touched.

Just then, the noise of bare feet was heard, and with a jerking rattle, like the panting of a ferocious beast when running in pursuit, on the threshold of the third gallery, between the ivory door-posts, a man appeared, pallid, terrible, with outstretched arms, and screamed:

"My child!"

With a bound Hamilcar fell upon him, covering his mouth with his hands, and cried out, even louder:

"He is the old slave who brought Hannibal up! he calls him 'my child'! he will become mad!

Enough! enough!" And pushing out by the shoulders the three priests and their victim, he went out with them, and closed the door behind him with a tremendous kick.

For some time Hamilcar listened attentively, still fearing to see them return. He next thought of ridding himself of the slave, to make quite sure of his not speaking; but the peril had not completely passed, and his death, if the Gods were angered at it, might return upon his own son. Then changing his purpose, he sent to him by Taanach the daintiest things from his kitchen—a quarter of a goat, some beans, and some preserved pomegranates. The slave, who had not eaten for a long time, flung himself upon the food, whilst his tears fell into the dishes.

Hamilcar at length returned to Salammbô, and unknotted Hannibal's fastenings. The child was in such a state of exasperation that he bit the Suffete's hand until he drew blood; he repressed him with a caress.

To keep the boy quiet Salammbô tried to frighten him with stories of Lamia—an ogress of Cyrene. "Where then is she?" he asked. Then he was told that the brigands would come to put him in prison; to which he replied, "When they come I shall kill them."

Hamilcar then told him the frightful truth, but he grew furious with his father, declaring that he was able to utterly destroy all the people, since he was the master of Carthage.

At last, exhausted by his struggles and anger, he slept a savage sleep, talking in his dreams, as he lay with his back propped up against a scarlet pillow, his head thrown a trifle backwards, and one of his little arms extended out straight from his body in an imperious attitude.

When the night grew dark Hamilcar lifted the child softly up in his arms, and descended the stairway of the galleys without a torch. In passing through the commercial house he took a bunch of grapes and a jug of pure water. The child awakened before the statue of Aletes, in the vault filled with gems, and smiled, as the other child had smiled, in the arms of the Suffete, at the play of splendours surrounding him.

Hamilcar was very certain that no one had now the power to take his son. It was an impenetrable spot, communicating with the shore by a subterranean passage, that he alone knew: he cast his eyes about him, respiring a long breath, and placed the boy on a stool beside the golden bucklers.

No one at present saw them; he had nothing more to heed, and he gave way to his feelings. Like a mother who finds her lost firstborn, he embraced his son, pressing him to his heart; he laughed and cried at the same time, called him by the most endearing names, and covered him with kisses. The little Hannibal, frightened by this terrible tenderness, remained quiet.

Hamilcar returned with silent steps, by feeling along the walls around him, until he reached the large hall, wherein the moonlight streamed through one of the slits in the dome · in the middle the sated slave slept, lying at full length on the marble slabs. He regarded him, and was moved by a kind of pity. With the toe of his buskin he pushed a rug under his head. Then he lifted his eyes to contemplate Tanit, whose slender crescent was shining in the sky; and he felt himself stronger than the Baals, and full of contempt for them.

The preparations for the sacrifice had already begun.

A section of the wall of the temple of Moloch was removed in order to pull the brazen God through without disturbing the ashes on the altar. As soon as the sun rose the sacred slaves of the temple pushed him to the square of Khamoûn.

He moved backwards, sliding over cylinders; his shoulders overtopped the walls; from the farthest point the Carthaginians who perceived him fled with speed, for it was impossible to contemplate with impunity the Baal save in the exercise of his wrath.

An odour of aromatics was wafted through the streets. All the temples were thrown open simultaneously, and tabernacles upon chariots, or on litters which pontiffs carried, issued forth. Great plumes of feathers nodded at their corners, and rays flashed from their pointed spires, terminated by globes of crystal, gold, silver, or copper.

These were the Canaanite Baalim, reproductions of the supreme Baal, returning towards their essence to humble themselves before his power, and be lost in his splendour. The canopy of Melkarth, of fine purple, sheltered a flame of bitumen oil; while upon that of Khamoûn, which was of hyacinth colour, was erected an ivory phallus bordered with a circle of gems: between the curtains of Eschmoûn, blue as the ether, a Python slept, describing a circle as it bit its tail; and the *Dii-Patæci*, held in the arms of their priests, their heels dragging on the ground, resembled large babies in swaddling clothes.

Following came all the inferior forms of divinity: Baal-Samin, God of celestial spaces; Baal-Peor, God of sacred mounts; Baal-Zeboub, God of corruption; and those of the neighbouring countries and of cognate races: the Iarbal of Libya; the Adrammelech of Chaldea; the Kijun of the Syrians; Derceto, with the maiden's face, ramping upon her fins; and the body of Tammouz was transported on a catafalque between torches and heads of hair. To subject the kings of the firmament to the sun, and prevent their individual influence from impeding his, metal stars of divers colours were brandished on the ends of long staves. In this collection all varieties were found, from the black Nebo, which was the genius of Mercury, to the hideous Rahab, which was the constellation of the Crocodile.

The Abaddirs, stones fallen from the moon, turned in silver filigree slings; small loaves reproducing the female sex were carried in baskets by the priests of Ceres; others brought their fetiches, their amulets; forgotten idols reappeared; and they had even taken from the vessels their mystic symbols, as though Carthage was desirous to collect herself completely in one thought of death and desolation.

Before each of the tabernacles a man balanced on his head a vase, in which fumed incense; cloudlets hovered here and there, and through the dense vapours could be discerned the hangings, the pendants, and the embroideries of the sacred pavilions.

In consequence of their enormous weight, they

advanced slowly. The axle-trees of the chariots sometimes got caught in the narrow streets; then the devotees profited by the opportunity to touch the Baalim with their clothing, which they ever afterwards treasured as something sacred. The brazen statue continued to move towards the square of Khamoûn. The Rich, carrying sceptres with emerald apples, started from the far end of Megara; the Elders, crowned with diadems, assembled in Kinisdo; and the masters of finance, the governors of provinces, merchants, soldiers, sailors, and the numerous horde employed at funerals, all displaying the insignia of their magistracy or the instruments of their avocations, converged towards the tabernacles that descended from the Acropolis between the colleges of pontiffs.

In deference to Moloch, they were all bedecked with their most splendid jewels. Diamonds sparkled over their black apparel; but their rings, now too wide, loosely fell from their emaciated hands, and nothing could be more lugubrious than that silent concourse, where brilliant ear-rings struck against pallid faces, and where gold tiaras encircled foreheads wrinkled by an atrocious despair.

Finally the Baal attained the centre of the square. His pontiffs made an enclosure with trellises to keep back the multitude, and remained themselves at his feet, surrounding him.

The priests of Khamoûn, in reddish woollen robes, alligned before their temple under the columns of the portico; those of Eschmoûn, in white linen mantles, with collars of the heads of hoopoes, wearing conical tiaras, established themselves on the steps of the Acropolis; the priests of Melkarth, in violet tunics, took their position on the western side; the priests of the Abaddirs, swathed in bands of Phrygian stuffs, placed themselves on the eastern side; and ranged on the southern side with the necromancers, all covered with tattooings, were the howlers in patched mantles, the priests of the *Dii-Patæci*, and the Yidonim, who divined the future by placing a bone of a dead body in their mouths. The priests of Ceres, habited in blue robes, had prudently stopped in Satheb street, intoning in a low voice a thesmophorion in Megarian dialect.

From time to time files of men arrived, completely naked, with arms stretched out, holding each other by the shoulders, giving vent from the depths of their chests to hoarse, cavernous intonations; their eyes turned toward the Colossus, which glittered through the dust, and at intervals they swayed their bodies all together, as if shaken by a single movement. These men were so furious, that in order to establish quiet among them, the sacred slaves struck them roughly with clubs, making them lie flat on the ground with their faces against the brazen trellises.

At this moment, from the back part of the square, a man in a white robe came forward. As he slowly pierced through the throng, he was recognised as a priest of Tanit—the high-priest Schahabarim. Yells were raised, for the tyranny of the male principle prevailed upon this occasion in all minds, and the Goddess was so completely forgotten that no one had even noticed the absence of her pontiffs. But the amazement redoubled when her high-priest was seen to open one of the gates of the trellis, intended only for those to enter who would offer victims for the sacrifice.

The priests of Moloch, believing that he came to offer an insult to their God, with violent gestures endeavoured to expel him. Nourished as they were by the viands of the holocausts, clothed in purple like kings, and wearing triple crowns, they spat upon this pale eunuch priest, attenuated by macerations, and a contemptuous laughter of rage shook their black beards, spread out over their breasts in the sunlight.

Schahabarim, without response, continued to walk forward, and crossing, step by step, the whole enclosure, he arrived beneath the legs of the Colossus; then he threw out his arms and touched it on both sides: this was a solemn act of adoration.

For a long period the Rabbet had tortured him, and in despair, or perhaps in default of a God completely satisfying his thoughts, he had decided at last to accept Moloch.

The concourse were shocked by this apostacy, and uttered a prolonged murmur. There was a feeling that the last tie had been severed that attached their souls to a clement Deity.

But Schahabarim, because of his mutilation, could not participate in the cult of the Baal. The men in red mantles expelled him from the enclosure; then, when he was outside, he turned around to all the other colleges successively, and the priest, now without a God, disappeared in the crowd, that scattered at his approach.

Meantime a fire of aloes, cedar, and laurel wood

burned between the legs of the Colossus. His long wings buried their points in the flame; the unguents with which he had been rubbed now trickled like sweat over his brazen limbs. About the round stone upon which his feet rested, children, enveloped in black veils, formed a motionless circle; and his inordinately long arms allowed the palms of his hands to reach down to them, as if to seize this crown and convey it to the sky.

The Rich, the Elders, the women, and in fact the entire multitude, thronged behind the priests, and on the terraces of the houses. The large, painted stars revolved no longer; the tabernacles were placed on the ground, and the smoke from the censers rose on high perpendicularly, like gigantic trees spreading their bluish boughs to the centre of the azure. Many of the spectators fainted; others became inert and petrified in their ecstasy; an infinite agony pressed heavily upon their hearts. The clamours one by one died out, and the people of Carthage panted in silence, absorbed in the terror of their desire.

At last the high-priest of Moloch passed his right hand beneath the children's veils, and pulled out a lock of hair from each of their foreheads, which he threw into the flames. Then the men in red mantles intoned a sacred hymn:

"Homage to thee, O Sun! King of the two Zones! Creator, self-begotten! Father and Mother! Father and Son! God and Goddess! Goddess and God!" and their voices were lost in the explosion of countless instruments, sounding all together to smother the cries of the victims. The scheminith with eight strings, the kinnor with ten, and the nebel with twelve, all twanged, whistled, and thundered forth. Enormous leather bottles stuck full of tubes emitted a sharp, rolling noise ; the tambourines, beaten with all possible force, resounded with heavy, rapid blows ; and despite the fury of the clarions, the salsalim clicked like the wings of locusts.

The sacred slaves with a long hook opened the seven compartments ranged in the body of the Baal. Into the highest division farina was introduced ; into the second, two turtle-doves ; into the third, an ape ; into the fourth, a ram ; into the fifth, a lamb; and into the sixth, as they did not possess an ox, a tanned hide from the sanctuary was substituted ; the seventh aperture remained gaping.

Before a human victim should be offered, it was deemed best to test the arms of the God. Slender chainlets, passing from the fingers over his shoulders, descended at the back, which men pulled downwards, raising to the height of his elbows his two open hands, that, in approaching each other, came opposite his belly. They worked them several times successively with little jerks. Then the musical instruments were hushed, and the fire roared fiercely.

The pontiffs of Moloch walked to and fro on the large stone slab, examining the multitude.

The first offering must be an individual sacrifice, an oblation perfectly voluntary, which would be effectual to incite others. But no one came forward, and the seven alleys leading from the barrier to the Colossus remained completely empty. To stimulate the people, the priests pulled from their

A A

girdles little stilettoes, with which they slashed their faces. The Devotees, who had been stretched on the ground outside, were introduced into the enclosure, and a packet of horrible irons was thrown to them : each one chose his torture. They passed spits through their breasts, slit their cheeks, put upon their heads crowns of thorns; then they enlaced their arms together, and surrounding the children, they formed another great circle, ever contracting and expanding. Having reached the balustrade, they threw themselves back, only to eddy outwards again, continually attracting to them the crowd, by the vertigo of their movements, full of blood and cries.

Gradually the people, thus incited, came into the end of the alleys, and threw into the flames, pearls, gold vases, cups, all their treasures, and flambeaux.

These offerings became more and more splendid, and kept multiplying. Presently a man who staggered, a man pale and hideous from terror, pushed forward a child; then could be distinguished between the hands of the Colossus a little black mass—it sank into the dark opening. The priests leaned over the edge of the large slab, and a new chant burst out, celebrating the joys of death and the renascence of eternity.

The children mounted up slowly, and as the smoke rose in lofty, whirling masses, they seemed from afar to disappear in a cloud. Not one moved. All had been securely bound hand and foot, and the dark drapery prevented them from seeing anything, and from being recognised.

Hamilcar, in a red mantle, like that of the priests

of Moloch, remained near the Baal, standing before the great toe of his right foot. When the fourteenth child was put in, all the people saw that he made a demonstrative gesture of horror; but quickly resuming his attitude of composure, he crossed his arms, and gazed on the ground. On the other side of the Colossus the grand pontiff likewise remained motionless, bowing his head, upon which was an Assyrian mitre, and observing on his breast the gold plaque covered with prophetic stones, which threw out iridescent lights as the flames struck across them. He grew pale and abstracted.

Hamilcar inclined his head, and they were both so near the pyre that the hem of their robes in rising from time to time swept it.

Moloch's brazen arms moved more rapidly; they no longer paused. Each time a child was placed upon them, the priests of Moloch extended their hands over the victim to charge upon it the sins of the people, vociferating:

"These are not men, but oxen!" and the multitude around repeated, "Oxen! Oxen!" The Devotees screamed out, "Lord! Eat!" and the priests of Proserpine, conforming in terror to Carthage's need, mumbled their Eleusinian formula: "Pour forth rain! conceive!" No sooner were the victims placed on the verge of the aperture than they vanished, like a drop of water on a red-hot plate, and whiffs of white smoke curled up through the scarlet glow.

Yet the appetite of the God was not appeased: he still wanted more. In order to supply him, the children were piled on his hands, and were retained there by a great chain.

In the beginning, Devotees tried to count them, in order to note if the total number corresponded to the days of the solar year; but now so many were piled on that it was impossible to distinguish them during the dizzy movements of those horrible arms. All this lasted a long time, until nightfall. Then the interior divisions gave a most sombre glare. For the first time, the burning flesh was visible. Some people even fancied that they recognised hair, limbs, and entire bodies.

The day fell; clouds gathered over the head of the Baal. The pyre, now flameless, made a pyramid of glowing embers that reached to his knees; and all crimson, like a giant covered with blood, with head bent backward, he seemed to reel under the weight of his intoxication. According as the priests urged haste, the frenzy of the people augmented; as the number of victims decreased, some cried out to spare them, others that Moloch must have more. It seemed as though the walls, with their masses of spectators, would crumble beneath the yells of horror and of mystic voluptuousness. Then came into the alleys some faithful ones, dragging their children, who clung to them; and they beat the little hands to make them loose their hold, that they might deliver them to the red men.

Occasionally the musicians paused from sheer exhaustion; and in the lull could be heard the screams of mothers and the crackling of the grease spattering on the coals. The mandrake-drinkers crept on all-fours around the Colossus, roaring like tigers. The Yidonim prophesied; the Devotees chanted with their cleft lips. The railings were broken, for now all wanted to participate in the sacrifice; and fathers whose children were deceased, cast into the yawning furnace their effigies, toys, and preserved bones. Those who possessed knives rushed upon the others; they cut each other's throats in their voracious rage, maddened by the holocaust. The sacred slaves, with bronze winnowing-baskets, took from the edge of the stone slab the fallen cinders, which they tossed high in the air, that the sacrifice should be dispersed over the entire city, and attain to the region of the stars.

The tumultuous noise and vast illumination had attracted the Barbarians to the very foot of the walls. Climbing upon the ruins of the *helepolis*, they looked on, gaping with horror.

CHAPTER XIV.

THE DEFILE OF THE BATTLE-AXE.

THE Carthaginians had not re-entered their dwellings before the clouds gathered thickly, and those who turned their faces up towards the Colossus felt great drops upon their foreheads—and the rain fell.

All night it rained profusely—in floods; the thunder growled like the voice of Moloch triumphant over his vanquishment of Tanit; and now pregnant, she opened from high heaven her vast breast. Occasionally she was seen in a luminous light extending over pillows of clouds, then the darkness reclosed, as though, yet too weary, she would sleep again. The Carthaginians all believed water to be a production of the moon, and uttered cries to facilitate her labour.

The deluging rain beat upon the terraces, overflowing everywhere, forming lakes in the courts, cascades over the stairways, and whirlpools at the street corners. It poured down in heavy, warm masses and spouting streams; from the corners of all the buildings leaped great, foaming jets; against the walls it was like white sheets vaguely suspended, and

THE DEFILE OF THE BATTLE-AXE. 359

the roofs of the temples were cleansed till they shone brilliantly black under the flashes of lightning. By a thousand channels torrents descended from the Acropolis ; houses suddenly crumbled ; beams, rubbish, and household furniture swept by in the resistless streams gushing impetuously over the pavements.

People exposed amphoras, jugs, and canvases to catch the water : the torches became extinguished ; and to light their pathways they took brands from the pyre of the Baal. In order that they might drink, they turned their faces upwards and opened their mouths. Some, by the edges of miry pools, plunged their arms in up to their armpits, and gorged themselves so copiously with the water that they vomited it like buffaloes.

Gradually a freshness spread abroad ; all breathed the humid air, giving full play to their limbs ; and in the happiness of their intoxication an immense hope sprang up. All their miseries were forgotten. Their country was once more revived.

They experienced the desire to throw back upon others the excess of their fury, which they had been unable to employ against themselves. Such a sacrifice ought not to be useless—even though they had no remorse, they found themselves carried away by that frenzy created by complicity in irreparable crimes.

The storm fell upon the Barbarians in their badly closed tents ; and the next day all, still benumbed, were floundering about in the deep mud, searching for their munitions and weapons, spoiled and lost.

Hamilcar himself went to seek Hanno, and, in

pursuance of his full powers, confided to him the command. The old Suffete hesitated some minutes between his rancour and his appetite for authority; however, he consented.

Subsequently Hamilcar sent out a galley, equipped with a catapult on both ends, and anchored her in the gulf, facing the raft. Then on all the disposable vessels he embarked the most robust of his troops. Then he was flying; and making sail towards the north, he gradually disappeared in the mist.

But three days after, when they were about to renew the attack, the people from the Libyan coast arrived in a tumultuous state. Barca had come upon them. He had levied for provisions on all sides, and spread his troops throughout the country.

The Barbarians were as indignant as if he had betrayed them. However, those who were most wearied of the siege, especially the Gauls, did not hesitate to leave the walls in order to endeavour to join the Suffete. Spendius wanted to reconstruct the *helepolis*. Mâtho had traced an imaginary line from his tent to Megara. This course he pledged himself to follow, and not one of their men stirred. But Autharitus' soldiers departed, deserting the western portion of the ramparts. The indifference was so profound, that no one even dreamed of replacing these men.

Narr' Havas spied them from the distance in the mountains. He moved his troops during the night on the exterior side of the Lagoon by the sea-coast, and he thus entered Carthage.

He presented himself like a saviour, with six thousand men, all carrying under their mantles farina, and bringing forty elephants freighted with forage and dried meats. Soon the people flocked around them, giving them names. The arrival of such a succour rejoiced the Carthaginians even less than the spectacle of these strong animals consecrated to the Baal : it was a pledge of his sympathy, a proof that at last he came to defend them, and to intervene in the war in their behalf.

Narr' Havas received the compliments of the Elders ; then he went up towards Salammbô's palace. He had not seen her since the time when, in Hamilcar's tent, standing between the five armies, he had felt her little, cold, soft hand bound to his. After the betrothal she had gone to Carthage. His love, diverted by other ambitions, had come back to him, and now he counted on enjoying his rights by marrying and taking possession of her.

Salammbô did not understand how this young man could ever become her master! Though she prayed nightly to Tanit for the death of Mâtho, her horror for the Libyan was diminishing. She dimly felt that the hatred with which he had persecuted her was something almost religious ; and she would gladly have seen in Narr' Havas some reflection of that violence which still held her enthralled. She yearned to know more of him; nevertheless, his presence would have embarrassed her, and she sent word that she could not receive him.

Besides, Hamilcar had forbidden his people to admit the Numidian king to his daughter; he withheld this compensation till the conclusion of the war, hoping thereby to preserve his devotion;

and Narr' Havas, fearing Hamilcar's displeasure, retired.

But he carried himself haughtily towards the Hundred, changing their plans, and demanding prerogatives for his men, and had them appointed to important posts.

With wide-open eyes, the Barbarians discerned the Numidians on the towers.

However, the Carthaginians' surprise was even greater when there came sailing into their port an old Punic trireme bearing four hundred of their men, who had been taken prisoners during the war in Sicily. In fact, Hamilcar had secretly sent back to the Quirites the crews of the Latin vessels taken before the defection of the Tyrian cities, and Rome, in exchange for this fair dealing, had now returned to him these captives. Rome disdained the overtures of the Mercenaries in Sardinia, refusing even to recognise as subjects the inhabitants of Utica.

Hiero, who ruled at Syracuse, was led on by this example. In order to preserve his states, he required a balance of power between the two peoples; hence he was interested for the safety of the Canaanites, and he declared himself their friend by sending to them twelve hundred head of cattle and fifty-three thousand nebel of wheat.

A deeper reason caused help to be sent to Carthage: it was thoroughly perceived that, if the Mercenaries triumphed, all, from the soldiers to the scullions, would rise in revolt, and that no government, no household, would be able to resist the movement.

During this time Hamilcar reduced the eastern

countries. He drove back the Gauls; and all the Barbarians found themselves besieged on every side.

Then he set himself to work to harass them. He would march up, then depart; and continually renewed this manœuvre, until gradually he drew them out from their encampments. Spendius was obliged to follow; then Mâtho as well, in the end, yielded.

He did not pass beyond Tunis. He shut himself within the city walls. This obstinacy was full of sagacity; for soon they saw Narr' Havas leave by the gate of Khamoûn with his elephants and soldiers. Hamilcar recalled him. But already the other Barbarians were wandering about the provinces in pursuit of the Suffete.

At Clypea he had received three thousand Gauls. He had horses brought from Cyrenaica and suits of armour from Bruttium, and recommenced the war.

Never had his genius been so impetuous, so fertile as now. During five months he drew them in his track. He had a goal to which he desired to lead them.

The Barbarians had at first tried to surround him by small detachments, but he always escaped them. They split up no more. Their army now numbered forty thousand men all told, and they frequently rejoiced to see the Carthaginians driven to retreat.

That which tormented them most was the cavalry of Narr' Havas. Often in the most oppressive hours of the day as they traversed the plains, dozing under the weight of their weapons, a great line of dust would rise on the horizon, and horsemen galloped up, and from out of the depths of a cloud full of flaming eyeballs, a shower of darts was launched upon them. The Numidians, covered in their white mantles, uttered loud yells, lifted up their arms, pressing their knees against their rearing stallions, made them wheel suddenly, and thus disappeared. They always held in reserve provisions and javelins, at some distance off, packed upon dromedaries; and they returned more terrible, howling like wolves, flying like vultures.

The Barbarians who were posted on the edge of the files, fell one by one: this continued till the evening, when they endeavoured to enter the mountains.

Although the mountains were perilous for the elephants, Hamilcar had involved himself in them. He followed the long chain which extended from the promontory of Hermæum to the summit of Zagouan. This was, in their belief, a plan to hide the weakness of his troops. But the continual uncertainty in which he kept them ended by exasperating them more than a defeat. Nevertheless, they were not discouraged, but marched behind him.

One evening, behind the Silver Mountain and the Lead Mountain, in the midst of huge rocks, and at the mouth of a defile, they surprised a corps of velites, and thought that certainly the whole Punic army was before them, for they could hear the tramp of feet and bluster of clarions; at once the Carthaginians fled through the gorge. This defile sloped down to a plain, formed like an iron axe, environed by high cliffs. To overtake the velites the Barbarians made a charge, dashing into it; and right at the further end, other Carthaginians were rushing about tumultuously among galloping cattle. A man wear-

THE DEFILE OF THE BATTLE-AXE. 365

ing a red mantle could be discerned: it was the Suffete, at the sight of whom the pursuers yelled out, transported by an increase of fury and joy. However, many, either from languor or caution, had remained at the entrance of the defile; but cavalry, debouching from a wood, with blows of lances and sabres drove them back on the others, until speedily all the Barbarians were below in the plain.

After this vast mass of men had fluctuated about for some time, they halted, but could not discover any outlet.

Those who were adjacent to the defile turned back, but the passage had in the meantime entirely disappeared. They hailed those in the van to make them proceed; the latter crushed themselves against the mountain, and from afar they abused their comrades, who knew not how to refind the passage.

In fact, scarcely had the Barbarians descended, before men lying in ambush behind the rocks had heaved them up with beams and overset them; and as the pitch of the ground was very abrupt, the enormous blocks of rocks, rolling down in confusion, completely choked up the narrow orifice.

At the other extremity of the plain lay a long passage, here and there split by crevices, that led to a ravine beyond, rising to the superior plateau, where the Punic army was stationed. In this passage, against the walls of the cliff, scaling-ladders had previously been arranged; and, protected by the circuitous turnings of the crevices, the velites, before being overtaken, were able to seize the ladders and scale the walls; nevertheless, many became entangled at the bottom of the ravine, and were pulled aloft with cables, as the earth in that quarter was covered by live sand, and of such a pitch that it would be impossible for any man to crawl up, even on his hands and knees.

Almost immediately the Barbarians reached this spot; but a portcullis, forty cubits high, made to exactly fit in the space, suddenly dropped before them, like a rampart that had fallen from the sky.

Thus the strategic combinations of the Suffete were successfully accomplished. None of the Mercenaries knew the mountain, and, marching at the head of the column, they had thus blunderingly led the others into the trap. The rocks, a little narrower at the base, were easily knocked over, and whilst they all were running, his army in the horizon had yelled as if in distress. Hamilcar, it is true, might have lost all his velites,—half of them only remained down there; and he would willingly have sacrificed twenty times as many men for the success of such an enterprise.

Until morning the Barbarians marched in compact files, from one end to the other of this circumscribed plain. They tapped the mountain with their hands, trying to find some passage; but all to no purpose.

Finally, day broke; they then saw a large white wall, perpendicularly scarped; and not a visible means of escape, not a hope! The two natural passages from this entanglement were closed by the portcullis on one side, and choked by rocks on the other.

They all looked at each other without a word.

They collapsed, feeling an icy cold in their reins, and an overwhelming weight upon their eyelids.

They rose up and bounded against the rocks; but those at the base, pressed down by the uppermost, were immovable. Then they tried to clutch on to the rocky sides to attain the top; but the tun-bellied form of these huge masses refused all hold. They tried to split the earth at the sides of the gorge, but their weapons broke; then, as a last resort, they made a vast fire with their tent-poles, but the mountain would not burn.

Now they turned back to the portcullis; it was garnished with long spikes, thick as boar-spears, and sharp as porcupine quills, set closer together than bristles in a brush. But their rage animated them so blindly, that they threw themselves upon it: the first were spiked to the very backbone, the second fell backwards over each other, the whole recoiled, and left human shreds and blood-stained scalps caught on the horrible spikes.

When their discouragement was a little abated, they examined their provisions. The Mercenaries, whose baggage was lost, possessed hardly enough supplies for two days, and all the others found themselves absolutely destitute, as they had been waiting for a promised convoy from the southern villages.

Meanwhile, the cattle loosened by the Carthaginians in the gorge to decoy the Barbarians into this trap, wandered about: these they killed with their lances; after eating until their stomachs were full, their thoughts became less dismal.

The next day, they slaughtered the mules, in all forty; then scraped their hides, boiled their entrails, and pounded up the bones. As yet they did not despair: the army at Tunis would assuredly hear of their dilemma, and come at once to their rescue.

But the evening of the fifth day their hunger redoubled: they gnawed the shoulder-belts of their swords, and devoured the little sponges edging the bottoms of their helmets.

These forty thousand men were crowded in a kind of hippodrome formed by the mountain; some of them persistently remained before the portcullis, or at the base of the rocks; others confusedly covered the plain of the basin. The strong avoided each other, and the weak sought the brave, who, however, could not save them.

From fear of the infection, the bodies of the velites had been quickly buried, and the location of the pits remained no longer distinguishable.

Lying on the ground, all the Barbarians languished. Here and there between their lines, a veteran sometimes passed, and they shouted curses against the Carthaginians, against Hamilcar, and also against Mâtho. Although he was innocent of their present disaster, it seemed to them that the calamity would have been less if he had also shared it. Then they moaned; some even wept softly and low, like little children.

They would go to the captains and beg them to give them something to appease their sufferings. The officers made no reply, or, seized with a fit of rage, picked up stones and threw them into their faces.

In truth, many kept carefully hidden in the ground a reserve of food, possibly only a few handfuls of

THE DEFILE OF THE BATTLE-AXE. 369

dates, or a little farina, that they ate stealthily during the night, with their heads cautiously covered under their mantles; those who possessed swords held them drawn, and the more defiant stood upright, with their backs to the wall.

They accused and threatened their chiefs. Autharitus had no fear in showing himself, and with that tenacity peculiar to the Barbarians, which nothing could rebut, twenty times a day he sallied forth to the rocks, each time hoping perhaps to find them displaced, and, swinging his heavy shoulders covered with furs, he reminded his companions of a bear, that leaves its cavern in the spring to see if the snow has melted.

Spendius, surrounded by Greeks, hid himself in one of the crevices; and, as he was afraid, he caused the report of his death to be noised about.

They all had become hideously meagre; their skin was mottled with bluish patches. The evening of the ninth day three Iberians died, whereupon their frightened comrades quitted the place. The bodies were despoiled, and the white, naked corpses remained on the sand exposed to the sun.

Then some Garamantes commenced to prowl about these bodies. They were men accustomed to a life in the desert, and reverenced no God. At length the oldest one of the band made a sign, and bending over the corpses, with their knives they cut off strips and devoured them, squatting on their heels. The others looked on, standing aloof. Cries of horror were raised. Many, notwithstanding, in the depth of their hearts were jealous of their courage.

In the middle of the night some of the others

approached, and, dissimulating their real desire, asked for a tiny morsel, only to taste. Some braver ones followed; their number increased; soon a crowd collected. But almost all, feeling the cold flesh on their teeth, let their hands fall; others, on the contrary, devoured their portions with delight.

In order to be encouraged by example, they mutually stimulated each other. Those who had at first refused, came to see the Garamantes, and did not leave; their morsels were cooked over the embers on the point of a spear, and salted with the dust; they even disputed among themselves as to the best bits. When there remained not a morsel of the three corpses, their eyes roved over the plain to find others.

But did they not possess some Carthaginians—twenty captives taken in the last skirmish—and whom no one until now had noticed? They disappeared; it was a piece of revenge, to boot. Then, as they needs must live, and the taste for such food developed itself, and as they were dying, they killed the water-carriers, the grooms, and all the servants of the Mercenaries. Daily some of them perished. A few ate lustily, regained their strength, and were no longer sad.

Soon this resource failed them; then their appetite turned towards the sick and wounded: since they could not recover, it was as well to deliver them from their sufferings. Hence, as soon as a man tottered, all cried out that he was lost, and should serve the others. To accelerate their deaths they employed all manner of ruses. They stole from them the last remnants of their unclean portion: as if by accident, they trampled upon them. The dying, to raise a belief in their strength, endeavoured to lift their arms, or to rise up, or to laugh. People in swoons were roused by the cold contact of a notched blade sawing off a limb; and they killed still-more out of ferocity, without need, in order to appease their fury.

On the fourteenth day a warm, heavy fog, such as frequents those regions at the end of winter, settled down upon the army. This change of temperature produced many deaths, and corruption developed with frightful speed in the warm humidity retained by the mountain walls. The drizzle, which fell upon the dead and softened them, soon made of the whole plain one great mass of rottenness. White vapour floated above, stinging their nostrils, penetrating their skin, and troubling their eyes: and the Barbarians fancied that they saw in the breaths that they exhaled the souls of their dead comrades. An immense disgust overwhelmed them. They would have no more of it. They would rather die.

Two days later the air became pure again, and hunger reseized them. It seemed at times that their stomachs were clawed with hooks; then they rolled over in convulsions, stuffing their mouths full of dirt, biting their own arms, and then burst into frantic spasms of laughter.

Yet more, if possible, did their thirst torment them, as they had not a drop of water—for the water-bottles since the ninth day had been completely dry. To deceive this want, they resorted to the trick of applying on their tongues, the metal scales of their sword-belts, the ivory hafts, or the iron of their glaives, while experienced camel-drivers compressed their bellies with ropes; others sucked a stone, and some drank urine cooled in their brazen helmets.

And they ever looked for the army from Tunis! The length of time that it took to come, according to their conjecture, made its speedy arrival certain. Besides, Mâtho, who was so brave, would not forsake them. "He will come to-morrow!" they said to each other. The morrow came and passed, but he came not.

At the commencement they had prayed, made vows, and all sorts of incantations; but at present they did not feel for their Divinities other than hatred, and out of vengeance endeavoured not to believe in them.

Men of violent characters perished first; the Africans resisted better than the Gauls. Zarxas, amid the Baleares, remained extended full length, his hair tossed above his arms, inert. Spendius had found a plant with broad leaves full of juice, and, in order to scare the others, declared it to be poisonous; then he fed himself upon it.

They were too weak to knock down with a stone the ravens that flew about. Sometimes, when a bearded-vulture perched on a corpse, and had been for a long time tearing it, a man would crawl towards it with a javelin between his teeth, lean upon his arm, and, having taken a good aim, throw the weapon. The bird with white plumage, disturbed by the noise, would pause, look all about in a tranquil manner, like a cormorant on a reef, then, when satisfied no harm awaited it, plunged again its hideous yellow beak into its prey ; and the man, in despair, would fall flat on his face in the dust. Some succeeded in discovering chameleons and serpents. But it was the love of life that kept them alive. They held their minds exclusively fixed on this idea—and clung to existence by an effort of will that in itself prolonged it.

The most stoical gathered near together, sitting about in the middle of the plain, here and there between the dead ; and, wrapped in their mantles, abandoned themselves silently to their sorrow.

Those who had been born in cities recalled the bustling streets full of clatter, the taverns, the theatres, the baths, and the barbers' shops, where stories were told : others, again, saw fields at sundown, where the yellow grain waved and the huge oxen ascended the hills with the ploughshares on their necks. The travellers dreamed of cisterns, the hunters of their forests, the veterans of their battles ; and in the torpor that stupefied them, their fancies jostled each other with all the power and clearness of dreams. Suddenly hallucinations came over them ; they sought a gate in the mountain side to escape, and desired to pass through. Others, believing that they were navigating in a tempest, gave orders for handling a ship ; some even recoiled in terror, perceiving in the clouds Punic battalions ; then again, others fancied that they were figuring at a feast, and sang songs.

Many in a strange mania repeated the same word, or continually made the same gesture ; then, when they came to raise their heads and look at one another, sobs suffocated them, on discovering the horrible ravages depicted on their faces. Some ceased to suffer, and sought to employ the tedious hours by recounting the various perils from which they had escaped.

Death seemed certain and imminent for all. How often had they not tried to open a passage! As for imploring terms from the conquerors, by what means could they? They did not even know where Hamilcar was.

The wind blew from the direction of the ravine, continually making the sand flow over the portcullis in cascades, and the mantles and hair of the Barbarians were completely covered over with falling sand, as if the rising earth was desirous to engulf them. Nothing budged; the eternal mountain each morning seemed higher. Sometimes flocks of birds flew swiftly overhead, spreading out their wings across the open blue sky, in the freedom of the air: they closed their eyes to avoid seeing them. They felt at first a buzzing in their ears; their finger-nails blackened; the cold seized their breasts. They lay down upon their sides, and expired without a cry.

On the nineteenth day, two thousand Asiatics were dead, and fifteen hundred men from the Archipelago, eight thousand Libyans, the youngest Mercenaries, and complete tribes—in all, twenty thousand soldiers, one half of the army.

Autharitus, who had only fifty Gauls surviving, was about to kill himself, thereby putting an end to it all, when at the summit of the mountain facing him, he believed he saw a man. The great height made this man look like a dwarf. However, Autharitus recognised on his left arm a trefoil-shaped buckler, and cried out, "A Carthaginian!" In the fer, and sought to employ the tedious hours by recounting the various perils from which they had escaped.

Death seemed certain and imminent for all. How often had they not tried to open a passage! As for imploring terms from the conquerors, by what means could they? They did not even know where Hamilcar was.

The wind blew from the direction of the ravine, continually making the sand flow over the portcullis in cascades, and the mantles and hair of the Barbarians were completely covered over with falling sand, as if the rising earth was desirous to engulf them. Nothing budged; the eternal mountain each morning seemed higher. Sometimes flocks of birds flew swiftly overhead, spreading out their wings across the open blue sky, in the freedom of the air: they closed their eyes to avoid seeing them. They felt at first a buzzing in their ears; their finger-nails blackened; the cold seized their breasts. They lay down upon their sides, and expired without a cry.

On the nineteenth day, two thousand Asiatics were dead, and fifteen hundred men from the Archipelago, eight thousand Libyans, the youngest Mercenaries, and complete tribes—in all, twenty thousand soldiers, one half of the army.

Autharitus, who had only fifty Gauls surviving, was about to kill himself, thereby putting an end to it all, when at the summit of the mountain facing him, he believed he saw a man. The great height made this man look like a dwarf. However, Autharitus recognised on his left arm a trefoil-shaped buckler, and cried out, "A Carthaginian!" In the plain below the portcullis, and under the rocks, instantly all rose to their feet. The soldier marching on the edge of the precipice was eagerly watched by the Barbarians.

Spendius picked up an ox skull, and with two girdles fashioned a diadem, placing it on the horns at the end of a pole, in witness of peaceful intentions. The Carthaginian disappeared. They waited expectantly.

At last, in the evening, like a stone detached from the cliff, there suddenly fell from above a baldric made of red leather covered with embroidery and three diamond stars; in the centre it bore stamped upon it the seal of the Grand Council—a horse under a palm tree. This was Hamilcar's response, the safe conduct that he sent.

They had nothing to fear; any change of fortune brought an end to their ills. A measureless rapture agitated them; they embraced and wept. Spendius, Autharitus, Zarxas, four Italians, one Negro, and two Spartans, offered themselves as envoys. They were at once accepted; however, they knew no way by which to gain exit.

In the midst of this dilemma, a crash resounded in the direction of the rocks, and the topmost crag, having swayed on its base, bounded down to the bottom. In fact, though from the side of the Barbarians the rocks were immovable—for it would have been necessary to ascend an inclined plane: besides, they were closely packed by the narrowness of the gorge—from the other side, on the contrary, it was enough to push them vigorously to make them descend.

The Carthaginians pushed them forward, and at daybreak they had shifted into the plain, resembling the steps of a gigantic stairway in ruins.

Yet the Barbarians could not climb up, so ladders were thrown over. All rushed for these; but the prompt discharge of a catapult forced them back; and only the Ten were taken up.

These marched between Clinabarians, leaning their hands on the cruppers of the horses to sustain themselves. Now that their first joy was over, they began to experience uneasiness. The demands of Hamilcar would be cruel; but Spendius reassured his companions, saying:—

"It is I who will speak!" Then he vaunted his knowledge of admirable things to say for the welfare of the army.

Behind all the bushes they encountered sentinels in ambush; all, however, prostrated themselves before the baldric Spendius had put over his shoulder.

When finally they arrived at the Punic encampment, the crowd pressed about them, and they heard significant whispers and laughter.

The door of a tent opened; Hamilcar was at the back part, sitting on a bench near a low table, on which shone a naked blade. His captains stood about him. When he saw these men, he started backwards, then leaned forward to examine them.

The pupils of their eyes were extraordinarily large, and a wide black ring encircled them, extending to the lower part of their ears; their bluish noses projected between their hollow cheeks, furrowed by deep wrinkles; the skin of their bodies, too loose for their flabby muscles, was hidden under a coat of slate-coloured dust; their lips stuck against their yellow teeth; they exhaled an infectious odour, imparting the idea that they were half-open tombs, living sepulchres.

In the middle of the tent, on a mat, round which the captains were about to sit down, there was a smoking dish of pumpkins. The Barbarians rivetted their gaze on it, quivering in every limb, as the tears started to their eyes. Nevertheless they restrained themselves.

Hamilcar turned round to speak to some one, when instantly they all rushed upon the dish, throwing themselves flat on the ground, their faces steeped in the grease; noises of deglutition mingled with sobs of delight, which they could not suppress. Rather from astonishment than in pity, they were permitted to finish the contents of the bowl. Then, when they again stood up, Hamilcar commanded by a sign that the man who wore the baldric should speak. Spendius was frightened, and stammered.

Hamilcar, in listening, constantly twirled around on one finger a large gold ring, the same which had imprinted the seal of Carthage on the baldric; he accidentally dropped it on the ground. Spendius at once stooped down and picked it up: before his master the habits of a slave returned to him. The others shuddered indignantly at this baseness.

But the Greek raised his voice, and recounted the crimes of Hanno, whom he knew to be a foe of Barca. He tried to move Hamilcar's pity with the details of their sufferings, and spoke on for a long time in a style rapid, insidious, and violent. Towards the end he forgot himself, and was carried away by the fervour of his imagination.

Hamilcar replied that he accepted their excuses. Peace, therefore, was about to be concluded, and this time it would be final! But he required that ten Mercenaries chosen by himself, without weapons and without tunics, should be delivered to him.

They had not expected such clemency, and Spendius exclaimed:

"Yes! twenty, if you will, master!"

"No! ten suffice me," mildly replied Hamilcar.

In order that they could deliberate, they were dismissed from his tent. As soon as they were alone, Autharitus objected on behalf of his sacrificed companions, and Zarxas said to Spendius:

"Why did you not kill him?—his sword was within your reach!"

"Him!" exclaimed Spendius, and repeated frequently, "Him! him!" as if the thing had been an utter impossibility, and Hamilcar were a divinity.

So thoroughly were they overcome by their protracted fatigue, that they gladly stretched themselves on their backs upon the ground; sorely perplexed as to what course to determine upon.

Spendius persistently urged them to yield; after some parley they consented, and they returned to the Suffete.

Then the Suffete put his hand in the hands of the ten Barbarians one after another, and pressed their thumbs; afterwards he rubbed his hands on his clothes, for their clammy skins had presented to his touch a sensation harsh and soft, that made a slimy, creeping impression. Subsequently he said:

"You all, then, are the chiefs of the Barbarians, and you have sworn for them?"

"Yes!" they answered.

"Without reservation, from the bottom of your souls, with the intention of fulfilling your promises?"

They assured him that they would return to the others, and execute their pledges.

"Ah! well!" said the Suffete, "according to the convention which has passed between me, Barca, and you, the ambassadors of the Mercenaries, it is you whom I choose, and I shall keep you!"

Spendius fell fainting on the mat. The Barbarians, as if abandoning him, pressed close together; and there was not a word, not a murmur.

Their comrades who awaited them, when they did not return, believed that they were certainly betrayed. Without doubt the envoys had given themselves up to the Suffete.

They waited two days longer; then, on the morning of the third, their resolution was taken. With ropes, picks, and arrows fitted like rungs of a ladder between strips of canvas, they succeeded in scaling the rocks; and leaving behind them the weaker ones, about three thousand in number, they set out to rejoin the army at Tunis.

At the top of the gorge spread out a prairie, lightly sprinkled with shrubs, the buds of which the Barbarians devoured; then they came upon a field of beans: these also disappeared as if a cloud of locusts had passed over the region. Three hours later they came to a second plateau, bounded by a belt of green hills.

Between the undulations of these hillocks, sheaves the colour of silver shone, stacked at regular distances: the sun so dazzled the Barbarians that they could but confusedly discern under them, large, black masses, that sprang up, as though they were blooming out of the earth. They were the lances in the towers, on the backs of the formidably equipped elephants.

Besides the spear of their breastplate, the pointed ferrules on their tusks, the brazen plates which covered their sides, and the daggers fastened to their knee-caps, they had on the end of their trunks a band of leather, in which was fixed the hilt of a large cutlass. Starting all at the same time from the bottom of the plain, they advanced from each side in parallel lines.

A nameless terror froze the Barbarians; they could not take a step, to flee. Already they found themselves enveloped.

The elephants entered this mass, and with the spears on their breastplates clove it; the lance-like tusks overturned it like plough-shares. They cut, they hewed, they hacked with the scythes extending from their trunks; the towers full of fiery darts seemed like moving volcanoes. Nothing could be distinguished but a broad mass, on which were visible white patches of human flesh, grey spots of fragments of brass, and red splashes of blood. The horrible animals passed through it all, ploughing in it back furrows.

The most furious were led by a Numidian, crowned with a diadem of plumes. He hurled javelins with terrific rapidity, while uttering at intervals a long, shrill whistle ;—the monstrous beasts, docile as dogs, in the midst of the carnage kept turning an eye in his direction.

Their circle gradually narrowed. The weakened Barbarians could not resist: soon the elephants reached the centre of the plain. There was not room enough, and the animals crowded together, half rearing up, and clashed their tusks. Suddenly Narr' Havas quieted them, and turning round they trotted back towards the hills.

Meanwhile two syntagmas, taking refuge at the right in a hollow, had thrown down their weapons, and were now upon their knees: turning towards the Punic tents, with uplifted arms, they implored mercy.

Their arms and legs were shackled; then, when they were flat on the ground, close together, the elephants were led over them.

Their breast-bones cracked like coffers being broken; the huge animals at each step crushed two men; their cumbrous feet plunged into their bodies with a movement of their haunches, that made them appear lame. They continued to go in this way to the end of the group.

The level of the plain became motionless; night fell. Hamilcar was exultant before the spectacle of his vengeance, but suddenly he started.

He saw, and all saw, six hundred paces distant, on the left at the summit of a peak, yet more Barbarians! In fact, four hundred of the stoutest Mercenaries, Etruscans, Libyans, and Spartans, early in the beginning of the fray had gained the heights, and until now had been uncertain what to do.

After the massacre of their comrades, they had resolved to cut through the Carthaginians; already they were descending in close columns in a marvellous and formidable fashion.

A herald was instantly sent by the Suffete, stating that he required soldiers, and would receive them without condition, so much had he admired their bravery. They could even, added the man of Carthage, come a little nearer, to a certain spot, which he pointed out, and where they would find provisions.

The Barbarians ran thither and passed the night in eating; then the Carthaginians burst out into murmurs against the partiality of the Suffete for the Mercenaries. Did he yield to the promptings of an insatiable hatred, or was it possibly a refinement of perfidy?

The following day he came himself, unarmed, bareheaded, with an escort of Clinabarians, and declared to the Barbarians that, having more men than he could afford to feed, his intention was not to retain them. However, as he required good soldiers, and knew not by what method to choose the best, they must fight among themselves till death, and he would admit the victors to his own body-guard. Such a mode of death was preferable to any other. Then he parted his troops—for the Punic standards hid the horizon from the Mercenaries—and showed them Narr' Havas's one hundred and ninety-two elephants, forming a single straight line, and brandishing with uplifted trunks cutlasses, like giants' arms poising axes over their heads.

The Barbarians scrutinised each other silently. It was not the fear of death that made them pale, but

THE DEFILE OF THE BATTLE-AXE.

the horrible duress they found themselves reduced to.

The community of their hazardous existence had established between these men profound, singular friendships. For the most part the camp replaced their country; and living without families, they transferred to a comrade their instincts of tenderness, and they slept side by side under the same mantle, beneath the starlight. In this perpetual wandering, as they traversed all sorts of countries, full of murders and adventures, they formed strange loves—unnatural unions as serious as marriage, wherein the stronger protected the younger amid the din of battle, aided him to leap across precipices, sponged from his brow the sweat of fevers, stole food for him; and the other, a child picked up on the roadside and become a Mercenary, would repay this devotion by a thousand delicate cares, and by the complaisances of a wife.

In the hours of their intoxication they exchanged their necklaces and ear-rings, gifts they had formerly bestowed upon each other after some great peril.

All begged to die, but no one would strike the blow. Here and there a youth said to another man, whose beard was grey: "No! no! you are more robust! You will revenge us! Kill me!" And the elder answered: "I have fewer years to live! Strike to the heart, and think no more about it!"

Brothers contemplated each other, with hands clasped; lovers uttered to lovers eternal farewells, standing upright, weeping on each other's shoulders. They took off their breastplates, that the points might bury themselves more quickly, revealing the scars of terrific blows received for Carthage, resembling historic inscriptions on columns.

Placing themselves in four rows, in the fashion of gladiators, they began by timid engagements; some even bound up their eyes, moving their swords gently, like the staves of the blind. The Carthaginians gave vent to yells, crying out that they were cowards. The Barbarians grew excited, and soon the conflict became general, headlong, and terrible.

Occasionally two men stopped covered with blood, fell into each other's arms, and expired kissing. Not one recoiled. They rushed determinedly upon the extended blades. Their delirium became so furious that the Carthaginians even at a distance experienced fear.

At length they stopped. A loud, hoarse noise was emitted from their chests; and their eyeballs could be seen amidst their long hair, which hung down as if they had emerged from a bath of purple dye. Some turned rapidly round and round, like panthers wounded in the forehead. Others stood motionless, regarding a corpse at their feet; then suddenly they tore their faces with their finger-nails, seized their swords with both hands, and buried them in their abdomens. Sixty yet remained. They asked for drink. They were bidden to throw down their swords; when they had done so, water was brought to them.

While they were drinking, their faces buried in the vessels, sixty Carthaginians leaped upon them, and slew them, by stabbing them with stilettoes in the back.

Hamilcar had permitted this, to gratify the in-from Tartessus, and Punic guinea-fowls, fluttered about. The gardens, uncultivated for so long a time, had grown rank with verdure; the colocynth sprang up through the branches of the cassia trees; the dragon-wort sprinkled the rose-fields; all species of vegetation formed tangled bowers, and the sun's rays, descending slantingly, outlined here and there upon the ground, as in a wood, the shadow of a leaf.

The domestic animals having become wild, bounded away at the slightest noise. Sometimes a gazelle might be seen dragging with its little black hoofs the peacocks' feathers scattered about. The noise of the distant city was lost in the murmur of the waves. The sky was perfectly blue; not a sail appeared on the sea.

Narr' Havas ceased speaking. Without responding, Salammbô looked at him. He wore a linen robe over which flowers were painted, with a golden fringe at the hem; and two silver arrows held back his hair, braided close against his ears. He rested his right hand on the wooden shaft of a pike ornamented with bands of electrum and tufts of hair.

In contemplating him a host of thoughts absorbed her. This young man, with a sweet voice and feminine figure, captivated her eyes by the grace of his fine person, and he seemed like an elder sister sent by the Baals to protect her. The memory of Mâtho seized her; she did not resist the desire to inquire what had become of him.

Narr' Havas responded that the Carthaginians were advancing on Tunis, in order to capture him.

While he explained their chances of success and Mâtho's weakness, she appeared to rejoice with an extraordinary hope; her lips quivered, her breast palpitated. When at last he vowed to kill Mâtho himself, she cried out:

"Yes! Kill him! It must be so!"

The Numidian replied that he ardently desired his death, inasmuch as when the war was once terminated he should marry her.

Salammbô trembled, and bowed her head.

But Narr' Havas went on to compare his love and his desires to the flowers that languished for rain; to travellers lost in the night awaiting the dawn. He also told her that she was more beautiful than the moon; more to be preferred than the morning breezes, or than the face of the host. He would have rare objects, not to be found in Carthage, brought for her from the country of the Blacks, and the apartments of their mansion should be sprinkled with gold dust.

Evening fell. Balmy odours filled the air. For a long time they looked at one another in silence, and Salammbô's eyes, in the depth of her long, ample draperies, had the appearance of two stars, seen through a rift in a cloud. Before sunset, he retired from her presence.

The Elders felt relieved from a vast anxiety when he left Carthage, for the people this time had received him with even more enthusiastic acclamations than upon the former occasion. If Hamilcar and the Numidian king triumphed alone over the Mercenaries, it would be impossible to resist them. Then they resolved to weaken Barca, by making old

Hanno, the one whom they loved, participate in the honours of the deliverance of the Republic.

Hanno went immediately towards the western provinces, so as to revenge himself in the same regions which had witnessed his shame: but the inhabitants, as well as the Barbarians, were either dead, or hiding, or had taken flight. Then his wrath poured itself forth upon the country; he burned the ruins of ruins, leaving not a solitary tree, not a spear of grass: the children and the infirm whom they met were tortured; he gave the women to the soldiers, to violate before slaying them, having the most beautiful always thrown into his own litter—for his atrocious malady inflamed his desires, and he would gloat over his victims with all the rage of a madman.

Often, on the crest of the hills, black tents sank down, as if overthrown by the wind, and broad discs with shining edges, which were recognised as the wheels of chariots, revolved with a doleful sound as they gradually disappeared in the valleys.

The tribes which had abandoned the siege of Carthage were thus wandering through the provinces, waiting for an opportunity, for some victory of the Barbarians, to return. But from terror, or because of famine, they all retraced the roads leading to their own countries, and disappeared.

Hamilcar was not jealous of Hanno's successes, nevertheless he hastened to end them, ordering him to fall back on Tunis; and Hanno, who loved his country, on the appointed day was found under the walls of that city.

Tunis had for her defence her aboriginal population, twelve thousand Mercenaries, and all the Eaters-of-Unclean-Things. They, like Mâtho, had their eyes rivetted on the horizon of Carthage, and the populace, as well as the *Schalischim*, beheld her lofty walls from afar, dreaming of the infinite joys behind them. In the agreement of hatred, the resistance was quickly organised. Leather-bottles were used to make helmets, all the palms in the gardens were hewn down to furnish lances, cisterns were excavated; and as for food, they fished along the lake shore, catching large white fish which fed on the corpses and filth.

Their ramparts, kept in ruins by the jealousy of Carthage, were so weak that one might throw them over with a push of the shoulder. Mâtho ordered the breaches to be filled up with the stones from dwellings. It was the supreme struggle; he hoped for nothing, and yet, he said to himself, that Fortune was fickle.

As the Carthaginians drew near, they noticed a man on the rampart, who from his waist overtopped the battlements. The arrows flying about him seemed not to frighten him more than a flight of swallows. Most extraordinarily, not one touched him.

Hamilcar pitched his camp on the southern side; Narr' Havas on his right occupied the plain of Rhades; Hanno was stationed on the lake shore; and the three generals were bound to retain their respective positions so that all should attack the walls at one and the same time.

But Hamilcar, in the first place, desired to show the Mercenaries that he would chastise them like slaves, therefore he had the ten ambassadors crucified close together on a hillock facing the city.

At this spectacle the besieged abandoned the ramparts.

Mâtho had believed, that if he could pass between the walls and Narr' Havas's tents so expeditiously that the Numidians would not have time to sally forth, he would fall on the rear of the Carthaginian infantry, who would thus be caught between his division and the troops within the town. He dashed out with his veterans.

Narr' Havas saw him ; he crossed the lake shore, and went to warn Hanno to despatch his men to succour Hamilcar. Did he think Barca too weak to resist the Mercenaries ? Was this a perfidy, or a folly ? No one ever knew.

Hanno, desiring to humiliate his rival, did not hesitate ; he ordered the trumpets to be sounded, and all his troops rushed upon the Barbarians. They wheeled round and charged straight upon the Carthaginians ; they overthrew them, trampled them under foot, and driving them back, reached the tent of Hanno, who then was surrounded by thirty Carthaginians, the most illustrious of the Elders.

Hanno appeared stupefied by their audacity ; he called his captains ; the assaulters thrust their fists forward to seize him by the throat, vociferating abuse. The crowd pushed each other, and those who had their hands on him could scarcely hold him. However, he tried to whisper to them : "I will give you all you want! I am rich! Save me!" They dragged him away, and, heavy as he was, his feet did not touch the ground. They had also dragged away the Elders. His terror redoubled.

"You have defeated me! I am your captive! I will ransom myself! Listen to me, my friends!" and, carried along by their shoulders pressed against his sides, he repeated: "What are you going to do? What do you want? You see well, I do not resist! I have always been complaisant!"

A gigantic cross was erected at the gate; the Barbarians howled out, "Here! here!" Then he raised his voice louder, and in the name of their Gods he commanded them to take him to their *Schalischim*, because he had something to confide to him, upon which depended their welfare.

They paused, some declaring it would be wise to call Mâtho; and he was sent for.

Hanno sank down upon the grass, and he saw around him still more crosses, as if the torture under which he was going to perish had multiplied itself beforehand. He made strenuous efforts to convince himself that he was deceived, that there was only one cross, and even that there was not one. Finally, the Mercenaries lifted him up as Mâtho appeared.

"Speak!" cried Mâtho.

He offered to deliver over Hamilcar: then they would enter Carthage, and both be kings.

Mâtho turned away, making a sign for the men to hasten; he thought this was a stratagem to gain time.

The Barbarian was deceived, for Hanno was in one of those dire extremities where a man no longer considers anything but self-preservation. Besides, he hated Hamilcar so thoroughly, that for the slightest hope of safety he would have sacrificed him and all his soldiers.

At the foot of thirty crosses the Elders languished upon the ground; already ropes had been passed under their armpits. Then the old Suffete, fully realising that he was to be put to death, wept bitterly.

His captors pulled off what remained of his clothing, revealing the horrors of his person. Ulcers covered this nameless mass; the fat of his legs concealed his toe-nails; the flesh hung like green rags to his fingers; the tears which ran between the tubercles of his cheeks, made his visage something shockingly deplorable, and had the appearance of occupying more space than on any other human face. His royal bandeau, half untied, trailed with his long white hair in the dust.

Believing that the ropes were not sufficiently strong to swing him up to the top of the cross, they nailed him to it before it was erected, in the Punic mode. But his pride was aroused in his misery; he began to overwhelm them with abuse. He frothed and writhed like a marine monster stranded and killed on the shore. He predicted that they should all end even more horribly than he, and in that he should be revenged. He was right: for on the other side of the city, whence now escaped jets of flames mingled with columns of smoke, the envoys of the Mercenaries were in the agonies of death.

Some who had fainted at first, were revived by the coolness of the breeze; but they remained with their chins on their breasts, their bodies lagging a little, in spite of the nails through their arms, which were fastened above their heads. From their hands and feet blood slowly fell in big drops, like ripe fruit dropping off from the branches of a tree; and Carthage, the gulf, the mountains, and the plains, appeared to them to be all revolving as an immense wheel; sometimes a cloud of dust lifted from the earth, and enveloped them in its eddies. They were consumed by a horrible thirst; their parched tongues curled up in their mouths, and they felt an icy sweat trickling over them with their departing souls. Meanwhile, they saw at an infinite depth, streets, soldiers marching, blades waving; and, the tumult of battle came indistinctly to them, as the noise of the sea to shipwrecked sailors dying in the rigging of their ships. The Italiots, more robust than the others, continued to shriek; the Lacædemonians kept silent, with eyes closed; Zarxas, formerly so vigorous, drooped like a broken reed; the Ethiopian alongside of him had his head reversed backward over the arm of the cross; Autharitus, motionless, rolled his eyes; his heavy, long hair was caught in a crack in the wood and drawn straight over his forehead, and the death-rattle that escaped his lips seemed rather like a growl of wrath.

As for Spendius, a strange courage had come to him; now he despised life, because of the certainty that he should have an almost immediate and eternal release; he awaited death with impassibility.

In the midst of their swoonings, sometimes they shuddered at the touch of feathers as they grazed against their lips. Huge wings cast long, waving shadows about them, croakings sounded in the air; and as the cross of Spendius was the highest, it was thereon the first vulture alighted. Then he turned his face towards Autharitus, saying slowly, with an indefinable smile :

"Do you recall the lions on the road to Sicca ?"

"They were our brothers !" answered the Gaul, as he expired.

The Suffete during this period had broken through the walls, and attained the citadel. Under a gust of wind the smoke suddenly flew upwards, disclosing the horizon as far as the walls of Carthage ; he believed even that he could distinguish the people who watched from the platform of Eschmoûn ; then he turned his eyes, and perceived to the left, on the lake shore, thirty immense crosses.

In fact, to render the crosses more frightful, they had constructed them out of tent-poles lashed end to end ; so that the thirty bodies of the crucified Elders appeared high up in the sky. On their bosoms gleamed, like white butterflies, the feathers of the arrows shot at them from below.

On the summit of the tallest shone a broad, gold fillet ; it hung upon the shoulder of the crucified one, for the arm on that side was wanting ; and Hamilcar with difficulty recognised Hanno. His spongy bones giving way under the iron nails, portions of his limbs had become detached, and there only remained on the cross shapeless fragments, like portions of animals hung upon a hunter's door.

The Suffete had been unable to learn anything of Mâtho's sally : the city before him concealed all that lay beyond at the back ; and the captains sent successively to the two generals had not returned. Then the fugitives came, recounting the rout ; and the Punic army halted. This catastrophe falling in the midst of their victory, stupefied them. They no longer heeded Hamilcar's commands. Mâtho profited by it to continue his ravages upon the Numidians.

Hanno's camp having been overthrown, he had turned again on them. The elephants charged; but the Mercenaries, with firebrands snatched from the burning wall, advanced on the plain, agitating the flames; the huge animals were frightened, and fled, precipitating themselves into the gulf, killed each other in their struggles, or were drowned under the weight of their breastplates. Already Narr' Havas had ordered his cavalry to charge; the Mercenaries threw themselves flat down with their faces against the ground, then, when the horses were within three steps of them, they sprang under their bellies and ripped them open with poniards; half of the Numidians had thus perished when Barca unexpectedly came up.

The Mercenaries, now exhausted, could not hold out against his troops. They retreated in good order as far as the Hot-Springs Mountain. The Suffete had the prudence not to follow them. He moved towards the embouchures of the Macar.

Tunis belonged to him; but the city remained merely a heap of smoking rubbish. The ruins had tumbled down through the breaches in the walls out into the plain; beyond, between the shores of the gulf, the elephants' carcases, driven by the wind, intershocked, like an archipelago of black rocks floating on the water.

Narr' Havas, in order to sustain this war, had exhausted his forests, taking alike young and old, male and female elephants, and the military strength of his kingdom could not be reinforced. The people, who saw these animals perish from afar, were in despair; men lamented in the streets, calling them by their names, as deceased friends: "Ah! Invincible! Victor! Thunderbolt! Swallow!" And during the first day everyone spoke of only the dead citizens. The next day, seeing the Mercenaries' tents pitched on the Hot-Springs Mountain, their despair became so deep that many of the people, especially the women, hurled themselves headlong down from the top to the bottom of the Acropolis.

All were ignorant of Hamilcar's designs; he lived alone in his tent, having no one near him but a young boy, never admitting anyone, not even Narr' Havas, to eat with them. Nevertheless, he manifested towards him extraordinary attentions since Hanno's defeat; and the king of the Numidians had too much interest in becoming his son to be distrustful of them.

This inaction veiled crafty intrigues. By all sorts of artifices he won over the chiefs of villages; and the Mercenaries were hunted, repulsed, and tracked like ferocious beasts. As soon as they had entered into a wood, the trees were fired about them, the waters of the springs they drank from were poisoned, and they were walled up in caverns wherein they had taken refuge to sleep. People who had formerly protected them, even their recent accomplices, now pursued them; they could always recognise in these bands Carthaginian armour.

THE DEFILE OF THE BATTLE AXE. 397

Numbers of the Mercenaries' faces were eaten by red-tetter; this they thought had attacked them from touching Hanno. Others imagined it was because they had eaten the fish of Salammbô; and, far from repenting, they dreamed of yet more abominable sacrileges, that the humiliation of the Punic Gods might be greater. They would have liked to exterminate them.

Thus, for the term of three months, they marched wearily along the eastern coast, from behind the mountain of Selloum, and as far as the first sands of the desert, seeking a place of refuge, no matter where. Utica and Hippo-Zarytus alone had not been treacherous; but alas, Hamilcar surrounded both of these cities. Then they reascended to the north at hazard, without knowing the roads. By dint of miseries, their brains were disturbed.

Their only sentiment was one of exasperation, which continued developing itself. One day they found themselves again in the gorges of Cobus, once more before Carthage!

Then the engagements multiplied. Fortune inclined to neither side; both armies were so worn out that they wished, instead of skirmishing, to engage in a great pitched battle, provided that it should certainly be the last.

Mâtho had desired to carry the challenge himself to the Suffete. However, one of his Libyans devoted himself to the mission. At his departure all were convinced that he would not return.

He returned the same evening.

Hamilcar accepted the challenge. They would meet the next day at sunrise, on the plain of Rhades.

The Mercenaries wanted to know if he had said nothing more, and the Libyan added :

—" As I stood before him, he asked me why I waited. I answered,—'For some one to kill me!' Then he replied :—' No! go now; that shall be to-morrow, with the others.' "

This generosity astonished the Barbarians ; some were terrified at it, and Mâtho regretted that the envoy had not been killed.

Mâtho's army still contained three thousand Africans, twelve hundred Greeks, fifteen hundred Campanians, two hundred Iberians, four hundred Etruscans, five hundred Samnites, forty Gauls, and a band of Naffur—Nomad bandits met with in the date region : all told, seven thousand, two hundred, and nineteen soldiers; but not one complete syntagma. They caulked up the holes in their breastplates with the shoulder-blades of animals, and they replaced their brazen cothurnes with ragged sandals. Copper or iron plates weighed down their garments ; their coats-of-mail hung in tatters about them, revealing scars that seemed like purple threads, between the hair on their arms, and upon their faces.

The resentment for their dead comrades came back upon their souls, and increased their strength. They felt confusedly that they were the ministers of a God who dwelt in the hearts of the oppressed, like the pontiffs of a universal vengeance ! Then the misery of an exorbitant injustice enraged them, and especially as they gazed at Carthage on the horizon. They made solemn oaths to fight for one another to the death.

THE DEFILE OF THE BATTLE-AXE. 399

They slaughtered the beasts of burden, eating as much as possible in order to acquire strength; afterwards they slept. Some prayed, turning themselves towards different constellations.

The Carthaginians were first on the battle-field. They rubbed the surface of their bucklers with oil, to make the arrows glance off more easily; the foot-soldiers who had long hair, prudently cut it off close over the forehead; and Hamilcar, as early as the fifth hour, ordered his men to overturn all the bowls, knowing the disadvantage of entering a combat with too full stomachs. His army amounted to fourteen thousand men, about double the entire number of the Barbarians. Still he had never experienced an equal anxiety: if he succumbed, it would certainly be the annihilation of the Republic, and he would perish on the cross; if he triumphed, on the contrary, by the Pyrenees, Gaul, and the Alps, he would conquer Italy, and the empire of the Barcas would become eternal. Twenty times during the night he got up to survey everything personally, even to the most minute details. As for the Carthaginians, they were exasperated by the prolonged terror.

Narr' Havas doubted the fidelity of his Numidians; furthermore, he thought that the Barbarians might conquer them; a strange weakness possessed him, and every moment he quaffed large cups of water.

A man whom he did not know, opened his tent, and placed on the ground a crown of rock salt, ornamented with hieratic designs made in sulphur, and lozenges of mother-of-pearl. One sent sometimes to her betrothed his marriage-crown as a proof of love or manner of invitation.

Nevertheless, Hamilcar's daughter had no affection for Narr' Havas, for the memory of Mâtho embarrassed her in an intolerable way; it seemed to her that the death of this man could alone disentangle her thoughts: like seeking to cure the sting of a viper by crushing the viper on the wound.

The king of the Numidians was at her disposal. He waited impatiently for his marriage, and as it was to follow the victory. Salammbô had sent him this present in order to inspire his courage. Then his anxieties disappeared, and he thought only of the happiness of possessing so beautiful a wife.

The same vision had assailed Mâtho; but he rejected it at once; and his love, which he drove back, diffused over his comrades-in-arms. He cherished them like a portion of his own person— aye, of his hate—and he felt his genius loftier, his arm more powerful; all that he must execute appeared now clear before him. If occasionally sighs escaped from him, it was because he recalled the fate of Spendius.

He ranged the Barbarians in six equal lines, stationing the Etruscans in the centre, all attached to one bronze chain; the archers were kept in the rear, and on the wings he distributed the Naffur, mounted on camels with short-clipped hair and covered with ostrich plumes.

The Suffete disposed his soldiers in a similar order; outside of the infantry, beside the velites, he placed the Clinabarians, and beyond them the Numidians. When day appeared, the two armies were both thus drawn up in line of battle, face to face. All along these lines the foes contemplated each other with large, wild eyes. At first, there was evident hesitation; at length the two armies simultaneously were put in motion. The Barbarians advanced slowly, in order to avoid getting out of breath, beating the ground with their feet. The centre of the Punic army formed a convex curve. Then a terrible shock burst, like the crashing of two fleets running foul of each other. The first rank of the Barbarians was soon opened, and the archers, sheltered behind the others, hurled their balls, arrows, and javelins. Meanwhile, the curve of the Punic army gradually straightened: it became a right line, afterwards was inflected; next, the two sections of velites approached each other in parallel lines like the branches of closing compasses.

The Barbarians, charging the phalanx furiously, entered into the break: they were ruining themselves. Mâtho halted them, and whilst the Carthaginian wings continued to advance, he caused the three interior ranks of his army to retire outwardly; soon they overlapped his flanks; his army then appeared in a long line of three ranks. But the Barbarians placed at the two ends were the weakest, especially those on the left, who had exhausted their quivers; and the troop of velites, which had at last come hand-to-hand with them, slaughtered them freely.

Mâtho drew them back. His right wing contained the Campanians, armed with battle-axes; these he pushed against the left of the Carthaginians; the centre forces attacked the enemy, and those on the

2 D

other extremity, out of danger, kept the velites at bay.

Then Hamilcar divided his cavalry by squadrons, set the hoplites between them, and let them charge the Mercenaries.

These conical masses presented a front of horses, and their broader sides bristled with lances. It was impossible for the Barbarians to resist, for only their Greek foot-soldiers were equipped in brazen armour, all the others being merely armed with cutlasses on the end of poles, scythes taken from the farmhouses, and swords forged from the felloes of wheels; the blades, too soft, bent in striking; and while they were straightening them under their heels, the Carthaginians on the right and left easily massacred them.

But the Etruscans, rivetted to their chain, did not swerve. Those who were slain, unable to fall, made a barrier with their corpses; and this vast line of bronze alternately spread out and closed in, supple as a serpent, and as unshakable as a wall. The Barbarians came behind it to re-form, took breath for a minute, and rushed on again, with their shattered weapons in their hands.

Many already were weaponless, and sprang upon the Carthaginians, biting them in their faces like rabid dogs. The Gauls with pride stripped off their tunics, showing from a distance their fine, large, white bodies, and endeavoured to terrify the enemy by enlarging their wounds. In the middle of the Punic syntagma, the voice of the crier repeating the orders was no longer heard. The standards above the dust repeated their signals, and everyone moved along, impelled by the oscillation of the vast mass encompassing him.

Hamilcar commanded the Numidians to advance, but the Naffur precipitated themselves to meet the encounter. These men, habited in ample black robes, with a tuft of hair on the top of their heads, carrying rhinoceros leather-bucklers, wielded a blade without haft, held by a rope; and their camels, stuck all over with feathers, gave vent to long, loud, gurgling plaints. Their blades fell in exact places, and then were lifted up with a sharp stroke, each time carrying off a limb. The furious camels galloped through the syntagma; those with broken legs hopped awkwardly, like wounded ostriches.

The entire Punic infantry fell again on the Barbarians, and broke their line. Their maniples wheeled, separating one from another. The more glittering arms of the Carthaginians encircled them like crowns of gold; a swarming agitation filled the centre; the sun shone down on them, tipping the sword-points with white, dancing gleams. Some files of the slain Clinabarians lay stretched on the plain; the Mercenaries stripped off their armour and put it on themselves; then they returned to the combat. The Carthaginians, deceived, frequently entangled themselves in the midst of them. Stupefaction kept them motionless, or else they fell back and the triumphant cheers which arose from a distance seemed to drive them like wrecks in a storm. Hamilcar was in despair, for all was going to be wrecked by the genius of Mâtho and the invincible courage of the Mercenaries!

A noise of tambourines rang out on the horizon.

It was a crowd of old men, invalids, and youths fifteen years old, and even women, who, no longer able to restrain their anxiety, had left Carthage. In order to place themselves under the protection of something formidable, they had taken out of Hamilcar's park the only elephant in the possession of the Republic—the same one whose trunk had been cut off.

Then it seemed to the Carthaginians that their City, abandoning her walls, came to command them to die valiantly for her. Redoubled fury seized upon them, and the Numidians led on all the others.

In the middle of the plain the Barbarians were ranged with their backs to a hillock. They had no chance of success, nor even of surviving; but they were the best, the most intrepid, and the strongest.

The people of Carthage began to throw over the Numidians' heads, spits, larding-pins, and hammers; and those who had made consuls tremble, died under sticks thrown by women: the Punic populace exterminated the Mercenaries.

The Barbarians took refuge on the top of the hill: their circle at every fresh breach closed in. Twice they descended, but at each encounter were quickly driven back, and the Carthaginians, pell-mell, extended their arms, and reached out their spears between their comrades' legs, and thrust at random in front of them. They slipped in the blood, and the steep decline of the hill caused the dead to roll down. The elephant, endeavouring to climb the beleaguered hill, trod upon them up to his belly, and seemed to spread himself over them with delight.

The large end of his amputated trunk from time to time was lifted overhead like an enormous bloodsucker.

All halted. The Carthaginians ground their teeth, contemplating the top of the hill, where the Barbarians held their position, standing firmly ; finally, they rallied, and charged abruptly forward : the fray raged again.

Often the Mercenaries allowed the enemy to approach near, crying out that they would surrender, then with frightful sneers, at one blow they killed themselves; and as the dead fell, others jumped on them to defend themselves. The hill became like a pyramid that gradually grew higher.

Soon only fifty Barbarians were left, then twenty, then but three ; then two only survived—a Samnite armed with a battle-axe, and Mâtho, who still had his sword.

The Samnite, bent on his haunches, swung his battle-axe alternately from right to left, constantly warning Mâtho of blows directed at him : "Master! this way ! that way ! bend down !"

Mâtho had lost his shoulder-pieces, helmet, and breastplate, and stood completely naked, more livid than the dead ; his hair was perfectly straight, the corners of his mouth were covered with froth, and his sword whirled with such velocity, that it made an aureole about him. A stone shattered it close up to the guard ; the Samnite was killed ; the wave of Carthaginians closed in, touching him. Then he lifted his empty hands towards the sky, closed his eyes, and with arms thrown wide open, like a man about to spring from the summit of a promontory into the sea, he darted headlong into the midst of the lances.

The foe scattered before him. Frequently he rushed against the Carthaginians; but they always recoiled, turning away their weapons.

Mâtho's foot struck against a sword, and as he bent to seize it, he felt himself trammelled by the wrists and knees, and he fell.

Narr' Havas had followed him for some time, step by step, with a wide net used for trapping wild beasts, taking advantage of the moment when Mâtho bent towards the weapon to ensnare him in the toils.

He was then fastened on the elephant's back, his four limbs cross-wise, and all those who were not wounded escorted him, hurrying with great tumult on to Carthage.

The news of this victory had already travelled there—an inexplicable thing—as early as the third hour of the night, and the water-clock of Khamoûn marked the fifth hour as they arrived at Malqua. Here Mâtho reopened his eyes; there were such quantities of lights on the houses that the city appeared all in flames.

An immense clamour came vaguely to him, and lying on his back he gazed at the stars.

Then a door closed upon him, and darkness enveloped him.

The next day, at the same hour, the last of the men who had remained in the Defile of the Battle-axe expired.

The day that their comrades had departed, some

Zuæces who were returning home had rolled away the rocks. These men had supplied them with food for some time.

The Barbarians always expected to see Mâtho appear—and they would not quit the mountain, from dejection, from weakness, and that obstinacy of sick men who refuse to stir. At length, when their provisions were exhausted, the Zuæces went away. It was known that they scarcely numbered thirteen hundred, and that there was no need to employ soldiers to make an end of them.

Ferocious beasts, especially lions, in the three years of the duration of this war, had greatly multiplied. Narr' Havas made an extensive bush-beat, then chasing them, after having baited them by tethering goats at regular distances, he had drawn them into the Defile of the Battle-axe; and all these animals were still living there when the man arrived who had been sent by the Elders to find out who of the Barbarians remained.

Over the extent of the plain the lions and corpses were lying, and the dead were confounded with the clothing and armour. From almost all, the face, or else an arm, was missing. Some appeared still untouched; others were completely dried up, and the dusty skulls filled the helmets; fleshless feet stuck straight out of the greaves; skeletons kept their mantles; bones bleached by the sun made shining patches on the sand.

The lions lay, their chests against the ground, their two fore-paws stretched out, blinking their eyes in the glare of daylight, intensified by its reverberation from the white rocks. Others, sitting on their haunches, looked fixedly before them, or, half lost in their profuse manes, slept, rolled up like a ball. All appeared to be satiated, wearied, and listless. They were as motionless as the mountain, or as the dead. Night fell; wide red bands streaked the western sky.

In one of the heaps irregularly embossing the plain, something more weird than a spectre arose; then one of the lions commenced to move, cutting with his monstrous form a black shadow on the background of the impurpled sky. When he was near the man he felled him with a single blow of his paw. Then, stretched flat on his belly, with his fangs he slowly drew out the entrails.

Afterwards he opened his jaws wide, and for some minutes uttered a long, deep roar, which re-echoed in the mountains repeatedly, and was lost at last in the solitude.

All at once gravel rolled from above; then came the pattering of many rapid steps, and from the side of the portcullis and from the gorge appeared pointed snouts and straight ears, and yellow eyeballs gleamed. These were the jackals, come to devour the remains.

The Carthaginian who was watching as he leant over the edge of the precipice, returned to Carthage.

CHAPTER XV.

MÂTHO.

Joy—a profound, immoderate, universal, frantic joy—reigned in Carthage. The statues of the Gods had been repainted, the breaches in the ruins repaired, and the streets strewn with branches of myrtle; at the corners of the converging streets incense burned; and the multitude, pressing on the terraces in their motley apparel, resembled masses of flowers blooming in the open air.

The continual yelping of voices was dominated by the cry of the water-carriers as they sprinkled the streets. Hamilcar's slaves, in his name, distributed roasted barley and pieces of raw meat. People accosted each other, and embraced in tears; the Tyrian cities were taken, the Nomads were dispersed, and all the Barbarians were annihilated. The Acropolis was hidden beneath coloured canopies; the beakheads of the triremes, drawn up outside of the mole, glittered like a bank of diamonds; everywhere one felt order re-established, a new existence commenced. A vast happiness spread over all, for it was the wedding day of Salammbô and the king of the Numidians.

On the terrace of the temple of Khamoûn, gigantic gold plate laded three long tables, where the Priests, the Elders, and the Rich were to sit; and a fourth still higher table was arranged for Hamilcar, Narr' Havas, and Salammbô: for by the restoration of the Sacred Veil she had saved her country, therefore the people made her wedding celebration a national rejoicing, and on the square below they awaited her appearance.

But another desire, much keener, excited their impatience, for the death of Mâtho was promised for this ceremony.

It had been at first proposed to flay him alive, to run molten lead into his bowels, or to starve him to death; others wished to attach him to a tree with a monkey pinioned behind him, to beat his brains out with a stone—for he had offended Tanit, and it was but just that the cynocephales of Tanit should avenge her. Some even advised placing him on the back of a dromedary, and after having inserted in various parts of his body flaxen wicks steeped in oil, that he should be paraded about; and they were amused at the idea of the large animal wandering through the streets with this man writhing under the fire, like a lighted candelabrum agitated by the wind.

But to which of the citizens should his torture be committed, and why frustrate the others? They would wish to find a mode of death wherein the entire city could participate, that in every way all hands, all weapons, all Carthaginian things, even to the pavement stones of the streets, and the water of the gulf, should unite to rend him, crush him, annihilate him. Therefore the Elders decided that he should go from his prison to the square of Khamoûn without an escort, his arms fastened behind his back; but the people were forbidden to strike him to the heart, as it was desired to prolong his life; or to pierce his eyes, for they would have him see his torture until the end; or to throw anything against his person, or strike him with more than three fingers at a single blow.

Although he would not appear until the close of the day, frequently the crowd fancied they caught sight of him, and rushed towards the Acropolis, deserting the streets: then they returned with a prolonged murmur. Since the previous evening many people had remained standing in the same places, and from a distance called out to each other, significantly displaying their finger-nails, which they had let grow long to more surely lacerate the victim's flesh. Others walked about excitedly. Some were pale, as if they awaited their own execution.

Suddenly, behind the Mappals, great feather fans rose above the heads. It was Salammbô leaving her palace: a sigh of relief was exhaled.

But the cortège occupied a long time coming, it moving step by step.

At first, defiled the priests of the *Dii-Patæci*, then those of Eschmoûn, and those of Melkarth, successively followed by all the other colleges, with the same insignia and in the same order as they had observed at the time of the procession to the sacrifice. The pontiffs of Moloch passed by with heads lowered, and the multitude, as in a species of remorse, shrank back from them. But the priests of the Rabbetna advanced with a proud step, holding their lyres in their hands: the priestesses, wearing robes of yellow or black transparent stuffs, followed, uttering cries like birds, writhing like vipers, or to the sound of flutes they turned about, imitating the dance of the stars, and their light, fluttering vestments wafted delicate puffs of perfume softly through the streets. The people wildly applauded. Amid these women were hailed with cheers the Kedeschim with their painted eyelids, symbolic of the hermaphrodism of the Divinity; perfumed and clothed like the women, they resembled them, in spite of their flat breasts and their narrower hips.

The female principle dominated, overpowering all else. A mystic lasciviousness floated in the heavy air; already the flambeaux were lighted in the depths of the sacred woods, for during the night a grand debauchery would be held there;—three vessels had brought courtesans from Sicily, and others had come from the desert.

As the various colleges arrived they took up their places in the courts of the temple, on the exterior galleries, or on the length of the double stairway that ascended against the walls, approaching each other at the top. The rows of white robes appeared between the colonnades, and the entire architecture was peopled with human statues, motionless as stone.

After the priests came the master of finance, the governors of provinces, and all the Rich. Below, surged a vast tumult. From the neighbouring streets the throng poured forth; the sacred slaves beat them back with their staves; and in the midst of the Elders, crowned with gold tiaras, Salammbô was perceived upon a litter, over which a purple canopy was borne.

A tremendous cry arose; the cymbals and castanets sounded louder and louder, and the tambourines thundered as the grand purple canopy passed out of sight between the two gate-towers.

It reappeared on the first story. Salammbô paced slowly beneath it; then she crossed the terrace to take her seat at the back part, on a throne carved out of a tortoise-shell. An ivory stool of three steps was placed under her feet; on the edge of the first step two negro children kneeled, and occasionally she rested her arms, weighted with heavy bracelets upon their heads.

From her ankles to her hips she was enveloped in a network of tiny links, imitating the scales of a fish, and lustrous as polished mother-of-pearl. A blue zone compressed her waist, allowing her breasts to be seen through two crescent-shaped slashes, where carbuncle pendants hid their points. Her coiffure was made of peacocks' plumage, starred with jewels; a wide, ample mantle, white as snow, fell behind her;—her elbows close against her body; her knees pressed together; circlets of diamonds clasped high on her arms; she sat perfectly upright in a hieratic attitude.

Her father and bridegroom sat on two lower seats. Narr' Havas was robed in a golden-coloured simarre, and wore his rock-salt crown, from beneath which escaped two locks of hair, twisted like the horns of Ammon; Hamilcar was attired in a tunic of violet, brocaded with golden pampre, and wore his battle-sword girt to his side. In the space enclosed by the tables, the python of the temple of Eschmoûn lay on the ground between puddles of rose-oil, biting its tail, and thus describing a large black circle, in the centre of which was a copper column supporting a crystal egg, and as the sun shone upon it, prismatic rays darted out on all sides.

Immediately behind Salammbô spread the procession of the priests of Tanit, clothed in flaxen robes. At her right the Elders, bedecked with their tiaras, formed a great golden line. On the left, the Rich, with their emerald sceptres, made a great green line; and in the extreme background the priests of Moloch were ranged, and seemed, because of their mantles, like a purple wall. The other colleges occupied the inferior terraces. The multitude encumbered the streets or were mounted on the house-tops, and reached in long rows to the summit of the Acropolis.

Having thus the people at her feet, the firmament over her head, and around her the immensity of the sea, the gulf, and the mountains, and the perspectives of the provinces, Salammbô, resplendent, was confused with Tanit, and seemed herself the prevailing genius of Carthage—her soul incarnate.

The festival was to last all night, and candelabra with many branches were planted like trees upon the painted woollen tapestries that covered the low tables. Large flagons of electrum, amphoras of blue glass, tortoise-shell spoons, and small round loaves, crowded between the double row of plates bordered with pearls; clusters of grapes with their leaves like thyrsi entwined vine-stocks; blocks of snow were melting in ebony salvers; lemons, pomegranates, gourds, and water-melons, were piled in hillocks beneath the tall, massive argentries; wild boars with open jaws wallowed in the dust of spices; hares cooked whole, covered with their fur, seemed to leap between the flowers shells were filled with forced meats; pasties were baked in symbolic forms; and when the dish-covers were first withdrawn, live doves flew out.

Meanwhile, slaves with their tunics tucked up moved about on tip-toe; from time to time the lyres sounded a hymn, or a chorus of voices burst forth. The hum of the people, continuous like the roar of the sea, floated vaguely over the feast, and seemed to rock it in a vast harmony. Many recalled the banquet of the Mercenaries; they abandoned themselves to dreams of happiness; the sun commenced to decline, and the crescent moon had already risen in the other part of the sky.

Salammbô turned her head, as if some one had called her; the concourse, who watched her every act, followed the direction of her gaze.

At the summit of the Acropolis the door of the dungeon, cut in the rock at the foot of the temple, had just opened; a man stood on the threshold of this black hole.

He issued forth bent double, with the frightened air of a captive wild beast suddenly set at liberty. The light dazzled him; he remained some minutes motionless. All had recognised him, and held their breath.

The body of this victim was for the populace something specially their own, imbued with a splendour almost religious.

They leaned forward, straining to see him, particularly the women, who burned to contemplate the one who had caused the death of their children and husbands; but, despite of themselves, in the depths of their souls there arose an infamous curiosity—the desire to know him completely, a longing blended with remorse, which changed into an excess of execration.

Finally he advanced; the bewilderment of the surprise vanished. Numberless arms were raised, and for the moment he was no longer seen.

The stairway of the Acropolis had sixty steps; he descended them with a pitch forward, as if he was rolled in a torrent from the top of a mountain. Thrice he was seen to bound, then at the bottom he came down on his feet.

His shoulders bled, his chest heaved with deep pulsations, and he made such struggles to break the shackles, that his arms, which were crossed on his naked loins, swelled like the coils of a serpent.

The place into which he now walked presented many streets fronting him. Along each street a triple barrier of bronze chains, attached to the navel of the *Dii-Patœci*, extended in parallel lines from end to end. The crowd was packed back against the walls and houses; in the midst of the throng, the slaves of the Elders moved about, brandishing whipthongs.

One of these slaves pushed Mâtho before him with a powerful blow; he began to move forward.

The people stretched out their arms beyond the chains, remonstrating the while that he was allowed too wide a path. He passed along, struck, pricked, mangled by all these revengeful fingers; then when he reached the end of one street another appeared. Sometimes he threw himself to the side, striving to bite his tormentors; they would quickly draw back, and when the chains restrained him, they would burst out in peals of laughter at his thwarted efforts.

A child tore his ear; a young girl concealed under her sleeve a spindle, with the point of which she slit his cheek; they pulled out handfuls of his hair, tore strips from his flesh, and others held sticks on which were fastened sponges saturated in filth, with which they buffeted his face.

A stream of blood gushed from the right side of his throat; immediately a frenzy began. This last Barbarian represented to them all the Barbarians, all the army; they took revenge on him for all their disasters, terrors, and opprobrium. The rage of the people grew with its gratification; the chains strained too tight as they leaned against them, threatening to part asunder. They were insensible to the blows the servitors dealt to force them back; some clung to the projections of the houses; all the apertures in the walls were choked up by heads, and the evil they were incapable of doing to his person they howled out upon him.

Their maledictions teemed with atrocities of obscene abuse, with ironical encouragements and imprecations; and as they were dissatisfied with his present agonies, they announced to him others more terrible yet for eternity.

This vast howling filled Carthage with a stupid monotony. Often a single syllable, one intonation, harsh, profound, frantic, would be repeated for many minutes by the entire people. The walls vibrated from the base to the top, and the two sides of the streets seemed to Mâtho to come against him, and rise from the ground like two immense arms, which suffocated him in the air.

Meanwhile, he remembered that he had previously experienced something similar. It was the same crowd on the terraces, the same fierce looks, the same rage; but that other time he walked at liberty —all then scattered before him, for the power of a God shielded him. This memory, gradually becoming vividly distinct, brought to him a crushing sadness. Shadows passed before his eyes. The city whirled in a vertigo through his brain; blood jetted from a wound in his thigh; he felt himself to be dying; his legs doubled under him, and he sank softly upon the pavement.

Some of his persecutors took from a tripod in the peristyle of the temple of Melkarth a red-hot bar, slipped it through under the first chain, and pressed it against his wound. The scorching flesh was seen to smoke; the yells of the people drowned his voice; but again he stood up and advanced.

Six paces further on, and a third, and yet a fourth time he fell: always some new torture goaded him up and on. Boiling oil was squirted through tubes upon him; fragments of glass were strewn under his feet; yet he continued to walk. At the corner of the street Sateb he leaned beneath the pent-house of a shop, with his back against the wall, and moved no further.

The slaves of the Council struck him with whips of hippopotamus hide so furiously, and for so long a time, that the fringes of their tunics were soaked with sweat. Mâtho appeared insensible. Suddenly he took a fresh impetus, and started to run at hazard, emitting from his lips a shuddering noise, like one suffering from intense cold. Thus he passed through the streets of Boudès, the street of Scepo, crossed the vegetable market, and came into the square of Khamoûn.

From this point, now, he belonged to the priests, and the Elders' slaves scattered the crowd; here he had more space. Mâtho looked around him, and his eyes encountered Salammbô.

At the first step that he had taken she had arisen; then involuntarily, according as he drew nearer, she had advanced gradually to the edge of the terrace. Soon, for her, all other external things were effaced: she only saw Mâtho. A silence possessed her soul, one of those abysses wherein the whole world disappears under the impression of a single thought, of one memory—of one look. This man who walked towards her irresistibly fascinated her.

There remained nothing except his eyes which retained a human appearance: he was a long form completely red; his broken shackles, hanging the length of his thighs, were so bloody that they could no longer be distinguished from the tendons of his wrists, denuded of flesh; his mouth remained open; from his orbits issued two flames, which had the appearance of mounting to his hair:—and yet this wretched creature kept ever moving on.

He came just to the foot of the terrace. Salammbô was leaning on the balustrade; those frightful eyeballs were staring at her; and within her awoke the consciousness of all that he had suffered for her sake. Although he was now agonised in death-throes, she resaw him in his tent, on his knees as he encircled her waist with his arms, babbling sweet speeches; she yearned to feel those arms again, and hear those words once more. She did not wish that he should die. At this moment Mâtho was seized with a great tremor. She was about to cry out, when he fell backwards to the earth, and moved no more.

Salammbô almost swooned; she was carried back to her throne by the priests who pressed around her. They felicitated her: it was her work. All clapped their hands and stamped their feet, and yelled her name in universal acclamation.

A man darted upon the body; although he was beardless, he wore on his shoulders the mantle of the priests of Moloch, and in his girdle the sort of knife used to cut up the sacred viands, the haft terminating in a golden spatula.

By a single stroke he split open Mâtho's chest, then tore out his heart, placing it on the spatula; and Schahabarim—for it was he—raised his arm, offering it to the Sun.

The sun was sinking behind the waves; his rays struck like long arrows athwart the crimson heart. He sank beneath the sea as the throbbing diminished, and at the last pulsation disappeared. Then from the gulf to the Lagoon, and from the isthmus as far as the lighthouse, in all the streets, over all the house-tops, and over all the temples, there welled forth a single cry; sometimes it paused, only to reburst: the edifices trembled—Carthage was convulsed in the spasm of a Titanic joy, and a hope without bounds.

Narr' Havas, intoxicated with pride, passed his left arm about Salammbô's waist, in sign of possession; and in the right hand he took a gold patera, and drank to the genius of Carthage.

Salammbô arose, like her consort, grasping a cup in her hand, in order also to drink. She fell, with her head leaning over the back of the throne, pallid, stiff, her lips parted,—and her dishevelled hair hung to the ground.

Thus died the daughter of Hamilcar, for having touched the Veil of Tanit.

ANNOUNCEMENTS.

ALAMO:
AN HISTORICAL ROMANCE.

BY

M. FRENCH SHELDON.

TO BE ISSUED THIS YEAR.

CINCHONA-LAND:
A MONOGRAPH.

BY

HENRY S. WELLCOME.

BASED ON A PERSONAL JOURNEY THROUGH THE CINCHONA DISTRICTS OF SOUTH AMERICA.

TO BE ISSUED THIS YEAR.

www.ingramcontent.com/pod-product-compliance
Lightning Source LLC
Chambersburg PA
CBHW032139010526
44111CB00035B/621